THE REPORTER'S
ENVIRONMENTAL HANDBOOK

THE REPORTER'S
ENVIRONMENTAL HANDBOOK

BERNADETTE WEST
PETER M. SANDMAN
MICHAEL R. GREENBERG

RUTGERS UNIVERSITY PRESS
NEW BRUNSWICK, NEW JERSEY

"No fruit for me, buddy . . . I only eat food that lists its toxins on the package . . ." by Jim Borgman is reprinted with the special permission of King Features Syndicate.

"Funky Winkerbean" by Tom Batiuk is reprinted with the special permission of North America Syndicate.

"Bloom County" © 1994 is reprinted with the permission of The Washington Post Writers Group.

"After the discovery of fire, early man is exposed to the environmental hazards of burning garbage" by Carl Hennicke © 1989 *The Home News* is reprinted with his permission.

"Remember when they used to send us poverty programs! . . ." by Doug Marlette is reprinted with the permission of Doug Marlette and Creators Syndicate.

"Sally Forth" by Greg Howard is reprinted with the special permission of King Features Syndicate.

"Major Developments in Federal Legislative History" by Rae Zimmerman, from pages 237–240 of *Public Health and the Environment*, ed. Michael Greenberg, 1987, is reprinted with the permission of the Guilford Press.

LIBRARY OF CONGRESS CATALOGING-IN-PUBLICATION DATA

The reporter's environmental handbook / edited by
   Bernadette West, Peter M. Sandman, Michael R. Greenberg.
         p.   cm.
   Includes bibliographical references (p.) and index.
   ISBN 0-8135-2148-3 (cloth) —ISBN 0-8135-2149-1 (pkb.)
   1. Environmental protection in the press—United States—
   Handbooks, manuals, etc.   2. Environmental health—
   Reporting—United States—Handbooks, manuals, etc.
   I. West, Bernadette.   II. Sandman, Peter M.
   III. Greenberg, Michael R.
   PN4888.E65R46   1994
   070.4'4936317—dc20   94-25451
                                                   CIP

British Cataloging-in-Publication information available

CONTENTS

PREFACE AND ACKNOWLEDGMENTS

C hernobyl . . . Three Mile Island . . . Love Canal . . . Bhobal . . . Times Beach, Missouri . . . mercury poisoning in Minamata, Japan . . . radon-contaminated homes . . . dioxin dumping in the bay. . . . These arc the stories that make the front-page and nightly news headlines. Environment and health coverage is no longer relegated to the back of the paper or the tail end of the broadcast.

As the public becomes increasingly aware of and worried about the environment, editors and reporters cannot rely on a "seat-of-the-pants" approach when reporting on environmental issues. Stories must be technically accurate, responsible, objective, and balanced. The quality of reporting influences public perception, and from public perception, often, comes public policy. Yet, few papers and broadcast stations can assign a full-time reporter to environmental stories. Faced with a fast-breaking story, even beat reporters may not have time to consult a specialist. The aim of this book is to give every reporter and editor the background needed to report these complex and controversial stories effectively.

The Reporter's Environmental Handbook was first published by the Hazardous Substance Management Research Center (HSMRC) at the New Jersey Institute of Technology in 1988 under the title *The Environmental Reporter's Handbook*. The HSMRC is a National Science Foundation–industry–university cooperative research center which receives funding from the National Science Foundation, the state of New Jersey, and approximately thirty corporations. This second edition has been extensively revised, enlarged, and updated—and retitled *The Reporter's Environmental Handbook* to reflect the need of *all* reporters for sound background information on environmental issues.

The book is the result of the Environmental Risk Reporting Project. Initiated in 1985, the project is dedicated to improving the quality of environmental journalism and health-risk reporting throughout the United States. It has sponsored seminars for journalists, analyzed the content of environmental news in newspapers and on television, worked with state government to foster communication between reporters and news sources, and produced this book as well as a videotape and articles for writers and professionals in the environmental field. The project is a joint undertaking of Rutgers, the State University of New Jersey and the University of Medicine and Dentistry of New Jersey–Robert Wood Johnson Medical School; it is funded by the Northeast Hazardous Substance Research Center and the Hazardous Substance Management Research Center at New Jersey Institute of Technology, Newark, New Jersey, and housed at the Center for Environmental Communication (CEC) at Rutgers.

The concept for the *Handbook* emerged from Laurel Van Leer's (now with the *Central New Jersey Home News*) research for the Environmental Risk Reporting Project on the feasibility of various devices for getting environmental-risk information to reporters. The first edition included twenty-three briefs on specific environmental issues and the problems reporters might encounter in covering stories on them. The book won praise from reviewers and won a Special Award for Journalism from the Sigma Delta Chi Society of Professional Journalists in 1989.

The second edition retains eighteen briefs (with revisions) from the original edition and adds nine new topics: automobile-caused pollution, electromagnetic fields, endangered species, the greenhouse effect, green marketing, oil spills, ozone, right-to-know legislation, and toxic metals. The new briefs were suggested by our own research and by members of the Industrial Advisory Board (IAB) of the Hazardous Substance Management Research Center and representatives from the New Jersey Department of Environmental Protection and Energy (NJDEPE). We asked members of the HSMRC's Industrial Advisory Board and Public Policy Division as well as representatives of fourteen environmental organizations to review the choice of topics and the drafts of the new and revised briefs. We sent drafts to 127 people who had indicated a willingness to review them and got back sixty-seven sets of comments, some quite brief and some quite extensive.

Every attempt was made to incorporate the suggestions offered by our reviewers. All twenty-seven briefs in this book have been reviewed by at least one outside reader, and over half have been reviewed by two or more outside readers; the drafts were then revised and checked once more by ourselves and the HSMRC members. The general information sections on finding an expert, doing background checks on a company's environmental record, and covering an environmental emergency have not changed from the first edition. The information on resources—legislation, key telephone numbers, and acronyms—has, of course, been updated.

In this second edition, we wrote nine new briefs and revised all the briefs from the first edition, soliciting comments from experts in the field. Therefore, the authors are greatly indebted to all who helped prepare the first edition—the coeditor, David Sachsman, and Liz Fuerst, Annemarie Cook, and Laurel Van Leer who helped with the development of the first edition—and to the experts who contributed drafts of individual briefs to the two editions. For this edition, we must especially thank the following contributors: Joan E. Siederer (on birth defects), James Ross (on chemical emergencies), Richard S. Magee (on incinerators), Michael Gochfeld (on occupational exposure), Richard Fenske (on pesticides), James Detjen (on checking a company's environmental record), Bernard D. Goldstein (on finding an expert), and Rae Zimmerman (on federal legislation).

We are also deeply grateful to the reviewers in government agencies, companies, and trade associations, environmental advocacy organizations, and academia who gave us careful critiques of the briefs and invaluable suggestions for the second edition. In the notes to the individual briefs, we acknowledge by name those who provided extensive comments. We are grateful as well to the cartoonists and their publishers who granted permission to enliven this book with their work.

Once again, the research and writing were funded by the Northeast Hazardous Substance Research Center and the Hazardous Substance Management Research Center, New Jersey Institute of Technology. The HSMRC has also contributed additional funds to underwrite the publication and distribution of copies of this book to newsrooms around the country.

Major support has been provided by the United States Environmental Protection Agency's Office of Research and Development and Hazardous Substance Research Centers Program, Dale Manty, Director. Special thanks are also due to the Training and Technology Transfer Advisory Committee of the Northeast Hazardous Substance Research Center and its chairman, Ron DiCola, and director, Jerry McKenna, at NJIT. A special environmental educator's manual has also been prepared in cooperation with the Technology Transfer and Training Program of Great Lakes/Mid-Atlantic HSRC, directed by Tom Voice, of Michigan State University, and Mike Senew, chairman of its Advisory Committee, and the EPA-funded National Consortium for Environmental Education and Training, led by Paul Nowak at the University of Michigan.

We wish to acknowledge Karen Reeds and Judith Martin Waterman for their thoughtful and careful editing of the manuscript. We also wish to thank the centers at NJIT and their staffs and their Advisory Committees, not just for financial support but for their helpful advice at every stage of The *Handbook*'s revision. They will doubtless have further comments on the book as published; its errors and its opinions are those of the authors alone.

GETTING STARTED

HOW TO USE THIS BOOK

F irst read the chapters in the "Getting Started" section. "The Language of Risk" provides a necessary perspective on what is often misunderstood and often inflated: the way we talk about the risks of exposure. To accurately write a story one must be sensitive to the language of risk and hazard. You quickly will find that there are two very different ways of talking about risk: one quite technical and quantitative, the other very nontechnical and often emotion-filled. Scientists and ordinary citizens often talk at cross-purposes about risk. Paying attention to these distinctions will give your story far greater authority and win you credibility with all of your sources and your audience.

Then read "Handling an Environmental Emergency: A Case Study in Finding Sources." This chapter serves as a guide to covering all environmental stories through its detailed description of a reporter's movements while covering an environmental emergency. The process is roughly the same for covering an emergency and a nonemergency. This chapter illustrates the who, what, where, when, and why of an environmental incident; identifies the questions to be asked and how to find the answers; and suggests ways of finding sources.

Once you have the overall picture presented in this section, use the *Handbook* as a reference for background information and sources as each story arises.

The *Handbook* presents briefs on twenty-seven specific environmental and health issues. They are listed alphabetically from "Acid Rain" to "Water Pollution," and should be used like recipes in a cookbook: "Incinerators" for one story, "Radon (Indoor)" for the next. While each brief is self-contained, briefs on related subjects—for example, radon and indoor air pollution—are cross-referenced.

Each brief begins with a note on the risks of exposure. It identifies who is likely to be harmed, whether the risk is increasing or decreasing, and concisely describes the problems raised for communities and individuals and the approaches being used to correct these problems. Next, the briefs identify what you need to know to research the story and warn of pitfalls in reporting it. Finally, the briefs identify specific sources for researching your story, with phone numbers and addresses as current as we can make them.

Once you have read the brief, you should have a clear idea of the kinds of data you will need to gather, what experts and activists, organizations, resources, and legislation you will need to consult, and what questions to raise.

The chapters in the "Resources" section of the *Handbook* offer broad guidelines for tracking down the environmental record of a company and for finding an expert to interview. They also provide a summary of federal environmental legislation, key telephone numbers, key references, an extensive glossary, and a list of acronyms and abbreviations to help you through the alphabet soup of organizations and agencies that deal with the environment and environmental health and the terminology they use.

THE LANGUAGE OF RISK

A fundamental question in managing any risk—and in reporting it—is figuring out how risky it is. Big risks deserve big news stories, especially if the proper authorities are ignoring them. Small risks deserve small stories, or no stories at all. How do you decide which is which?

It helps to have some baseline information: about two million Americans die every year from all causes. Cigarette smoking and alcohol are the two most clearly identified risk factors. Smoking tobacco is estimated to be associated with 350,000–450,000 of the deaths, and alcohol abuse with about 200,000. None of the risks described in these briefs approaches the seriousness of smoking or alcohol abuse.

Unfortunately, the science of risk assessment does not allow us to say precisely how many people are killed or injured by any of the risks described in these briefs. In fact, for most environmental risks, the data on risk identification, dose-response, and exposure assessment are so limited that scientists have attempted risk assessments only for cancer. About 460,000 Americans die annually from cancer, which makes cancer the second leading cause of death (heart disease kills more people than cancer; tobacco smoking is a risk factor for both). So, in the briefs, we draw special attention to the risks of cancer associated with each hazard.

If we look at the relative risk of cancer as a measure of "how risky" something is, the briefs fall into three groups. Asbestos, indoor air pollution, radon, and exposures at work are responsible for the greatest number of cancers—though far fewer than cigarette smoking. (Asbestos is estimated to be responsible for 1,000–10,000 deaths per year, for example.) Benzene, chemical emergencies, dioxin, water pollution, hazardous household products, leaking underground storage tanks, municipal solid-waste incinerators, pesticides, and sanitary landfills are less important problems. The carcinogenic burden of acid rain cannot be estimated.

The question, "how risky?" has both a technical and a nontechnical side. On the technical side, we want to know how many people are likely to be injured, or made ill, or killed as the result of a given environmental health risk, or how much ecosystem damage is likely to be sustained. Scientists have come up with an assortment of methods for estimating the chances of such injury, and it's important for you, in reporting a story, to be aware of the advantages and drawbacks connected with those methods.

On the nontechnical side comes a somewhat different question: How upsetting, frightening, or enraging is the situation likely to be to the people who must endure it? Technical people sometimes argue that the nontechnical aspects of risk should play little if any role in risk policy. But even they would not like to live in a world in which, for example, coerced risks were handled the same way as voluntary risks. Just because hang-gliding—a voluntary risk—is legal, should a factory emitting pollutants be permitted to impose a comparable, but involuntary, risk on its neighbors? Or, conversely, just because the factory must reduce its dimethylmeatloaf emissions below the risk level of skiing, does that mean we have to outlaw skis? Figuring out how to balance technical and nontechnical considerations is a real dilemma—for risk managers and journalists alike.

A host of other thorny questions confront the risk-policy maker, and the reporter trying to make sense of risk. A few examples:

|||||| **HOW SHOULD WE DEAL WITH UNCERTAINTY?**

The answers to technical risk questions invariably come with a lot of uncertainty attached. If we wait for definite answers, we will end up ignoring serious problems for decades, just because the research isn't definitive yet. But if we act quickly, we may well be wrong—and it may be politically impossible to back off. If we base policy decisions on our best estimate of the risk, it is as likely to be too low as too high; that is, we will offer too little protection half the time. But if we base policy decisions on a high-side "conservative" estimate of the risk, the price we will pay for being confident that we are protecting people enough is a very high likelihood that we are over-protecting them.

||||| **DOES IT MATTER WHO IS AT RISK?**

Although some would argue that all lives are of equal value, most risk policies treat different people's lives differently. Risk to by-standers, for example, is usually taken much more seriously than risk to employees; the underlying assumption is that work involves some risk, for which the worker is presumably paid, but innocent bystanders deserve a higher level of protection. Other distinctions are even more controversial. Juries, for example, often base damage awards on how much potential income the plaintiff has lost, thus putting a higher value on the life and health of a young professional than on the life and health of an older and less prosperous victim. Similarly, risky facilities are likelier to end up in poor neighborhoods than in rich neighborhoods—the land is cheaper, the neighborhood may be more desperate for the jobs, and it may be less politically able to organize an effective opposition.

||||| **WHAT ABOUT THE COST OF RISK
REDUCTION, IN MONEY OR IN JOBS?**

Putting a price tag on human life is always, politically and morally, controversial—but not putting a price tag on human life may make sensible risk management impossible. If you are willing to spend whatever it takes, there are always more steps you can think of to "pad the world" and thus reduce risk. Some risk policies cost tens of millions of dollars for every life saved, while others cost only thousands; most would agree that the second bunch are wiser than the first—and, of course, money spent on the first bunch is no longer available to spend on the second. Similarly, most employees would rather endure small risks than lose their jobs; among other things, losing your job significantly damages your health and your family's health. On the other hand, those trying to avoid regulations often overstate their cost in money or jobs. And the discovery of a cost-effective way to prevent a particular risk usually comes after the decision to eliminate that risk, not before; if cost considerations were used to justify inaction, the cheaper solution might never be found.

⫼ **WHAT IF WE DON'T KNOW HOW TO REDUCE THE RISK?**

Basing risk-policy decisions on the size of the risk sounds sensible, but it assumes we know how to reduce any risk we like, and the only issue is which ones deserve our attention. In reality, of course, some risk-reduction technologies are well-established, others are experimental, and still others don't exist at all. In some areas, it may make sense to require the "best available technology" to reduce the risk in question, rather than setting a quantitative standard for tolerable risk.

We could extend this list of risk-policy problems for pages. The point is that deciding what to do about a risk isn't easy even after you have answered the technical "how risky?" question and the nontechnical "how risky?" question. Still, risk policy begins with the effort to answer those two questions.

⫼ **SO, HOW RISKY IS IT?: THE TECHNICAL ANSWER** ⫼

The focus of public and regulatory concern about environmental health is usually long-term, repeated chronic health risk. Of course explosions, spills, and other acute risks are also matters of concern. But most (though not all) of the *Handbook* will focus on chronic risk.

Since the mid-1970s, chronic human health risks associated with chemical, biological, and physical substances have been evaluated in a multistep process called quantitative risk assessment (QRA). QRA has begun to consider impacts other than human health—impacts on wildlife, vegetation, and other ecological systems. Historically, however, only human health effects were considered, and the *Handbook* will, therefore, focus most closely on these.

Quantitative risk assessment proceeds in four steps: 1. hazard identification—what's out there that might be dangerous? 2. dose-response assessment—how much of it will do how much harm? 3. exposure assessment—how much of it are people actually getting? and 4. aggregate risk assessment—given the three previous steps, how great is the overall risk?

ⅢⅢ   **HAZARD IDENTIFICATION**

The goal of the first step in QRA, hazard identification, is to determine whether a substance can cause human health effects. Scientists use both human and animal studies to make this determination.

The science that tries to deduce the existence of a hazard from human data is called epidemiology. Epidemiologists may follow a particular group of people over time, noting their exposure to particular potential hazards and trying to relate this to the incidence of particular diseases. More often, epidemiologists have to work backwards, noting who got sick and who stayed healthy, and trying to relate this information to people's past exposures to the hazard in question.

Workers are the most studied human group because they are exposed to high concentrations of many dangerous substances. For example, the extreme hazard posed by asbestos was recognized by observing excess respiratory cancers and asbestosis among shipyard workers and other building-trade workers who routinely handled asbestos. Likewise, uranium mine workers were observed to have higher rates of lung cancer and underground coal miners higher rates of chronic obstructive lung diseases.

Epidemiological studies have serious limitations. Humans are exposed to so many substances that only the most dangerous ones can be picked out and identified. For example, workers exposed to asbestos, radioactive materials, and coal dust were much more likely to manifest a health problem if they also smoked tobacco products. In other words, excess disease observed among human populations can often be explained by an exposure or pre-existing condition that may be independent of the exposure to the substance in question.

Another major limitation of the vast majority of human studies

"NO FRUIT FOR ME, BUDDY... I ONLY EAT FOOD THAT LISTS ITS TOXINS ON THE PACKAGE..."

is that people must contract the disease before the problem is discovered—obviously an undesirable way to learn about risk.

Furthermore, it is impossible to control human studies to the extent possible with animal studies. With animal populations, the experimenter can make sure the test animals have no relevant exposures except the one being tested. But for obvious ethical reasons, you can't "experiment" on human risk exposures—and so multiple factors always complicate the analysis. Instead of controls, epidemiologists must use statistics. They "factor out" the effects of smoking, age, and other "confounders" statistically, to determine how much of the effect being observed is attributable to the risk being studied (e.g., living near an incinerator).

This method is problematic for several reasons. First, it is intrinsically unconvincing to laypeople. Scientists estimate that radon results in a certain number of lung cancer deaths annually, but they cannot say specifically which people will be affected; the number is based on a statistical calculation of excess lung cancer deaths—not on counting the bodies of radon victims. This leaves people feeling free to mistrust the number, in either direction.

Second, for a clear effect to emerge from statistical analysis, the effect has to be large, or the sample has to be large, or the effect has to be concentrated in ways that make it easy to observe. If, for example, exposure to a certain chemical kills one person in three, scientists can tell with a small sample, regardless of confounding factors. If it kills one person in one thousand, scientists can tell only if the sample is large or if the effect is idiosyncratic. (If the chemical causes a rare disease we will be able to see the excess incidence in people living near the plant that manufactures the chemical, but if it causes a common disease we will miss it.) If it kills one person in a million, scientists will not be able to find it. In other words, even if a hazard is serious enough that risk managers would want to know and do something about it, it still may not be serious enough for epidemiologists to isolate its effects with confidence. Assume that dimethylmeatloaf may cause one exposed person in a thousand to get, say, pancreatic cancer. If it does, the substance is a significant carcinogen in need of control. But if only a few hundred workers and neighbors of the dimethylmeatloaf factory are exposed, no epidemiological study is going to be able to find the fraction of one cancer that would be statistically expected to result. The question is worth answering, but epidemiology won't be able to answer it. The fact that lots of other substances could also cause pancreatic cancer will only make the problem worse.

Laboratory studies of mice, hamsters, and other animals are also used to evaluate potential human health hazards. Large quantities of the substance under investigation are introduced into the animals. Effects are observed and then the animals are sacrificed to determine if they have developed tumors and other effects that cannot be observed otherwise. During the last decade, lower organism tests have been developed to screen substances for mutagenesis, which many scientists believe is necessary to cause cancer. Tests on lower organisms and on isolated cells are, of course, less expensive and ethically less problematic than tests on large animals.

Animal studies have significant advantages: they can be done in advance of human exposure, and they can be carefully controlled to isolate the effect under investigation. But animal studies also have important limitations. Animals are not necessarily perfect sentinels of human response to exposures. That is, humans may be affected, but animals may not be—and vice versa. In addition, in order to make animal studies timely and cost-effective, laboratory animals are bred to be highly susceptible to tumors or other health effects of concern; they are placed in controlled environments (unlike humans who are exposed to multiple substances); and they are given extremely high doses of the substance in question (and the potential impact of those doses is enhanced with solvents).

In other words, protocols used in laboratories do not resemble human exposure conditions. What we learn from an animal study is what happens when small numbers of rodents are exposed to huge quantities of one substance at a time for a short period of time. What we actually want to know is what happens when large numbers of human beings are exposed to small quantities of lots of substances at once over a long period of time. The two are, obviously, not the same.

Human studies, in brief, provide weak answers to the right questions. Animal studies provide strong answers to the wrong questions. Neither is ideal—but they're all we have.

|||||||| **DOSE-RESPONSE ASSESSMENT**

It is a truism of toxicology (the study of what's poisonous and what isn't) that "the dose makes the poison." Lots of substances are highly toxic at high doses, but harmless or even essential at low doses. Thus, the second step in QRA, dose-response assessment, estimates the human health effects of varying amounts of exposure to the substance in question. For example, is a person exposed to 16 grams of a chemical twice as likely to develop cancer as a person exposed to 8 grams? four times as likely as a person exposed to 4 grams? ten thousand times as likely as a person exposed to 0.0016 grams? These are not simple questions. In their efforts to come up with answers, scientists must try to take into account the age, gender, and lifestyle of exposed populations; the intensity of the exposure (four grams in five seconds versus four grams in five years); the pattern of exposure (inhalation, skin contact, ingestion); and other factors that affect response.

Threshold—the level below which risk is absent—is an important concept in dose-response assessment. Some risks have no threshold. In Russian roulette, for example, the risk of one bullet in a six-chamber gun is one in six; expand to a six million–chamber gun and the risk is one in six million. It is never zero, no matter how many chambers. But some risks are zero until a threshold exposure is passed. Drowning is a good example. You cannot drown standing up in a few inches of water; the risk climbs sharply as the water level rises above your head; then it levels off again (deep is deep). The dose-response curve for Russian roulette would be a straight line running through zero. For drowning, the curve would be an S-curve, with all the increased risk between two and seven feet.

However, we do not know the dose-response curve for most chronic human health risks. This has resulted in ongoing disagreement over two huge issues. First, what is the likeliest curve? And second, given that we don't really known the shape of the curve, how conservative should we be in making assumptions about its shape?

The first question is obviously very hard to answer. Dose-response assessment is almost always hindered by a paucity of data, especially dose-response observations at low doses. As we have already discussed, risks get harder to measure when the exposures get smaller, so we usually end up measuring the dose-response relationship at high levels of exposure (in animals, extremely high levels), then extrapolating the curve downwards. For example, we have data on the impact of high doses of asbestos exposure in shipyards and asbestos mines, but not much data on the chronic very low-dose exposures that an office worker might encounter in a public building from a ceiling containing asbestos. Scientists frequently make educated guesses (called extrapolations) from the data they do have (on shipyards or asbestos mines) to the risk they are trying to define (asbestos in homes and offices). These extrapolations are deservedly controversial because they are grounded in uncertain science and, often, in unacknowledged assumptions about the trade-offs between protecting public health and spending money.

Since the first question is so hard to answer, the second question becomes critical: how cautious should the guess be? Currently, QRAs tend to make very cautious guesses—and many people who acknowledge that the "real" risk is probably lower than the risk estimate arrived at in a conventional QRA argue that this is a good thing. The "best guess estimate," by definition, is going to be too low half of the time, and too high the other half. An estimate that is almost sure not to be too low will usually be too high; many experts believe this is a better way to protect public health. Other

experts, however, argue that conservative risk estimates are misleading, especially since people tend to forget they were conservative, and treat them as "best guess estimates."

Sometimes scientists find contradictory results. For example,
one research group finds a major health impact while another finds
no discernible impact. In such a case, still other scientists will
examine the two study designs to try to determine why they
reached such different results. But often no consensus conclusion
emerges; the studies really disagree, and so do the experts who
have looked at them. Further research may or may not resolve the
problem—and meanwhile a policy decision must be made. In this
very common predicament, scientists, policy makers, journalists,
and the public must all decide how to handle scientific disagreement. Once again, their answers contain implicit value judgments
about the trade-offs between public health and cost.

ⅢⅢ   **EXPOSURE ASSESSMENT**

Now that we "know" how much of the substance in question it
takes to do harm, we obviously want to know the levels at which
people are actually exposed. This is the third step in QRA, exposure
assessment. Using instruments, many of which have only recently
been invented, scientists try to measure how much radon is accumulating in a basement, or how much chromium is found in a
workplace. They multiply their measurements by the amount of
time people are exposed to arrive at a total dose.

Exposure assessment has been the weakest link in risk assessment because direct measurements have rarely been available.
Instead, scientists have tried to recreate exposure, which is an
extremely difficult task requiring numerous assumptions to replace the missing information. A workplace exposure to asbestos,
for example, might be recreated from blueprints of a facility and
other information about the structure, and some knowledge about
how many times workers went into the basement where they could
have come into contact with asbestos-covered pipes.

ⅢⅢ   **AGGREGATE RISK ASSESSMENT**

The fourth step in QRA characterizes the aggregate risk to the total
population and to various subpopulations of importance (e.g.,

workers, community residents). This is done by using census data and surveys to estimate where people spend their time.

In assessments of total risk, both individual risk and societal risk are important. If exposure to a certain chemical causes one death in a hundred each year, and a total of three hundred people have been exposed, it is a very serious individual risk for those three hundred people, but a very small overall societal risk (three deaths a year). If exposure to the chemical causes one death annually in a hundred thousand, and all 250 million U.S. citizens are exposed, it is a very small individual-level risk, but a fairly high societal risk (2,500 deaths a year). Risk assessors try to collect data on both kinds of risk. Policy makers and journalists should stay alert to them both.

Results of the QRA are forwarded to decision makers who explicitly add legal, economic, political, and social considerations to the results of the scientific analyses. As we have already noted, the results of many risk assessments are highly uncertain—that is, health effects are not known within a narrow enough range to strongly guide decisions. Consequently, decision makers usually have wide latitude to impose nonscientific decision-making criteria. For example, a multibillion-dollar asbestos removal program is underway in U.S. schools. Risk assessments do not justify removing asbestos where it is not damaged. In fact, some scientists believe that short-term risk is increased by removing undamaged asbestos. Yet tens of billions of dollars are being spent on asbestos removal, motivated by parents' concerns on behalf of their children, school officials' fear of future lawsuits, and other nontechnical factors.

Overall, supporters of quantitative risk assessment do not consider it a scientific panacea. They argue that some worthwhile information is usually available about hazard identification, dose-response assessment, and exposure assessment, and that using this information does narrow the range of reasonable management strategies for decision makers to consider. Often they complain that decision makers rely too little on the available data, responding more to nontechnical factors than to the QRA. Detractors contend that the results of quantitative risk assessments are so uncertain that they can often do more harm than good. Vested interests, they say, use risk assessment to try to dazzle decision makers into managing risk without taking public viewpoints into account.

Quantitative risk assessment is still in its infancy. The answers it offers to the technical "how risky?" question are still highly debatable. But researchers are getting better at estimating risk. The problem is that we do not seem to be getting any better at achieving a societal consensus about what should be done with the risk estimates.

ⅲⅲ RISK = HAZARD + OUTRAGE: THE NONTECHNICAL ANSWER ⅲⅲ

So far we have been talking about risk the way risk assessors do. To experts in risk assessment, "risk" is a multiplication of three factors: magnitude (how bad is it when it happens), probability (how likely is it to happen), and the number of exposed people. As we have seen, measuring risk is a difficult proposition, and experts do not often agree on the outcome—but at least they agree on what they ought to measure.

Unfortunately, what the experts are busy trying to measure is not really what risk means to most people. If you took a long list of hazards and ranked them in order of expected annual mortality or likely ecosystem damage and then reordered the same list by how upsetting the various risks are to people, the correlation between the two would be very low. In other words, the risks that kill people or damage ecosystems according to the experts are completely different from the risks that upset ordinary citizens, the people who read newspapers and watch television news programs.

To understand why, let's redefine our terms. Let's take what the risk assessor means by risk, magnitude times probability times the number of people exposed, and call it *hazard*. And let's take what the public means by risk, all the things that people are worried about that the experts ignore, and call it *outrage*. This gives us a new definition of risk:

$$\text{Risk} = \text{Hazard} + \text{Outrage}$$

This redefinition suggests a new way to frame the problem of disagreements between experts and the public over risk. The experts, when they talk about risk, focus on hazard and ignore outrage, while the public focuses on outrage and ignores hazard. That low correlation, then, isn't the result of public ignorance or misperception; it is the result of a definitional dispute.

In the research literature on risk communication, there are at least thirty-five variables that show up as what we are calling components of outrage. The following list of ten tend to dominate most controversies over the risks discussed in this book.

⦀ **IS IT VOLUNTARY OR COERCED?**

Consider two ski trips. For the first, you decide to go skiing; for the second, someone rousts you out of bed in the middle of the night, shanghais you to the top of a mountain, straps slippery sticks to the bottoms of your feet, and pushes you down the mountain. The experience on the way down the mountain is exactly the same— sliding down a mountain is sliding down a mountain. Nonetheless, the first trip is recreation and the second is assault with a deadly weapon.

The same distinction applies to community behavior. Imagine two different scenarios for siting a controversial facility. In scenario one, a company comes into town and says: "We're going to put our dimethylmeatloaf factory here, whether you want it here or not. If you don't like it you can move." In scenario two, the company says: "We'd like to put our dimethylmeatloaf factory here, but only if you want it here. If we can negotiate mutually acceptable terms, we'll sign a contract and build the facility. If we can't agree on terms, we won't build it." A voluntary siting process like this second scenario isn't guaranteed to work, of course. A coercive process like the first scenario often fails as well; it is hard to site controversial facilities. What is guaranteed is that under the second scenario the public is going to consider dimethylmeatloaf a lot less risky than under the first scenario. The right to say "no" makes saying "maybe" a much smaller risk.

⦀ **IS IT NATURAL OR INDUSTRIAL?**

A natural risk is much more acceptable than a coerced risk, but somewhat less acceptable than a voluntary risk. It is "God's coercion," and we are all more forgiving of God than we are of regulatory agencies or multinational corporations. A very good example is radon. In northern New Jersey, for example, roughly 30% percent of the homes have enough radon in their basements to represent an excess lifetime lung cancer risk of somewhere between one in a hundred and three in a hundred. That's a huge risk—but most people still will not spend $20 on a charcoal canister to test for radon. If some corporation were going door to door putting radon in people's basements, then they would test—and then they'd sue the company to pay for the monitoring, the mitigation, and the worry. But because it's God's radon, not a corporation's radon—because it's a natural risk, not an industrial risk—it generates enormously less outrage.

||||||| **IS IT FAMILIAR OR EXOTIC?**

The risks that people underestimate are usually familiar risks, while exotic risks provoke more outrage. A beautiful example is the Superfund cleanup. Just as they're about to reduce the hazard of a familiar waste lagoon, the outrage goes through the roof because unknown exotic technologies are introduced. They're sinking high-pressure injection wells; maybe they're bringing a rotary kiln incinerator to the site; people are walking around in moon suits. (Did you ever have anybody knock on your door in a moon suit? "Just testing your drinking water, nothing to worry about.")

||||||| **IS IT MEMORABLE OR NOT MEMORABLE?**

Memorable risks are the ones that linger in our minds. The best source of memorability is personal experience, but a good second-best is the news media, especially television. People who have never been to Bhopal or Chernobyl learned from those two events, via journalism, about the risks of chemical manufacturing and nuclear power. Symbolism is another important source of memorability. The symbol of chemical risks is the 55-gallon drum. The symbol of nuclear risks is the cooling tower. Closely connected to symbolism is the real, but not necessarily harmful, "signal" of risk: an odor, a flare, a particulate residue on cars and houses. These signals may actually be symptoms of something amiss, or they may be irrelevant to hazard. They nonetheless make the risk more memorable, and therefore make the outrage greater.

IS IT DREADED OR NOT DREADED?

All risks are not dreaded equally. Given the same number of deaths, cancer generates more dread (and therefore more public concern, media coverage, and regulatory action) than asthma or emphysema. Contaminated water generates more dread than contaminated air; air generates more dread than food; and food generates more dread than touch. High dread is a nearly universal response to radiation and to waste.

IS IT KNOWABLE OR NOT KNOWABLE?

Knowability is really several factors taken together. The public, for example, worries much more about uncertainty than the experts. But even more frightening than uncertainty is expert disagreement, what Lois Gibbs calls "dueling PH.D.s." One side's expert says, "I eat it for breakfast," while the other side's expert says, "even thinking about it will give you cancer." Another component of knowability is detectability. At the Three Mile Island nuclear power accident in 1979, for example, even journalists were frightened. A reporter who had been through endless wars and hurricanes and other risky situations explained that radiation and cancer are undetectable: "At least in a war, you know you haven't been hit *yet.*"

IS IT CONTROLLED BY ME OR BY OTHERS?

Control is related to, but different than, voluntariness. Voluntariness determines who decides; control, who implements. If your spouse asks you to go to the store for groceries, the trip may not be voluntary—but you're still in control because you're driving. Driving is, in fact, a good example. Eighty-five percent of Americans consider themselves better than average drivers. That's a sizable optimistic bias hooked to control. Agencies and companies typically have two messages for the public in a risk controversy. The first message is, "We're in charge here. Butt out." And the second message is, "Don't worry." It is very hard to disempower people and reassure them simultaneously; the reassuring message gets lost in the outrage generated by the disempowerment.

‖‖‖ **IS IT FAIR OR UNFAIR?**

Probably the most important component of fairness is the distribution of risks as it relates to the distribution of benefits. At a manufacturing facility, for example, the risks—whether they are large or small—are concentrated in the immediate vicinity of the plant gates. Unless local demographics are unusual, the benefits are not similarly concentrated. The people who live near major manufacturing facilities tend to be lower in income and socioeconomic status than the people who live farther away. The neighborhood accurately perceives that the risk is not fairly distributed. That makes the risk a serious outrage, and that, in turn, makes it a serious risk.

‖‖‖ **CAN I TRUST YOU OR NOT?**

Large numbers of people believe that major manufacturing industries are capable of endangering our health, endangering our environment, and lying to us about it—and that the government is either unable or unwilling to stop them. Trust in both industry and government is low. Moreover, people use trust as a stand-in for hazard; they may not be able to tell whether the effluent is carcinogenic, but if plant management has been evasive and untrustworthy, it seems reasonable to assume the worst.

‖‖‖ **IS THE PROCESS RESPONSIVE OR UNRESPONSIVE?**

There are several components of process that are important in determining public outrage—the distinction between openness and secrecy, for example, and the distinction between courtesy and discourtesy. Companies and agencies that apologize for their misbehavior generate less outrage than those that stonewall. Sharing or confronting the cultural values of the audience is also a factor: a plant manager who coaches Little League and goes to PTA meetings has more credibility than one who commutes from out-of-town and sends his kids to private school.

One of the biggest factors is whether the spokesperson for the company responsible for the risk sounds hypertechnical or concerned and responsive. Technical people, by disposition and training, don't much like dealing with "soft" issues that are all tied up in emotions and values. Ordinary citizens, on the other hand, don't much like dealing with technicalities. In a sense it boils down to different approaches to passion. The expert tries to be dispassionate and wants the concerned citizen to be dispassionate too. The citizen, on the other hand, is passionate and expects the expert to be compassionate.

What are the implications for journalists of this hazard-versus-outrage distinction? To start with, the media are not really very interested in hazard, unless it's huge. A one-in-ten-thousand risk, for example, is serious enough to matter greatly to public health experts, but it's not a very good news story. A villainous company or government official would make it newsworthy; a victim (dying and accusing) would make it newsworthy; a controversy would make it newsworthy. In other words, outrage is what makes risks newsworthy.

There are many reasons for reporters typically paying more attention to outrage than to hazard. It is, of course, an easier story to cover, especially if the reporter has relatively little technical training. It's more interesting to readers and viewers (and editors). And the sources of outrage information are far likelier to be available, cooperative, and quotable than technical sources.

This focus on outrage is legitimate. Outrage isn't just a distraction from hazard; it is a real issue in its own right. A community that is exposed to a risk it didn't agree to, doesn't benefit from, and wasn't told about has a right to be outraged—even if the risk is small. A news story that reports an outrage of this sort is a real public service. Outrage, in short, deserves the coverage it gets.

But hazard sometimes deserves more coverage than it gets. It would be a public service as well for journalists to pay more attention to hazard (not less attention to outrage). High-hazard low-outrage risks need the public's attention. And high-outrage low-hazard risks need to be put into context, so that readers and viewers begin to understand that the risks that make people angry or frightened may or may not be the risks that endanger their health and environment.

The main thrust of this book is to clarify the hazard side of high-outrage environmental risks. These risks are heavily covered because they are controversial, that is, because they are significant outrages. The briefs that follow should make it easier to judge and report their hazard.

ⅢⅢ **REFERENCES** ⅢⅢ

Doll, R. and Peto, R. 1981. *The Causes of Cancer.* New York: Oxford University Press.

Higginson, J. and Muir, C. 1979. Estimated carcinogenesis: Misconceptions and limitations to cancer control, *Journal of the National Cancer Institute.* 63:1291–1298.

U.S. Environmental Protection Agency. 1987. Report of the cancer risk work group, *Unfinished Business: A Comparative Assessment of Environmental Problems.*

Wynder, E. and Gori, G. 1977. Contributions of the environment to cancer incidence: An epidemiologic exercise. *Journal of National Cancer Institute.* 58:825–832.

HANDLING AN
ENVIRONMENTAL EMERGENCY
A CASE STUDY IN FINDING SOURCES

The following is a hypothetical incident designed to illustrate how a reporter might use news sources to cover an environmental crisis on deadline. Reporters should be aware that each environmental incident poses its own set of problems and that different approaches may be indicated. One rule of thumb is that reporters should always speak to at least two experts (at least one of whom is not aligned with a vested position) to verify consequences of toxic accidents, because scientists often get conflicting results from the same data.

A call comes into the newsroom late Friday morning from a local resident. He is very upset, but he manages to explain that a large tanker truck has had an accident near a drainage ditch that runs in front of his home. He says that the truck is spilling a foul-smelling liquid into the ditch. He tells the editor he is greatly distressed about possible contamination of the community's seven public wells. The editor hands the story over to the reporter who handles that geographic beat.

The resident informs the reporter that the incident has occurred in the small town of East Cityville, right off the town's main intersection. Telephoning police headquarters, the reporter learns that a policer officer is on the way to the scene of the accident. When the officer reports in to headquarters, the reporter learns that the truck bears a red warning label marked "flammable" with the U.N. code number 2762. The truck belongs to Move for Profit Co., and was dispatched from a chemical company. The police department has decided to evacuate residents to a nearby church.

Calls to the regional office of that state's environmental agency elicit the news that state emergency response personnel have been dispatched to the scene. An hour later, in a subsequent call, the agency spokesperson tells the reporter the Move for Profit truck was carrying the pesticide chlordane. "It's one of the pesticides used in great volume in the United States," says the public affairs officer. "As you know," the officer says, "it's what we used for termites. It's probably under all the homes in this state." He further explains that chlordane should not pose a real airborne hazard unless it is mixed with the wrong substances, which is highly unlikely. But it is acutely toxic in high doses and is a suspected carcinogen, the spokesperson adds. High concentrations in wells would necessitate closing them. Ingestion or skin contact would lead to medical problems.

The spokesperson says he is awaiting reports from the agency representative on the scene before he can determine just how serious the East Cityville spill is.

The reporter next calls the Scientists' Institute for Public Information (800-223-1730), a referral service designed for journalists working on science and environmental stories, and gets the name of a chlordane expert on the staff of a nearby university. Another call is placed to Chemtrec, an emergency information service operated by the Chemical Manufacturers Association (800-424-9300). Chemtrec helps identify U.N. numbers on trucks.

The chlordane expert, a toxicologist, explains that the chemical vaporizes, is not soluble in water (does not dissolve), and can travel through a waterway as a slug of toxic material. In addition, he says, "it certainly is toxic if people come into direct contact with it or ingest it." The reporter asks if it is dangerous to get chlordane on your skin. The toxicologist tells him if some people come into contact with chlordane and it gets onto their skin, they are very likely to be symptomatic and need medical attention. The most common symptoms, the toxicologist reports, are those that affect the nervous system.

It starts off being a depressant, he continues, but it can also be a stimulant. People have been known to go into convulsions, and in very high doses, it's fatal. The journalist asks what the danger is to the city's public well system, which is near the accident scene. The toxicologist tells him that if chlordane accumulates in the well water in substantial quantities and is ingested, there is a concern. If it's only present in a low dose and it's not likely to cause acute symptoms, then there may be some question as to the danger. He says there are some chronic symptoms associated with chlordane involving the liver and possibly the kidneys.

The state will order the wells sealed if levels higher than expected are found, according to the toxicologist.

The reporter leaves to go to the spill site. There, he learns that the 20,000-gallon truck is spilling chlordane, at a rate of 25 to 30 gallons per minute, into a ditch that leads to one of East Cityville's largest streams. The municipal water authority has been notified to divert water intake from the stream. Water authority officials tell the reporter that they are advising residents not to drink or bathe in the water until the state environmental agency can finish its analysis to determine the degree of risk. In the meantime, state police have gotten the environmental agency to divert the stream feed water around the affected area. They believe the on-rush of this water was moving the spill further downstream.

Locating a state environmental agency official at the site, the reporter verifies that the chemical is chlordane and that it was being shipped by the King Chemical Company. King has contracted with Clean Adventure Company to help with the cleanup.

The reporter also engages a federal Environmental Protection Agency (EPA) official in conversation to find out what the federal perspective is on the spill.

Police have evacuated twenty-seven people, the reporter learns. The truck driver and a police officer who slipped and fell into the chlordane spill during his investigation have been taken to Cityville General Hospital.

The reporter finds a telephone and calls in the latest information to his editor. Before heading back to the newsroom, he telephones the hospital's spokesperson, who tells him the truck driver has suffered a concussion and the patrolman is being washed down with soapy water. Back at his desk, the reporter calls King Chemical and finds the president of the company evasive. After several minutes of questioning, the president will confirm only that the product in the truck is a mixture of solvents that was en route to a port for shipment overseas where it would be used for insect control. On advice of counsel, he refuses to make the truck's manifest—the cargo list—available to the reporter. Neither will he let the reporter talk to the chief company chemist.

For additional background, the reporter telephones the state's poison control center where a scientist explains that chlordane is relatively common since it was once used in termite control. However, he is most concerned about the wells and the drinking water because there is an immediate hazard with the sandy soil and the stream. He explains that chlordane does not travel well in water. "It's not too soluble," says the scientist, "so we have found throughout the state it is found in sediment and in fish but not in the water itself. Apparently, it settles down out of the water. If it did reach the water column it would be in the parts-per-billion range because of its relative insolubility. That is the great unknown. What does one part-per-billion mean? Some limited animal testing indicates that chlordane is a potential carcinogen and right now I don't think there's a scientist in the world who could tell you what the part-per-billion contamination rate would mean." He gets additional information from the National Pesticide Telecommunications Network at Texas Tech University (800-858-7378).

Another reporter is dispatched to the church where evacuees have been taken. She interviews a number of residents, including the elderly and mothers with children. One resident complains, "I don't see why they have to use these small rural roads to bring these convoys of big trucks through here. They should be using the main highway." Another resident volunteers that there have been problems before with trucks coming down this rural road, with spills and near-spills, but never of this magnitude. The reporter makes a mental note to check this with the police and in the newsroom files.

A third resident, active in the local chapter of the Sierra Club, tells the reporter the club has been trying to restrict chemical-laden trucks to the main highways.

The first reporter returns to the spill site and, confronting state environmental officials, finds out that King Chemical is now telling the state that the substance is 40 percent chlordane and 60 percent formaldehyde, a flammable solvent. He consults the National Institute for Occupational Safety and Health's *Pocket Guide to Chemical Hazards* and determines that formaldehyde is an irritant which affects the skin, eyes, and respiratory system. Officials say they are not as worried about the formaldehyde threat as they are about the chlordane.

By now, the truck has been righted and the spill stopped. The state has determined that 5,000 gallons have spilled, most of it into the ditch. The reporter mentions that the spill site is six miles from the reservoir and asks officials whether those 5,000 gallons will settle out before they reach the reservoir. State officials respond that they do not think the chlordane will travel even a quarter mile.

A water resource specialist from the state is present and he tells the reporter that six dikes have been erected in the stream to contain the chlordane. But chlordane has also leaked into some duck ponds outside of East Cityville. The water resource official says the state fish-and-game department has rescued the ducks from pond sites and is studying them. Clean Adventure Company is removing the substance from the water and putting it into a containment truck as fish-and-game officials fence off the area to keep wildlife out. Spying fish-and-game officials fencing off the area, the reporter corners them and finds out that several hundred striped bass have died in nearby ponds. The reporter wants to know how far the ponds are from the city water supply and learns that they are six miles away. Officials are emphatic that people must avoid fishing in these ponds until Clean Adventure can drain them and remove the silt and residue from the bottom and haul it away in barrels.

Back at the newsroom, the editor decides the second reporter should contact a national environmental group for a different perspective on the chlordane spill. She contacts the Natural Resources Defense Council (NRDC) in New York (212-949-0049) and is told that if the chlordane gets into Cityville's major water supply, "there is the possibility that a continuing amount of chlordane could show up in the drinking water." The NRDC says that the EPA has put out a health advisory recommending a maximum of eight parts per billion in drinking water. The reporter is told to find out what the state is doing to make sure the cleanup is effective.

The NRDC also says that it is interested in knowing what is

being done to clean up the soil so that children in neighborhoods around the spill are not going to be absorbing chlordane through their skin. Once chlordane gets in the soil, it apparently remains there a long time because it bonds with soil particles. The reporter is informed there is no good way to get chlordane out of the soil, the contaminated earth itself must be removed. Removal experts will not have to dig far below the surface, the reporter is told, because the chemical does not move very fast or very far.

The NRDC impresses upon the reporter the seriousness of communicating the problem to her audience. "I think it is serious," an NRDC official says. "Chlordane was widely used for so long. The EPA banned it because tests done by the Food and Drug Administration found that 99 percent of the meat supply had measurable residues of chlordane or its by-products. It was also found in human tissues. Every time someone is subject to an autopsy or surgery, a little sample is taken and the government keeps a registry. They found that virtually the entire U.S. population has measurable amounts of chlordane or its metabolites. Chlordane is a carcinogen in one animal species, and that's a red flag for possible threat to human beings."

The reporters are on deadline now and the story has to be written. Angles to cover for the second day include interviewing people who were exposed and finding out how they were decontaminated, how their homes were decontaminated, what officials are advising the people who breathed the chlordane mix to do next, and how the hospital dealt with the situation. Reporters should find out when the people will be allowed to return to their homes and what is being done to keep the area secure. Other questions to ask of the state environmental agency are whether a health study will be done and if monitoring wells are going to be sunk to track the underground path of the chlordane.

Concentration should be on the long-term effects on the drinking water supplies, especially in other cities that get their water from the East Cityville stream where the spill occurred. Reporters can contact geologists to find out if there is a large aquifer beneath the East Cityville public wells which also might have been contaminated. Contact can also be made with private regional watershed associations, which monitor water resources and development in the East Cityville area. If there is a local epidemiologist at the university, he or she may be asked about genetic implications of long-term exposure.

The reporter should contact Clean Adventure Company to determine where the chlordane was taken after it was removed from the stream and where the water that was pumped out of the ponds will go. Questions should also be raised about the final destination of the chlordane-contaminated soil.

There could be follow-up stories on the environmental history of the principal players, Clean Adventure, Move for Profit, and King Chemical. Perhaps the state environmental agency has had problems with one of them. The municipal government of East Cityville should be reached and asked if it intends to move against King Chemical on legal grounds.

Stories about companies or institutions that have been involved in an environmental controversy can be challenging. While some may not lead very far, others can prove to be very productive, especially when the reporter considers all possible angles of the story.

BRIEFS

ACID RAIN

Few recent issues are as complicated as acid rain. It epitomizes the intersection of public health and environmental sciences, politics, economics, ethics, and law in decision making. It may or may not be an extremely serious long-term environmental problem, and it may or may not seriously exacerbate respiratory problems.

|||||| IDENTIFYING THE PROBLEM ||||||

Acid rain occurs when combustion by-products from power plants, smelters, and motor vehicles (including aircraft) react chemically with air and water in the presence of sunlight to form mineral acids, which are washed out of the atmosphere by rain. Acidic chemicals come from nature as well as air pollution.

Sulfur dioxides and nitrogen oxides are the chemicals primarily responsible for acid rain. Most of the sulfur dioxide comes from the burning of coal or oil in power generation and industrial processes. Nitrogen oxides are present in automobile exhaust and emissions from burning processes. In the atmosphere, sulfur

|||||| This article is based on an earlier version by Liz Fuerst, Department of Journalism and Mass Media, Rutgers University, in the first edition of *The Environmental Reporter's Handbook*. Additional comments were received from Jed Waldman, University of Medicine and Dentistry of New Jersey–Robert Wood Johnson Medical School and Leonard Lapatnick of Public Service Electric and Gas Company. ||||||

dioxide and nitrogen oxide are converted to sulfuric acid and nitric acid, respectively. If present in large amounts, these acids cause the rain or snow to become acidic.

Acid rain is only one form of acid deposition, which can be wet (rain, snow, sleet, fog, or dew) or dry. Dry deposition occurs when gases or dry particles contact surfaces at the ground.

A common measure of acidity is pH, with pH values ranging from 0 (most acidic) to 14 (no acidity, an alkaline solution) with 7 being neutral. The lower the pH, the more acidic the solution. Even when the air is clean, rain water is slightly acidic with a pH of 5.6. This is because carbon dioxide, a natural part of air, forms a weak acid in water. Under certain conditions, natural emissions from such phenomena as volcanic eruptions, which emit sulfur, may control the acidity of rain. Acid rain is rain or snow that has a pH below 5.6. It should be noted that alkaline chemicals above 7 are hazardous as well. The acidity of rain depends on the type and amount of gases and particles present in the air.

Acid rain is a big political issue largely because the sources and the victims are often in different places. Since pollutants can travel great distances before depositing, it is difficult to pinpoint the exact sources of pollutants contributing to acid rain in a particular area. In North America, deposition usually occurs to the north and east of the source because of prevailing winds on the North American continent. For example, emissions from the industrialized Ohio River Valley states, including Missouri and Tennessee, are carried east and north toward New England and Canada. This situation often has resulted in people taking strong stands, that is, pitting *your* industry/jobs/economy against *my* health/ environment.

Acid rain is much less of an issue on the West Coast because there are no upwind sources of acid gases for thousands of miles. Here, the major cause is automobile exhaust. However, some of the largest sulfur-emitting generators are located in the West and Southwest, and there has been a great deal of controversy, including some in Mexico, over the impact these generators have on visibility in the Grand Canyon and other scenic areas.

Acid rain poses several environmental and health problems. One is the effect of the acidity itself. Highly acidic water can kill fish and make water undrinkable. The other is that acid in rainwater increases the rainwater's ability to leach heavy metals out of the soil. Thus, by the time acid rain makes it to a river or lake, it is not only too acidic, but it is also carrying more hazardous pollutants than it would have normally picked up if it were not acidic. Sensitive areas in which the waters already have become acidic are in Canada, New England, and New York's Adirondack Mountains as well as lakes in Wisconsin and Minnesota, the Pacific Northwest, and the Pine Barrens in New Jersey, which is naturally acidic.

There is conflicting evidence of the effect of acid rain on forests and crops. Because of the complexity of a forest, it may take years to determine the effects of acid rain on it. However, some research shows that, over time, acid rain can remove some important nutrients from the leaves or soil around trees. Acid rain is a prime suspect in the decline in forest growth in the Black Forest in Germany. In the United States, acid rain is a suspected cause of the lack of forest growth in the eastern United States and the acid neutralizing capacity of sensitive soils in the West, including the Cascade Mountains in Washington and the Colorado Rockies. Several factors affect the sensitivity of forests and crops to acid rain, including the amount of rainfall, the makeup of the soil or sediments, the geology, and way land is used.

There is increasing concern about the possible effects of dry acid particles (the seeds for acid rain) on human health. Some sulfates and nitrates that do not combine with rain, sleet, or snow may float back to earth as "acid dust." Some research shows there may be a link between breathing these particles and some lung diseases.

There is concern about the possible effect of acid rain on the quality of drinking water. Water for human consumption should be in the pH range 6-9. Acid rain may dissolve toxic metals from the soil and contaminate water supplies. In addition, acidic water can leach copper and lead from pipes made with these materials. This is less of a concern in areas served by public water supply systems, where metal contamination and acidity can be monitored and controlled. It is a greater concern in rural areas where private water systems are used and people are unaware of the quality of the water they drink.

|||||| CORRECTING THE PROBLEM ||||||

Studies have shown that effects of acid rain on lakes and forests can be reversed when the sources of the acid are reduced. Several approaches have been applied. Many utility companies have installed taller smokestacks that are capable of ejecting emissions higher into the atmosphere. This has satisfied local air-quality standards, but it has not addressed the long distance spread of acid deposition.

The federal Clean Air Act of 1970 required all new power plants to install scrubbers to cut down on sulfur dioxide emissions. Scrubbers—equipment using wet lime or limestone—remove much of the sulfur before it can be emitted. While scrubbers are effective, they are also very expensive. For older plants, with relatively short remaining life-spans, the costs of installing scrubbers may be excessive. Consequently, some older plants have chosen to use cleaner, low-sulfur coal as a less costly alternative to the use of scrubbers. But there are problems associated with low-sulfur coal. Because it is mined primarily in the western part of the country, transportation costs are higher; and because it is found in arid places, strip mining is the norm, and reclamation is difficult.

While this approach is directed toward industry, others (e.g., Warren Brooks) have suggested another approach. Rather than installing scrubbers on smokestacks, they suggest neutralizing an acidic lake by simply adding lime or other alkaline substances. They point out that water companies adjust the acidity of drinking water all the time. Of course, this would not solve the heavy metal problem or the forest and crop problems.

The 1990 amendments to the Clean Air Act placed additional limits, designed to further reduce emissions of sulfur dioxide, on coal-burning power plants. The amendments required 111 power plants in 22 states to reduce emissions to specified levels by 1995 and all utilities to meet an even stricter standard by the year 2000. They also required reductions of nitrogen oxides in tailpipe emissions levels in new cars starting with the 1994 model year; and in all cars by 1996.

New coal-burning technologies are helping to keep the lid on sulfur emissions. In a technique called fluidized bed combustion, a mixture of powdered coal and limestone is fed into a furnace where jets of air suspend the particles as the coal burns. The calcium in the limestone combines with sulfur in the coal to form calcium sulfate, a harmless dry waste product. There are more than forty of these boilers in the United States. Another technique used to remove sulfur involves the conversion of coal to clean burning gas and is called gasification.

ⅢⅢ **PITFALLS** ⅢⅢ

ⅢⅢ Reporters should not go out to cover a story on acid rain without keeping in mind two important controversies. First, there is disagreement with regard to the seriousness of the acid rain problem. Second, there is disagreement over how to best approach the problem (i.e., make the rain less acid or neutralize the lake).

ⅢⅢ When calculating pH, remember that the scale is logarithmic, meaning that a change of one point represents a tenfold change in acidity. For example, if a lake shows an acidity of pH 5, that is ten times more acidic than a reading of pH 6. The lower the reading, the more acidic the contents.

ⅢⅢ The tendency has been to blame utility companies for the problem. But as sulfur emissions have been reduced over the years, nitrogen oxide has become a greater part of the acid rain problem. The major source of nitrogen oxide emissions is motor vehicle exhaust not energy-producing facilities. Furthermore, emissions of this compound are more evenly distributed around the country than are sulfur dioxide emissions.

ⅢⅢ Acid rain affects many parts of the United States, not just the Adirondacks, Maine, New Hampshire, and Massachusetts. Acidification of streams and lakes can be taking place in local communities. Check with municipal and county environmental commissions and watershed associations.

ⅢⅢ **SOURCES FOR JOURNALISTS** ⅢⅢ

ⅢⅢ States' environmental agencies usually have an Office of Air Quality.

|||||| The U.S. Environmental Protection Agency is a good source for figures on emissions.

|||||| The Environmental Defense Fund, 257 Park Avenue South, 16th Floor, New York, New York 10010; 212-505-2100.

|||||| The Natural Resource Defense Council, 40 W. 20 St. New York, New York 10011; 212-727-2700.

|||||| The Acid Rain Foundation, Inc., 1410 Varsity Dr., Raleigh, North Carolina, 27606-2010; is 919-828-9443

|||||| *The Acid Precipitation Digest* is a publication of the Center for Environmental Information, Inc., 46 Prince St., Rochester, New York 14607; 716-271-3550.

|||||| The National Coal Association represents that industry's side in the acid rain debate. Its address is 1130 17th St. N.W., Washington, D.C.; 202-463-2625.

|||||| The Clean Coal Technology Coalition is an ad hoc group of utilities and coal companies that wants to promote new technologies in the field. Its address is 1050 Thomas Jefferson St. N.W., Suite 700, Washington, D.C. 20007. Its telephone number is 202-342-3368.

|||||| National Research Council. 1990. *Haze and the Grand Canyon: An Evaluation of the Winter Haze Intensive Tracer Study.* Washington, D.C.: National Academy Press.

|||||| Office of Technology Assessment. U.S. Congress. 1984. *Acid Rain and Transported Air Pollutants: Implications for Public Policy.* OTA-0-204, Washington, D.C.

AIR POLLUTION (INDOOR)

Exposure to indoor pollution produces a range of possible effects, including lethargy, headache, dizziness, eye irritation, respiratory problems, cardiovascular problems, and, in some cases, death. In most cases, however, indoor air-quality battles are about feeling sick, not about dying. Scientists estimate that secondary tobacco smoke and other household products cause 3,500–6,500 cancers, and radon another 5,000–30,000 lung cancers, annually. When compared to press coverage of chemical emergencies, outdoor air and water pollution, indoor air pollution gets much less coverage than it deserves.

|||||| IDENTIFYING THE PROBLEM ||||||

Indoor air pollution is the accumulation of substances within the home, workplace, or public space to such a degree that they can become a threat to human health. Some types of indoor air pollution are caused by vapors or particles given off by combustion, insulation, personal care and household cleaning products, solvents, or paint. Still other types are caused by substances from outdoors which migrate inside. Finally, many people are allergic to

|||||| This brief was based on information provided by Dr. Paul Lioy of the Exposure Assessment Measurements Division of the University of Medicine and Dentistry of New Jersey–Robert Wood Johnson Medical School. Additional comments were provided by senior attorneys at the Environmental Law Institute and Hugh Toll of Hoffmann–La Roche. ||||||

pollens and animal dander, which are airborne and concentrated in furniture and rugs.

Overall indoor air quality (IAQ) is often poorer than outdoor air quality. This is partly because structures concentrate contaminants that dilute or spread out-of-doors. With no winds to disperse them, indoor contaminants can occur in concentrations up to one hundred times greater than out-of-doors. This effect is compounded by the fact that most people spend more of their time inside, especially those most vulnerable—the sick, babies, and the elderly. Furthermore, there are many pollutants whose source is indoors. The problems of indoor air quality are not confined to factories. In fact, many homes and offices have worse indoor air quality than factories.

Sources of indoor air pollution include radon and asbestos, found especially in older homes and buildings in such products as insulation, vinyl floor tiles, and cement. [See the briefs on "Asbestos" and "Radon (Indoor)."] Lead in paint and in dust tracked in from the outside is another serious indoor air contaminant. Huge battles over de-leading homes and buildings loom on the horizon, making de-leading the "asbestos" reaction of the 1990s. (See the brief on "Toxic Metals.")

Primary and secondary (or passive) cigarette smoke contain carbon monoxide, tar, and nicotine. A 1990 University of California at San Francisco report, prepared for the U.S. Environmental Protection Agency, that summarized the research, concluded that the effects of cigarette smoke among nonsmokers included as many as 32,000 heart-disease deaths annually.

Other indoor contaminants include combustion products from gas stoves and poorly vented furnaces. Chemicals used in consumer and building products can be sources of poor indoor air quality. Formaldehyde, for example, common in resins used in wallboard, furniture, paneling, and certain types of insulation, can cause eye irritation, lethargy, and dizziness. It may also be carcinogenic. The growth of microbial contaminants such as spores and bacteria in poorly ventilated areas is another source of indoor air pollution.

"Sick building syndrome" is a term applied to a variety of pollution problems inside buildings where people work. The National Institute for Occupational Safety and Health (NIOSH) analyzed over five hundred studies of sick buildings and found that their problems fell into three categories: inadequate ventilation, chemical contamination, and microbial contamination. IAQ is more often attributable to multiple sources than to a single source. The phrase sick building syndrome is used to describe buildings that have poor air quality from a variety of sources. Typical symptoms include headaches, nausea, drowsiness, and eye, nose, and throat irritation.

||||| CORRECTING THE PROBLEM |||||

Inadequate ventilation is most often the culprit in situations of indoor air pollution. Many homes and offices have poor ventilation, partly because of energy conservation measures that have been taken to insulate buildings, partly because of overcrowding in some areas, and partly because of poor maintenance. For example, many homeowners fail to change or clean the filters on their air conditioners. Then, while keeping them on recycle instead of vent (to avoid cooling hot outdoor air), they concentrate whatever pollutants are present in ever-staler, but nice-and-cool air. In fact, it is often easier to solve an IAQ problem with improved ventilation, than it is to diagnose the pollutant.

It is no accident that labels on paint thinners and other substances direct usage in a well-ventilated area only. Without the frequent interchange of air—called the turnover rate—particles and vapors in a structure become trapped and pose a health hazard. Over-insulation, while cutting down on heating or cooling bills, prevents fresh air from seeping in, causing occupants to breathe stale, contaminated air. Many local building codes have a requirement for minimum ventilation rate.

To avoid nitrogen dioxide contamination in the home, clothes dryers must not be vented back into the residence for heat exchange unless the appliances are equipped with a specialized device.

To avoid exposure to formaldehyde, people should allow new wallboard to air outside before being brought into the building.

Radioactivity from decaying radium or uranium can be curtailed in a variety of ways, most of which involve being vented to the exterior. To reduce plant pollens and animal allergens, people should consider eliminating rugs, not having pets, and using air conditioning.

To avoid "sick buildings," they should be carefully inspected, regularly maintained, and designed better in the first place.

||||| **PITFALLS** |||||

||||| The core task for the reporter in an IAQ controversy is to find out what is thought to have caused the problem, then to determine [a] whether scientists think the substance is likely to cause that problem, and [b] what else might cause it.

||||| In cases of indoor air pollution, consider the impact of out-of-doors pollution and vice versa. Outside contaminants such as sulfuric acid from smokestack emissions may be seeping inside. Likewise, neighbors of an industrial facility or a Superfund site may attribute to external causes a myriad of negative health effects that are, in fact, caused by IAQ problems.

||||| The typical IAQ *problem* is low-level illness brought about by inadvertent, but essentially voluntary, exposures—poorly ventilated houses with poorly maintained furnaces, for example. Often the problem is missed entirely or attributed to something else (like a nearby factory or "allergies"). But there are two typical IAQ *controversies*, both involving an involuntary exposure. One is the individual or family with serious health problems; the other is the large group (workers in an office building, for example) with modest health problems. In both cases, people look for a cause and find a suitable culprit in the new carpet, or a new paint job, or the insulation in the walls. It is always possible that the assigned culprit is really guilty; it is also quite likely that we simply do not know and cannot find the real cause of the problem. Reporters, therefore, must walk a fine line between paying enough attention to noncontroversial IAQ problems, while bringing enough skepticism to bear on high-controversy IAQ battles.

||||| Don't draw conclusions based on complaints of only one per-

son. Try to check with a large sampling of people. Be sure to check with neighbors and other tenants in an office building to determine whether a complaint of suspected indoor air pollution is an isolated one or whether it may be part of a cluster. Dizziness, for example, may be caused by paint thinner in a basement, by smog seeping in from the outside and affecting large numbers of people, or by any of a host of other things. Make sure you talk with health and safety officials directly involved in the investigation.

ⅢⅢⅢ Occasionally, an IAQ problem explodes into a major confrontation. In such high-visibility controversies, the problem is likely to be exaggerated and is often misdiagnosed. A homeowner with very serious physical symptoms after painting the house may believe that volatile organic compounds in the paint are responsible; workers at an overcrowded office building may believe all their health complaints are caused by new carpeting. These charges are usually unprovable and probably unfounded. On the other hand, smaller but still serious IAQ effects are well-established—and usually ignored. It is important for journalists to understand the paradox. IAQ is probably responsible for a huge amount of undiagnosed "malaise," "colds," "allergic reactions," and the like and is probably not responsible for the occasional devastating illnesses of which it is accused. The point is, big controversies are likely to lead to exaggerated public impressions of a risk that, in most other circumstances, gets far too little attention.

ⅢⅢⅢ SOURCES FOR JOURNALISTS ⅢⅢⅢ

ⅢⅢⅢ Experts on indoor air pollution can be found through NIOSH, EPA, the National Institute of Health Sciences, and state departments of health. The U.S. Consumer Product Safety Commission is a good place to obtain information on indoor air pollution. Also try trade organizations like the Chicago-based Gas Research Institute for information on natural gas.

ⅢⅢⅢ Local health departments are the first agencies, usually, to check out complaints of indoor air pollution in the home or workplace. Department investigators may install sampling devices to check the interior air in a home or public place. Filters are then collected from monitors and the residue weighed and analyzed to determine the type and degree of exposure to pollutants. Water samples may also be taken from wells and basement seepage.

|||||| HAZARDOUS HOUSEHOLD PRODUCTS ||||||

The following products are considered hazardous by the U.S. Environmental Protection Agency because they are toxic, reactive, corrosive, or flammable. Information about household waste is contained in "Subtitle D Study Phase I Report," the U.S. Environmental Protection Agency's Office of Solid Waste and Emergency Response, October 1986.

These products also pose a threat as chronic indoor pollutants. Based on limited monitoring of American homes, scientists estimate 1,000–2,500 additional cancer deaths per year due to long-term exposure to common household products.

|||||| HOUSEHOLD CLEANERS

disinfectants
drain openers
general purpose cleaners
oven cleaners
toilet bowl cleaners
wood and metal cleaning agents and polishes

|||||| HOME MAINTENANCE PRODUCTS

adhesives
paints
paint removers and strippers
paint thinners
stains, varnishes, and sealants

AUTOMOTIVE PRODUCTS

air-conditioning refrigerants
body putty
carburetor and fuel-injection cleaners
general lubricating fluids
grease and rust solvents
oil and fuel additives
radiator fluids and additives
starter fluids
transmission additives
waxes, polishes, and cleaners

LAWN AND GARDEN PRODUCTS

fungicides or wood preservatives
herbicides
pesticides

MISCELLANEOUS

batteries
electronic items
fingernail polish remover
photo-processing chemicals
pool chemicals

ASBESTOS

Scientists estimate that 1,000–10,000 Americans die each year from the legacy of work-related asbestos exposures. Most were exposed during the period 1930–1960, when there was little regulation. Exposures have dramatically decreased during the last decade. But occupational and public exposures to airborne asbestos, when they occur, are a major health risk. The combination of asbestos exposure and tobacco smoking is particularly hazardous.

|||||| IDENTIFYING THE PROBLEM ||||||

Asbestos is a fibrous natural mineral characterized as being durable, waterproof, and fireproof. It is known to be present in about three thousand manufactured products, including roofing and insulation materials in schools and other public buildings. Asbestos has been used in car brake linings and other friction products. It was commonly used in the building construction and shipbuilding trades. For the past ten years, asbestos has been absent from nearly all building materials and has been eliminated from most consumer products.

|||||| This brief is based on information provided by Irving Selikoff, M.D., director, Environmental Science Laboratory, Mt. Sinai School of Medicine, The City University of New York with additional comments from Howard Kipen, Department of Environmental and Community Medicine, University of Medicine and Dentistry of New Jersey–Robert Wood Johnson Medical School and Paul Arbesman of Allied Signal. ||||||

Little is known about the effects of asbestos when ingested. But when submicroscopic fibers are inhaled, they can cause harm in two ways.

Scarring of the lung, also known as *asbestosis* is one in a general category of dust-related diseases called pneumoconioses. In Greek, *pneumon* means lung; *konis* means dust. Asbestosis is a restrictive lung disease. Similar diseases can result from inhaling other types of dust. One, "black lung," is common to coal miners. Scarring is caused by the inhaled dust and results in diminished lung capacity with related shortness of breath and possible eventual suffocation.

Cancers, such as *mesothelioma* and *lung cancer,* are another way in which asbestos fibers can cause harm. Mesothelioma is named for the mucous membrane lining of the chest—the mesothelial lining, where tumors are likely to develop. This type of cancer can also affect the lining of the heart and abdomen. It is usually preceded by asbestosis and is almost always fatal. Cancer of the lung is also caused by asbestos. There is controversial evidence of increased risk of cancer of the esophagus, stomach, colon, rectum, oro-pharynx, larynx, and kidney. A person exposed to asbestos may develop both asbestosis and one of the cancers. Both diseases have a latency period of twenty to thirty years or more. This means that the illnesses people are getting now result from asbestos exposures of decades ago—exposures that are rare today.

Other environmental and personal habits can increase the risk of developing cancer associated with asbestos exposure. For example, smoking greatly enhances respiratory cancer production.

There are six major types of asbestos fiber, and they vary in their hazard. Some scientists argue that the risk associated with chrysotile (white asbestos) is less than the risk associated with amphibole asbestos fibers. Asbestos-related diseases occur in proportion to the magnitude and length of exposure. In scientific terminology, this is a linear dose response. There is no established threshold for a safe level of asbestos exposure. Because amphibole asbestos tends not to break down in the body and stays in the lung area, even a small dose over time may be lethal.

The lethal capacity of asbestos in general has been widely recognized since the early 1960s. However, some scientists suggest it was recognized in the early 1900s. The key court battle involving asbestos took place between workers and their families and a manufacturer of asbestos—a company that was then called Johns-Manville (later called the Manville Corporation). The case hinged on what was known about the risks involving asbestos and when it was known. The court decided that Manville executives in the 1930s knew, or should have known, that asbestos was an occupational hazard, and, therefore, allowed workers' and workers' families' claims. As a result, the company went into bankruptcy. It emerged—no longer in the asbestos business—with the asbestos victims as its largest stockholder block, with several representatives on its board, and a huge claim on its profits. Today, asbestos victims essentially run the company, trying to earn the profit with which to pay the victims' claims. This represented one of the key legal decisions in the country about a company's responsibility for "due diligence" in protecting workers' and the public's health.

Today, Manville manufactures fiberglass, another fiber used in insulation, and the company has once again become a major player in a new controversy involving questions about the safety of fiberglass. Like asbestos, fiberglass is made up of long, thin, fibers that can be inhaled into the lungs where they may cause scarring and cancer. But there are key differences—fiberglass tends to break cross-wise instead of lengthwise, so the fibers are likelier to be less long and less thin—making them harder to breathe in and easier for the lungs to eject. Fiberglass, apparently, is also easier for the lungs to absorb than asbestos; the fiber itself is less durable.

Studies of animal inhalation have so far failed to produce fiberglass-related cancers. Epidemiological studies on fiberglass workers are ambiguous, in part because fiberglass workers in the old days were usually also asbestos workers. Animal implantation studies, on the other hand, have shown that a fiberglass fiber can cause cancer—if it is implanted, as opposed to inhaled.

Because of the implantation studies, several government agencies and international research bodies have listed fiberglass as a possible or probable human carcinogen. Because of the mostly negative inhalation studies and ambiguous epidemiological studies, fiberglass is not tightly regulated. However, the trend is toward more regulation and more controversy. While it is probably safer than asbestos, it is not absolutely safe, especially if blown into walls rather than used in batts. Because of the connection to asbestos—fiberglass is a similar sort of fiber, used in similar ways, and produced by some of the same companies—this may make fiberglass a bigger issue than the data justify.

Asbestos may be found in water as well as in the air. Sources of asbestos contamination include natural mineral deposits and asbestos cement pipes in water distribution systems.

‖‖‖‖‖ CORRECTING THE PROBLEM ‖‖‖‖‖

The U.S. Environmental Protection Agency regulates asbestos in the environment and in manufactured goods. It recently banned the use of asbestos in asbestos-cement pipe and fittings, in roofing and flooring felts, in vinyl asbestos floor tile, and in fireproof clothing. These items, as well as previously banned consumer patching compounds and artificial emberizing compounds that release asbestos fibers, can no longer be sold. Asbestos use in all other products is to be phased out over a seven-year period. Asbestos is listed as a "hazardous air pollutant" in the 1990 Clean Air Act, requiring EPA to set emission standards. It is also listed on the EPA's "community right-to-know" list. The EPA is setting standards for removal of asbestos in public schools. The Occupational Safety and Health Administration (OSHA) regulates workplace exposures. The OSHA limits in workplace air are currently set at 2 fibers/cm³. Proposed OSHA limits are 0.5 or 0.2 fiber/cm³. The asbestos level in public water supplies is regulated by the EPA at 7 million fibers/ liter exceeding fiber lengths of 10 microns.

School and other public officials must check construction records of public buildings to determine whether asbestos has been used as an insulator. Most state environmental agencies have a division that deals solely with asbestos detection and testing. If asbestos is friable, meaning that it is flaking or otherwise coming apart, it may pose a threat to human health if people are exposed and must be either contained or removed. The hazard can be reduced if the friable asbestos is encapsulated or encased in a tough, impermeable plastic coating. Removal is preferred by the public and is usually accomplished by firms certified to do business in the state. The removed material is then hauled away to specified waste sites.

FUNKY WINKERBEAN   BY TOM BATIUK

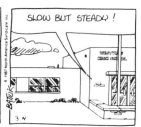

If asbestos is present, but not friable, it may be less hazardous to leave it in place undisturbed. Asbestos has been removed from thousands of American schools during the last five years as a result of federal and state legislation. Some of these efforts were poorly done, resulting in highly publicized cases of school closings and greater exposure to asbestos dust. Asbestos dust should always be removed upon demolition of a building.

Many people think that the EPA overreacted to asbestos. The EPA pushed the issue to the point at which thousands of school districts and managers of public buildings felt they had no choice but to mitigate—in the absence of evidence of friability and in the absence of competent mitigators. Some EPA officials now privately admit that they wished the agency had moved more slowly. Asbestos is bad in the air (which means, inevitably, in the lungs)—but it is not necessarily bad when wrapped around pipes or in the walls.

Today there is a lot of poor asbestos removal being done—do-it-yourself removal by homeowners and removal by unlicensed or untrained removal companies. The result can be—and often has been—a serious health hazard. The process of removing asbestos can put many more asbestos fibers into the air than were there in the first place, especially if the asbestos is not friable (e.g., asbestos tiles). This is why an air test for fibers is critical after any removal or encapsulation effort.

⦙⦙⦙⦙⦙ IMPORTANT POINTS FOR RESEARCHING A STORY ⦙⦙⦙⦙⦙

⦙⦙⦙⦙⦙ The risk *is* airborne fibers measured in fibers per centimeter of air; asbestos in nonfriable form is not a risk until it becomes airborne (or until people start touching it, hacking through it, etc.).

||||| Find out the source of asbestos exposure (where it is located) and the condition of the material containing asbestos.

||||| Determine the frequency and length of exposure.

||||| Remember, for purposes of measuring the amount of asbestos in water, the measurement is in fibers per liter.

||||| See whether the exposure has been reported to governmental or regulatory agencies. It is crucial to learn whether the material will be removed, encapsulated, or left alone. If it is to be removed, find out where it is going and if the transportation is adequate. Are carriers and routes good? If it is being left in place, find out the plan to monitor the asbestos to make sure it does not become friable.

||||| In exposures involving occupational settings, find out whether a respiratory disease and cancer study has been done of the potentially exposed group.

||||| Check to see if residential owners are hiring asbestos detection services, especially for homes built prior to 1960.

||||| Check the credentials and training of asbestos remediators.

||||| Check to see what the air measurements are after remediation. When there are doubts about measurements, a different company than the one doing the remediation can take measurements.

||||| See also the briefs on "Air Pollution (Indoor)" and "Occupational Exposure to Toxic Chemicals."

||||| **PITFALLS** |||||

||||| Reporters frequently write that fibers look like asbestos before the fibers are tested. Because the term asbestos scares people, before you report an asbestos problem make sure the substance is, in fact, asbestos. The term asbestos refers to a class of magnesium aluminum silicate compounds that are usually classified as amphibole or serpentine crystalline varieties.

||||| Although most schools and community buildings have been

checked for asbestos, don't assume automatically that a private company is negligent because it has not determined the presence of asbestos in its buildings. Asbestos monitoring is done by very few private companies and remediation plans require careful thought in addition to proper planning and budgeting.

|||||| Remember, it is equally important to measure air quality before *and* after remediation.

|||||| Demolitions or fires at an older building are likely to have asbestos implications. For example, walls lined with asbestos pose a problem when fire departments axe through them in a fire or when demolition companies tear them down. These are situations in which the fibers are going to get into the air and the risk, therefore, is worth taking seriously.

|||||| SOURCES FOR JOURNALISTS ||||||

|||||| Information on asbestos can be found at the Centers for Disease Control and Prevention in Atlanta, the National Institute for Occupational Safety and Health, the Occupational Safety and Health Administration, and other state and federal health and environmental agencies.

|||||| Because of the volume of legal actions generated by asbestos-related claims, it might be useful to check for experts at law schools and state bar associations. Court records are excellent sources of information on asbestos. In addition, labor organizations may be valuable contacts if they represent workers once exposed to asbestos. The Asbestos Information Research Coalition in Washington, D.C. (202-659-8550), and the Asbestos Institute in Montreal, Canada (514-844-3956), are affiliated with the asbestos industry. They will provide current scientific data. The TASCA Assistance Information Services in Washington, D.C. (202-554-1404) provides general information about asbestos. Manville, in Denver, Colorado, is another unique source of information given their past history and current ownership.

|||||| Regulations governing asbestos in water and methods for testing water are outlined in the *Federal Register* (January 30, 1991). The EPA Safe Drinking Water Hotline is a source of general information (800-426-4791).

AUTOMOBILES AND POLLUTION

Automobiles are the single most ubiquitous cause of pollution discussed in this volume. They contribute to air, noise, land-based (soil), and water (due to run-off) pollution.

|||||| **IDENTIFYING THE PROBLEM** ||||||

S ince World War II, the number of cars and trucks in the world has multiplied tenfold. Automobiles contribute heavily to air pollution; they account for more air pollution than any other human activity. Pollution from automobiles comes not only from smoking exhaust pipes, but also from the crankcase, carburetor, and gas tank. Because the automobile is familiar, and because people need and love their cars, we often underestimate their contribution to pollution.

Cars produce many types of pollutants. They are responsible for a substantial proportion of atmospheric exposure to carbon monoxide, nitrogen oxides, volatile organic compounds, and, in urban areas, suspended particulate matter. Atmospheric organic compounds and nitrogen oxides derived from auto emissions also contribute significantly to the formation of ozone. (See the brief on "Ozone.")

|||||| Comments on this brief were received from Jed Waldman of the University of Medicine and Dentistry of New Jersey–Robert Wood Johnson Medical School, Cliff Weisel of the University of Medicine and Dentistry of New Jersey–Robert Wood Johnson Medical School, Hartmut Kurzke of Degussa Corporation, and Robert Farrauto of Engelhard Corporation. ||||||

Carbon monoxide is a colorless, odorless gas found in car exhaust. It is formed when a car's fuel (gasoline, for example) does not burn completely. In the body, carbon monoxide prevents blood from carrying oxygen. Low levels may put a strain on people with respiratory diseases and heart problems. High levels can cause dizziness, headaches, clumsiness, and eventually death. Nearly 90 percent of carbon monoxide in the United States is produced by automobiles.

Carbon dioxide is another colorless, odorless gas found in car exhaust. It poses no direct risks to health. However, it is a major contributor to the process of atmospheric global warming. (See the brief on the "Greenhouse Effect.") Levels of carbon dioxide have increased 25 percent since the Industrial Revolution.

High temperatures in the engine combine oxygen with nitrogen to form the nitrogen oxides in car exhaust. Nitrogen oxides, in combination with hydrocarbons, form ground-level ozone in the presence of sunlight. Nitrogen oxide can damage lung tissue, worsen lung conditions such as asthma, and reduce the body's resistance to lung infections. More than half of the nitrogen oxide in the United States comes from automobiles. (See the brief on "Ozone.")

The incomplete burning of fuel in a car also causes the release of hydrocarbons. Hydrocarbons are also released as gasoline vapors at the pump. More than 50 percent of hydrocarbon emissions in the United States come from automobiles. Hydrocarbons react in sunlight with nitrogen oxide to form ground-level ozone. Ozone is a major ingredient in smog. It is a strong irritant to the eyes, lungs, and breathing passages. It is especially harmful to people with respiratory problems. (See the brief on "Ozone.")

Particulates are small bits of solid and liquid matter released from car exhaust. They can be toxic compounds themselves. In addition, other toxic and radioactive materials can attach themselves to particulates.

Benzene is used as an anti-knock compound in all gasolines. It is the only compound in gasoline that is a known carcinogen. Studies have linked benzene exposure to various blood diseases including leukemia. (See the brief on "Benzene.") Dose-response levels are not clear. Benzene is emitted when gasoline is pumped, and it is also found in noncombusted gas released from car exhaust systems. During the last twenty years, the levels of benzene in gas have been reduced from approximately 5 to 10 percent to 1 to 2 percent.

Two auto-emission problems that have been eliminated are chlorofluorocarbons or CFCs and lead. CFCs have been used as coolants in car air conditioners. They destroy the upper ozone layer that shields the earth from the sun's harmful ultraviolet rays. Installing or recharging a car air conditioner can release up to 2.5 pounds of CFCs. Under 1990 amendments to the Clean Air Act, CFCs will soon be out of auto air conditioners. However, the effects are still with us, and it will be decades before the ozone layer recovers from the effects of CFCs.

Lead is a toxic metal that can cause brain and nerve damage. Cars using leaded gasoline were the second largest source of lead pollution at one time (after lead paint). Today, lead is banned in gasolines. However, it is going to take a long time to get rid of the lead dust it has already put into the air. (See the brief on "Toxic Metals.")

|||||| CORRECTING THE PROBLEM ||||||

Automotive exhaust emissions from burning fuels are controlled by catalytic converters located in the exhaust system so that all exhaust gases pass through them. Catalytic converters change the carbon monoxide and hydrocarbons produced by incomplete fuel combustion into carbon dioxide and water. Catalytic converters were installed on all gasoline-fueled automobiles in the United States in 1975 to meet the standards of the 1970 Clean Air Act. Further improvements were made with the three-way converter, adopted in 1981 to meet the federal 1-gallon per mile nitrogen oxides standard. Catalyst and engine manufacturers are now making further improvements to meet new standards established under amendments to the 1990 Clean Air Act. Beginning in 1994, many diesel trucks sold in the United States will be equipped with catalytic converters to abate particulate emissions.

Despite improvements, many environmentalists claim that the internal combustion engine is doomed. The electric car is one alternative. Under the 1990 amendments, car manufacturers must begin to offer "zero-emission vehicles" for sale. By 2003, 10 percent of vehicles sold will have to emit no pollution. Electric cars are the only "zero-emission vehicle" we have and automakers around the world are pouring money into the development of electric cars. Electric motors do not spew the chemical by-products of burning gasoline that produce smog. General Motors has developed the Impact, a prototype electric sports car with a top speed of more than 100 mph and acceleration from 0 to 60 mph in eight seconds. Critics of the electric car have said that if the cars themselves do not pollute, the power plants that produce the electricity certainly do. Proponents respond that unlike gas-driven cars with which every one is a source of pollution, pollution generated by the electric car will be produced at a particular point, a generating station. There emission controls will be easier.

Use of mass transit and car pooling are two methods of reducing pollution from automobiles. Unfortunately, use of both strategies has been declining in the 1990s. According to recent census data, approximately 87 percent of the American population drove to work alone in 1990, up from 80 percent in 1980.

The 1990 Clean Air Act amendments imposed tighter restrictions on car exhaust. The amendments also mandated less volatile gasoline. They identified key pollutants emitted at the tailpipe and set targets for reducing them. They also required reductions in tailpipe emissions of hydrocarbons and nitrogen oxides and installation of more durable pollution control equipment on all new cars starting in 1998. In addition, automakers were required to equip automobiles with onboard diagnostic controls that ensure proper functioning of the pollution control equipment.

Under the amendments, states must require gas stations to install refueling controls called Vapor Recovery Nozzles on gas pumps. These nozzles capture the gas vapor that normally escapes when the tank is filled. This vapor adds hydrocarbons into the air, which contributes to the ozone problem. Other regulations call for the use of gas that is less volatile (i.e., less likely to evaporate during the summer). Some states require the use of leakproof fiberglass or stainless steel underground gas tanks. Old tanks that leak must be replaced. (See the brief on "Water Pollution.")

The amendments also call for oil companies to develop alternative, cleaner burning kinds of gasoline. Methanol and ethanol are two alternative fuels that would reduce the emission of many pollutants. However, methanol and ethanol may pose other risks.

California has written even stricter clean-air guidelines than those imposed by federal clean-air standards. The plan adopted by California will eventually require cars to run on alternate fuels like natural gas, methanol, and electricity. The California plan also phases in tighter controls on hydrocarbons and nitrogen oxides. Congress gave California the right to make its own rules to comply with federal clean-air standards. The other forty-nine states are allowed to follow the national program or adopt California's program. Delaware, the District of Columbia, Maine, Maryland, Massachusetts, New Hampshire, New Jersey, New York, Pennsylvania, Rhode Island, Vermont, and Virginia have agreed to use the California plan. Together they have formed the Northeastern States for Coordinated Air-Use Management.

||||||| PITFALLS |||||||

||||||| While new, less polluting fuels such as methanol and ethanol would reduce the emission of some pollutants, they would increase emission of other pollutants. Electric cars would transfer the burden of pollution to power plants. In other words, alternative fuels are not a panacea.

||||||| While a smoky exhaust pipe is an important source of pollution, the crankcase, carburetor, and gas tank contribute up to 40 percent of a car's pollution.

||||||| While less than 5 percent of the current fleet of automobiles in use are old out-of-tune cars, these cars are responsible for most of the uncontrolled automobile pollution.

||||||| Though automobiles continue to be a major source of air pollution, major improvements have occurred during the last two decades. Lead has been taken out of gasoline. Carbon monoxide and hydrocarbon emissions have been lowered by a factor of more than ten since passage of the Clean Air Act in 1970. However, reductions in nitrogen oxide (related to the ozone problem) have only been reduced by a factor of 3 or 4. In addition, most improvements in emissions have been offset by increases in the number of cars on the road and increased mileage resulting from longer commutes.

||||||| People resist efforts to regulate their lifestyles in the interest of air quality. In the interest of maintaining our individual

mobility, we often prefer to attribute pollution to industrial behavior rather than accepting our role in the problem. As a result, car-pooling laws, for example, have mostly failed. It is a tribute to the seriousness of the health hazard presented by cars that we have made serious efforts to reduce automotive air pollution—not by restricting driving but by requiring changes in car design and fuels. In fact, the government would prefer to take on the oil companies and car manufacturers than go against the American love affair with cars. Journalists, too, are vulnerable to the same tendencies—wanting to avoid confrontation over lifestyle issues. And yet journalists can perform a service by overcoming these biases and presenting a more complete understanding of the problem along with solutions that are directed at the individual, industry, and government.

|||||| SOURCES FOR JOURNALISTS ||||||

|||||| The American Lung Association (both the New York office and state offices) is a good source of information. The New York office is located at 1740 Broadway, New York, New York 10019; 212-315-8700.

|||||| The state agency for environmental protection usually has an office or bureau of air quality.

|||||| The EPA has an Office of Air Quality Planning and Standards located in Research Triangle Park, South Carolina; 919-541-5615.

|||||| The Safe Energy Communication Council, 1717 Massachusetts Ave., N.W., Suite LL-215, Washington, D.C. 20036; 202-483-8491.

|||||| U.S. Department of Transportation has a Public Affairs Office for National Public Highways Traffic Safety. It is located at 400 7th Street S.W., Washington, D.C. 20590; 202-355-4000.

|||||| The Air Pollution Control Council, P.O. Box 2861, Pittsburgh, Pennsylvania 15230, is another source of information. Its number is 412-232-3444.

|||||| The Natural Resource Defense Council is located at 122 E. 42 St., New York, New York 10168; 212-949-0049.

BENZENE

Benzene potentially poses a health problem as an indoor air pollutant or groundwater contaminant as well as an occupational hazard. However, no one can accurately estimate the extent of the risk. Benzene is probably not as serious a threat as asbestos and indoor radon exposure. Nevertheless, it should be pursued whenever there is evidence of major and sustained exposures. Scientists believe that someday they will be able to explain why some people are sensitive, and others are not sensitive to benzene, if they can explain the mechanisms by which benzene produces its toxic impacts. This understanding is important because eliminating benzene would have a seriously deleterious impact on the economy.

IIIIII IDENTIFYING THE PROBLEM IIIIII

B enzene is a volatile hydrocarbon liquid that is both an essential industrial chemical and a hazardous air pollutant. It is present in crude oil and in light petroleum derivatives such as solvents and gasoline. It is a normal product of the combustion of organic materials, and thus it is found in such things as cigarette smoke and auto exhaust. People can be exposed to benzene while

IIIIII This brief is based on information supplied by Robert Snyder, Department of Pharmacology and Toxicology, College of Pharmacy, Rutgers University with comments from James Hildrew of Mobil Oil Corporation. IIIIII filling the gas tank or cleaning paint brushes. As a result, benzene in low concentrations is universally distributed through the human environment. Because everyone is involuntarily exposed to some extent, knowledge of its toxicity is important.

For a century, benzene has been used commercially as a quick-evaporating solvent for rubber, producing rubber coatings, and rubber cement, and recently has found a place in the production of the plastic polystyrene. In small amounts, benzene is also used as an anti-knock compound in gasoline.

Historically, industrial overexposure to benzene vapors has had disastrous effects on human health. In the early 1900s, three young female cannery workers in Baltimore died after exhibiting symptoms that included extreme fatigue and hemorrhage. Using rubber cement in a small, unventilated room, they had worked at gluing lids to tin cans. Autopsies performed by doctors at Johns Hopkins University revealed that the women's normal bone marrow had disappeared and been replaced by fat and scar tissue. This condition is known as aplastic anemia. Scientists duplicated the rubber cement exposure and found that animals exhibited the same results. A decade later, the same condition was prevalent among rotogravure press workers exposed to colored printing inks that contained benzene, and in the 1940s and 1950s, large numbers of cases of aplastic anemia and leukemia were diagnosed in Italy among shoe factory workers who used rubber cement in their work. Overexposed workers in an Ohio rubber film production plant during World War II suffered a similar fate.

Adverse effects from benzene exposure may be acute or chronic. Acute effects from short-term exposure include headaches and dizziness. Chronic effects are related to the absorption of benzene in the bone marrow. This inhibits production of white and red blood cells and platelets. As these symptoms become manifest, a form of leukemia (acute myeloid leukemia) or aplastic anemia may develop.

The most common route of exposure to benzene is inhalation, because benzene vaporizes so easily. However, it is possible for groundwater to become contaminated by gasoline that has spilled or leaked from storage tanks. In such circumstances, drinking water supplies may contain benzene and closely related substances.

ⅢⅢ **CORRECTING THE PROBLEM** ⅢⅢ

Benzene is listed as a "hazardous air pollutant" in the amendments to the 1990 Clean Air Act, requiring the U.S. Environmental Protection Agency to set emission standards. The EPA has also established standards for benzene levels in drinking water and criteria for ambient fresh-water and saltwater. The maximum contaminant level in drinking water is 5 mg/L, but current regulatory limits are conservative. For the vast majority of the population, these limits can probably be regarded as safe levels, with a slight margin of error. While benzene in surface water readily evaporates into the atmosphere, it is a long-term contaminant of groundwater because it cannot evaporate underground, and since little microbial activity occurs in underground water, it does not break down.

The Occupational Safety Health Administration (OSHA) limits in workplace air have been set at 3.3 mg/m³. Short-term (5 minute) limits have been set at 16.5 mg/m³. Industries, such as those involved in coke production and the manufacture of plastics, petrochemicals, steel, and rubber, are trying to minimize occupational exposures to benzene through environmental controls and other means, and to limit environmental emissions. Land disposal of benzene products is prohibited under the Resource Conservation and Recovery Act (RCRA) of 1984. Benzene is also on the EPA's "community right-to-know" list.

Since benzene is an important component of oil-based paints and solvents, using substitutes for these products can reduce emissions and exposures. While a little "elbow grease" is more labor intensive, it is an effective substitute for paint removers. Local efforts to conduct hazardous-waste roundups of household products such as paint, oil, and gasoline cans help limit the dumping of these products into landfills. The EPA recommends commercial incineration as a suitable disposal method.

ⅢⅢ **IMPORTANT POINTS FOR RESEARCHING A STORY** ⅢⅢ

ⅢⅢ Determine the degree and duration of exposure, and evaluate its significance. How many people are implicated?

ⅢⅢ Identify the source of the benzene, who is responsible for it, what the remediation alternatives are, and how much they will cost.

ⅢⅢ Check to see what other sources of benzene affected persons may be exposed to on a regular basis.

ⅢⅢ See the brief on "Automobiles and Pollution."

ⅢⅢ PITFALLS ⅢⅢ

ⅢⅢ Benzene is ubiquitous in our environment: virtually everyone is exposed to it in low concentrations. One should not assume that all benzene exposures come from industrial sources. Smokers are known to carry elevated levels of benzene in their breath.

ⅢⅢ Do not automatically assume all benzene exposure will necessarily result in leukemia or aplastic anemia.

ⅢⅢ SOURCES FOR JOURNALISTS ⅢⅢ

ⅢⅢ When writing about benzene spills, contact state and federal health and environmental agencies, including the National Institute for Occupational Safety and Health. Labor unions that represent steel and petrochemical workers may be good sources. Trade organizations such as the American Petroleum Institute (202-682-8000) and the Chemical Manufacturers Association (202-887-1100) are other sources of technical information. University departments of environmental medicine and toxicology are other possible sources of information. Also check with the local chapter of the American Cancer Society for information on benzene-related leukemia.

ⅢⅢ Agency for Toxic Substances and Disease Registry. 1987. *Toxicological Profile for Benzene*. Washington, D.C.: U.S. Public Health Service.

BIRTH DEFECTS

Some environmental scientists believe that birth defects and low birth weight babies are associated with exposure to environmental contaminants. However, it has been difficult to establish the relationship because few reliable birth defect registries exist and because of confounding by smoking, drugs, alcohol abuse, and other behavioral risk factors.

IIIIII IDENTIFYING THE PROBLEM IIIIII

Birth defects are anatomical or biochemical abnormalities that are present at birth. They include cleft palate, dwarfism, underdeveloped limbs, spina bifida, and internal anomalies. Although many kinds of birth defects are apparent immediately, some manifest themselves only later in life.

There are two basic causes of birth defects: genetic changes and teratogenic changes.

IIIIII GENETIC CHANGES

These are present at conception, either inherited from a parent or represent a random or spontaneous change. Genetic changes are the result of a failure to transmit correct genetic information and can occur in three ways: aneuploidy, clastogenesis, and mutagenesis.

IIIIII This brief was written by Joan E. Siederer, an independent consultant in Issquah, Washington, with additional comments from Dorothy Warburton, College of Physicians and Surgeons, Columbia University. IIIIII

|||||| Aneuploidy—a gain or loss of a whole chromosome. Down's syndrome is a result of an additional chromosome and is also referred to as Trisomy 21.

|||||| Clastogenesis—microscopic addition, deletion, or rearrangement of the parts of a chromosome. This can result in mental retardation.

|||||| Mutagenesis—mutagenic changes (also called point mutations) are small changes in the DNA sequence. These can result in congenital malformations, mental retardation, and syndromes with variable ages of onset. Mutagenesis has environmental causes. However, the cause and effect relationship between radiation and various industrial chemicals and mutagenesis is controversial. Possible outcomes from exposure include failure to conceive and miscarriages. Men, as well as women, can be affected by exposures. For example, males with occupational exposure to some organic solvents have exhibited low sperm counts, abnormal sperm, and varying degrees of infertility.

|||||| **TERATOGENIC CHANGES**

A teratogen causes a malformation of a normal fetus while it is developing in the uterus. For example, ingestion by the mother of certain drugs like thalidomide can result in a deformity of the fetus. Consumption of alcohol by the mother can cause mental retardation in the fetus. Diethylstilbestrol (DES) has been shown to cause reproductive cancer in female children of women who ingested it.

Some characteristics of teratogenic effects are:

|||||| Sensitivity of developing embryo—any detrimental effect produced by exposure to a teratogen during the embryonic stage of development. Developmental toxicants can produce adverse effects on the developing organism at exposure levels that are not severely toxic or dangerous to the mother. One example would be alcohol or drug exposure at low dosages.

|||||| Importance of time and dose of exposure—developing organisms undergo rapid and complex cell changes in a relatively short period of time. Susceptibility to teratogens varies during the span of developmental stages—the pre-implantation, embryonic, fetal, and neonatal periods. Exposure to teratogens at certain stages in

prenatal development may be more harmful than at other points in the developmental process. The duration and timing of exposure predict the damage. It is not possible to generalize about the mechanisms of change teratogens take. Each agent appears to operate uniquely.

ⅲ CORRECTING THE PROBLEM ⅲ

At the level of the individual, pregnant women can avoid the risk of certain birth defects by avoiding the activities that have been known to cause them. Cigarette smoking by pregnant women has been found to cause low birth weight (itself a major risk factor for increased mortality and morbidity) but not birth defects. It is recommended that other products like caffeine and alcohol be consumed in moderation or not at all.

Prenatal diagnoses are made so that fetuses with severe birth defects can be aborted if the parents so choose. Some birth defects can be diagnosed by testing samples of the amniotic fluid to determine the fetus' genetic make-up. Other means of detection include using ultrasound techniques and maternal blood tests.

Some women are at higher risk than others for a particular birth defect. Women older than 35 are at increased risk for giving birth to children with Down's syndrome. Women age 40 or older have a 1-in-100 chance of bearing a Down's syndrome child, compared to a 1-in-1,000 chance for women under 25.

On a societal level, regulation of occupational and community exposure to potential mutagens and teratogens is important for reducing the risk of possible birth defects. Community and worker right-to-know laws have been valuable in making people aware of potential dangers from materials they work with or that may be used in manufacturing locations within their communities.

ⅲ PITFALLS ⅲ

ⅲ Reporters often confuse the distinction among carcinogens, teratogens, and mutagens. The same substance can be all three, or one, or two. It is possible that a substance is established as one and suspected of being another. It might be a strong carcinogen but a weak mutagen. Making the distinction can be difficult. The Ames test for mutagenicity in bacteria and cells is often used as a rough measure of carcinogenicity in humans. It serves as a useful screening test, but there are cases of false positives as well as false negatives.

ⅢⅢⅢ Birth defects are studied much less than carcinogenesis. Often there is no evidence either way—because there has been little effort to collect the evidence. In stories on possible carcinogens, reporters should be sure to ask what is known about birth defects. In stories about birth defects, do not accept "no evidence of risk" as equivalent to "no risk" without asking what research has been done.

ⅢⅢⅢ If you are tracking a story, determine how many cases have been reported and get federal or state officials to estimate the population size, the birth-population size, and expectancy of miscarriage or birth defect rate. Miscarriages and birth defects occur more regularly than one might think. For example, one in seven pregnancies ends in a miscarriage, the death of a fetus before it is fully developed. It is important not to automatically associate reports of miscarriages and birth defects with exposure to chemicals or to some other public health threat.

ⅢⅢⅢ Do not jump to conclusions. Those directly involved in the miscarriage or birth defect are likely to provide important leads about problems, and they should not be ignored. However, confirmation should be sought from uninvolved third parties.

ⅢⅢⅢ If there is exposure to chemicals, be sure to quantify it. If you are dealing with a radiation leak, be sure to get normal, daily background radiation levels for comparison.

ⅢⅢⅢ Be sure alarm is really over birth defects—not symptoms related to exposure. Exposure symptoms, even in infants and children, are not necessarily birth defects. For example, at Love Canal in upstate New York, infants and children seemed to have frequent nosebleeds and headaches, but while these may have been exposure-related, they were indeed not birth defects. The distinction is whether the children were exposed or the parents. Parental exposures (including exposures while pregnant) lead to birth defects. Of course, children and parents might be exposed, and both sets of problems could exist at the same time.

|||||| There are birth defects clusters just as there are cancer clusters. Many of the problems in investigating cancer clusters apply to birth defect clusters—false clusters, coincidental clusters, uncertain clusters, and clusters probably due to lifestyle but attributed to industry. Reporters and headline writers should not draw conclusions that have not been substantiated by sound scientific studies. Review the brief on "Cancer Cluster Claims" that describes how disease clusters are investigated.

|||||| Occupational exposures to teratogens have raised difficult questions about equal opportunity employment. If a particular job involves teratogen exposure, can an employer restrict the job to men in order to protect possibly pregnant female employees? Current law holds that the employer is liable for the risk but forbidden to control for the sex of workers; it is, therefore, obligatory to eliminate the teratogen exposure, even though there are many workers (males) not at risk.

|||||| SOURCES FOR JOURNALISTS ||||||

|||||| The federal Centers for Disease Control and Prevention (CDC) in Atlanta has a birth defects section which collects and disseminates information. Its direct line is 404-488-4967.

|||||| The University of Connecticut Medical Center, in Farmington, Connecticut, maintains a Pregnancy Exposure Risk Line to answer questions about exposure to materials with possible adverse effects. In Connecticut, the phone number is 800-325-5391; out-of-state, 203-679-1501.

|||||| Other sources of information include state health departments, the Food and Drug Administration (FDA), and the National Institute for Occupational Safety and Health (NIOSH).

‖‖‖ Local March of Dimes chapters and genetic clinics at hospitals and medical schools are important sources for news of research.

‖‖‖ Support groups for parents of children with particular birth defects can be located through the social services departments of most hospitals.

‖‖‖ Determine whether there is a geneticists' task force in your state which meets periodically to discuss birth defects problems. Start with a university genetics department and follow up with contacts in the pharmaceutical industry.

‖‖‖ In some cases, journalists may want to review medical journals for reports on contemporary research. In the 1960s, U.S. journalists brought the story of thalidomide in England and Australia to the attention of U.S. regulators after groups of pediatricians noticed a greater than normal occurrence of a rare birth defect involving limb deformity.

CANCER CLUSTER CLAIMS

Apparent cancer clusters frighten the public and, therefore, are routinely covered by the media. Most journalists are frustrated in their efforts
to build a story because cancer cluster investigations take a long time to
conduct and results are almost always inconclusive.

|||||| IDENTIFYING THE PROBLEM ||||||

"Cancer cluster" describes a situation in which there are
more cases of cancers within a short period of time,
for a small group of people, or in a small area than
would be expected from comparative state and national cancer
rates. For example, twenty cancers of a particular type are found in
a town where only six would be expected if the town had the same
cancer rate as its state or region. The cluster usually occurs within
a specific area, which can be as small as a single block or as large
as a county. When cases of the same type of cancer occur at
approximately the same time as well as in the same place, it is
called a time-space cluster.

Clusters have a focal point—a school, religious meeting place,
common water source, factory, or other location. Finding the focal
point is vital to the search for the cause. Moreover because there
are more than two hundred types of cancers, finding that eight of

|||||| Comments on this brief, written by Michael R. Greenberg, were provided by
Ellen Silbergeld of the University of Maryland for the Environmental Defense
Fund and Leonard Lapatnick of Public Service Electric and Gas Company. ||||||

ten cancers discovered in a neighborhood are the same type is strong evidence of a cluster. A finding that most of the cases are among a specific subpopulation is further evidence that a cluster exists. For example, a finding that eight of ten cancers among young high-school students are leukemias is much stronger evidence of a cluster than a finding of six different types of cancer among an entire community population. It must be remembered that cancer is a common disease, with many causes, including genetics.

|||||| **CORRECTING THE PROBLEM** ||||||

About fifteen hundred annual requests are made to state agencies in the United States for cancer cluster investigations. More than three-fourths of these requests end with a phone conversation and/ or a letter from the health department to the caller. This occurs because of very limited resources and the great expense involved in conducting a complete investigation. A health department can spend a lot of money investigating possible clusters that are very unlikely to lead to a definitive identification of a cause, or it can miss a few that are truly there and spend its resources on activities with a much higher likelihood of benefiting public health.

In determining whether to conduct a scientific investigation, health departments consider five factors:

1. How likely is there to be a cluster?
2. How serious is it if it is there?
3. How verifiable is it—that is, even if it is there, is the kind of cancer common enough and the population large enough that we can find it?
4. How big is the budget for cancer cluster investigations, and what other demands are being made on that budget?
5. How much political pressure is the community putting on the agency?

All are valid considerations.

There is no single protocol for investigating a cluster, but the process normally starts with verification of the cluster's existence. This is a labor-intensive process of reexamining records of mortality (death certificates) and incidence (found in state registries), talking to people with the disease, and checking with area attending physicians and coroners. The goal of this first step is to make sure the diseases have been accurately diagnosed and reported. Having verified this, scientists then determine the probability that the number of cases found could have occurred by chance. They do this by comparing them with the number that would be expected for a similar population in the state or nation. If misdiagnoses and inaccurate reporting have inflated the numbers, or if the number of cases observed is not higher than would be expected, scientists may chose to go no further.

Statistics, of course, have limits. If one in a thousand people normally gets a particular type of cancer, a neighborhood of two hundred people would normally expect no cases, or possibly, by coincidence, two cases. If, however, there are six cases, something is probably wrong. But if there is one case, it is not valid to conclude that 1/200 is five times 1/1,000 and, therefore, a cluster. It is important to keep in mind that unlikely things happen and are more likely to be noticed when one examines many communities. For example, if there is nothing special causing cancer in a given area, it is still possible to look at twenty kinds of cancer in ten communities—that is, at the distribution of two hundred cancer cases—and, by definition, one in twenty, or ten of the two hundred, will be statistically significant at $p < .05$. Given the large number of situations involving suspected clusters reported to the health department, they must make some important decisions as to which ones merit further investigation.

Therefore, in the first stage, the questions are whether the cluster is present and, if present, whether it has occurred by chance. If a true cluster is found, and the state government has sufficient financial and personnel resources, researchers will embark on the major project of finding the cause. This second stage of the investigation involves the search for all the possible causes. One component of this research may be a community survey in which detailed questions about the home, workplace, and recreational environments are asked to find common risk factors. Many studies stop here because investigators are unable to isolate a possible explanation or hypothesis for further research.

However, if the initial research does produce a working hypothesis, the study picks up momentum. If, for example, air pollution is a suspected cause, researchers will try to determine if the source is local pollutant-producing smokestacks, occupational exposures to chemicals such as benzene, or lifestyle exposure such as passive tobacco smoke. In addition, researchers will try to determine the likely dose-response relationship.

Having found a likely source, during the third stage of the investigation, researchers survey a comparison population or control group—persons similar in age, race, and sex to the affected group but having, say, different lifestyles, attending different schools, or drinking from a different water supply. This is called a cohort study. Only about 3 percent of requests for investigation lead to such in-depth cancer cluster field surveys.

‖‖‖ **IMPORTANT POINTS FOR RESEARCHING A STORY** ‖‖‖

‖‖‖ If diseases are assumed to be caused by community exposures to water, find out where the municipality or neighborhood gets its public water and whether it is near a hazardous-waste dump site or pollution source. If the cause is assumed to be air contamination, look at local pollutant-producing smokestacks.

‖‖‖ Find out whether clusters could be caused by common habits such as smoking, nutritional deficiencies, or occupational exposures.

‖‖‖ Evidence for the presence of a cluster is much more compelling if there is a known connection between the specific kind of cancer that is occurring in statistical excess and the kind of cancer your source is known to cause.

‖‖‖ There is an important distinction to be made between incidence and prevalence. The incidence in a given area of a particular type of cancer, for example, refers to the number of *new* cases of this type of cancer that were diagnosed during the present year. Prevalence refers to the cumulative total of cases of this type of cancer that currently exist in an area. Therefore, those who have died from the disease in the past are not part of the calculation used in either prevalence or incidence. Deaths due to a particular type of cancer constitute the mortality rate. In most cases, therefore, prevalence is larger than incidence because it includes cases diagnosed in previous years (but excludes those who have since died). The prevalence rate for breast cancer will be much higher than the incidence of new cases diagnosed each year. Reporters need to find out whether the cancers under investigation are cancer deaths and if not deaths, whether the cases were diagnosed during the year or whether they were diagnosed ten years ago. Knowing when the cancer actually occurred is key.

⁞⁞⁞⁞⁞ If a cluster is being investigated and researchers have not reached any conclusions, ask about methods used for the investigation.

⁞⁞⁞⁞⁞ Occasionally, officials have not heard about supposed clusters. Journalists should share what they know with researchers.

⁞⁞⁞⁞⁞ When officials know about supposed clusters but have not investigated, determine why there has been no investigation. Often the bottom line is a lack of budget since cluster research is labor-intensive. News stories may help the government find money for the research. Sensational stories, however, may cause panic.

⁞⁞⁞⁞⁞ **PITFALLS** ⁞⁞⁞⁞⁞

⁞⁞⁞⁞⁞ Most clusters are reported by community residents, so it is not unusual that some reporters write stories based only on this anecdotal evidence. Health surveys conducted by citizens are not worthless but neither are they a replacement for surveys conducted by trained health officials. If a story is based on data gathered by citizens, it should describe the limitations of such surveys and focus on the need for government studies. Use disclaimers where necessary.

⁞⁞⁞⁞⁞ Journalists should be careful about whom they consult for an "expert" opinion. Always verify the credentials of "experts." An advanced academic degree does not necessarily make someone an expert in a particular cluster investigation or in epidemiology.

⁞⁞⁞⁞⁞ Reporters and headline writers should not draw conclusions that have not been substantiated by sound scientific studies. Keep in mind that cluster studies rarely reach definitive conclusions about cause. This does not mean that local officials are incompetent or are covering up to protect polluters, nor does the failure to reach definitive conclusions mean that the problem is not real and that citizens are hysterical. Usually it simply means that the problem is too small to measure conclusively—even though it may be big enough to take seriously. Cluster investigations are hard, expensive, and *usually* inconclusive. (Which is why the reporter should consider whether one is worth doing every time there is a claim.)

|||||| In writing a story, consider whether there was exposure and whether there are alternative explanations to the one offered. These factors should not only go into the story, but they should also go into the decision as to how big to play the story. This is especially true when writing stories about neighborhoods affected by hazardous-waste dump sites.

|||||| Reporters should find out from the state or local health department how many cancers were found and how many would have been expected by chance. Often more cancers are found than would be expected to occur by chance, but the excess is not called a "statistically significant" cluster because the number is too small. A lack of statistical significance does not necessarily mean that a cluster is not real. It is appropriate to report the number of cancers observed, the number expected, and the fact that the results were not statistically significant because of a small number of cancer cases.

|||||| Agency unresponsiveness should not be confused with health risk; both deserve coverage, but a good risk story avoids treating one as a symptom of the other.

|||||| A news story can generate pressure and, thus, get a cluster investigation going. This can be good or bad, depending on the other factors that health departments must consider in making a determination as to whether or not to conduct a scientific investigation. (See above under Correcting the Problem for a list of these factors.) If there are much worse problems elsewhere in the state, and if the suspected prob-

lem is not really there, is not serious if it is there, or if it cannot be measured regardless of its presence, forcing an investigation is not a public service.

‖‖‖ Although this brief has focused on cancer clusters, many other chronic and infectious diseases can appear in clusters. For example, influenza and AIDS cases normally cluster in time and space. When a cancer cluster is suspected or found, ask about clusters of birth defects, low birth-weight babies, and other health outcomes that can be associated with the same type of exposures that produce cancers. *In other words, do not focus only on clusters of cancer.*

‖‖‖ SOURCES FOR JOURNALISTS ‖‖‖

‖‖‖ Local, county and, especially, state health departments should know what clusters are being investigated. Physicians who practice in the community, hospital administrators, and academic researchers are also sources of information but beware. They also may have strong opinions about causes but these should not be presented as facts unless there is hard evidence that they are more than speculations. Do not be fooled into thinking that evidence is "hard" when it is not. Assumptions can be fatal to credibility.

‖‖‖ Technical information can be gleaned from epidemiologists and academicians at nearby universities. State health departments are the best source of information in most states. But about half of all states have minimal programs and will not be able to help.

‖‖‖ U.S. Department of Health and Human Services, Public Health Services, Center for Disease Control and Prevention, *Guidelines for Investigating Clusters of Health Events*, MMWR 1990; 39 (No.RR-11). Massachusetts Medical Society, C.S.P.O. Box 9120, Waltham, Massachusetts 02254–9120; $3.00.

CHEMICAL EMERGENCIES

Chemical emergencies such as the accident at Bhopal and other large-scale chemical fire and explosion emergencies are significant hazards. Most of these emergencies pose a sizable acute risk to a small number of people right where they happen, and a smaller chronic risk to larger numbers of people close by. However, except for those living in the adjacent vicinity, they pose a smaller threat to public health than does asbestos, radon, and other indoor air pollutants, smoking, alcohol, and drug abuse. In fact, most fatalities connected with chemical emergencies are not chemical-related, but the result of related accidents (e.g., trucks crashing and people falling off scaffolding at emergency sites). Chronic public health risks like smoking are covered less widely by the media because they are less exciting, visual, and unusual.

IIIII IDENTIFYING THE PROBLEM IIIII

A warehouse catches fire, releasing toxic chemicals into the air. A tanker truck carrying chemicals fails to negotiate a turn on a country road and flips on its side, the contents start to pour out into a nearby stream. A freight train derails and a chemical tanker car begins to leak. These are the makings of a chemical emergency. Covering such an emergency can be difficult

IIIII This brief was written by James Ross, supervising program development specialist, Office of Site Safety and Health, Division of Publicly Funded Site Remediation, New Jersey Department of Environmental Protection and Energy. Additional comments were provided by Peter Hannak of Union Carbide. IIIII for many reasons: the scene is often tense and hectic, emergency personnel at the scene may not yet know the risk, and unfamiliar technical jargon is often used by emergency response teams.

The identity of the facility or transportation company is usually evident. A description of what material is involved may or may not be. Company representatives can provide the information but very rarely do because of the uncertainties of the legal consequences. If a state has enacted right-to-know legislation requiring all hazardous materials to be inventoried and recorded in an easy-to-find fashion, then the state or county health department more than likely has information on the material involved in the emergency. But even without right-to-know laws, state disclosure acts, licensing permits, and even zoning requirements may provide the needed information.

Information on what chemicals are involved can be found in several ways. For chemical emergencies occurring at a facility, toxic release inventories (TRIs) are the best key. For transportation accidents, the best sources are the U.S. Department of Transportation numbers displayed on the vehicle or held by the driver. These numbers identify the chemical being transported. For example, trucks carrying gasoline will have a placard with the DOT number and hazard class (DOT 1203-gasoline, hazard class number 3, flammable liquid).

Determining the effects of the material is more complicated. Finding out whether a material is toxic, explosive, or corrosive is usually easy because there are simple tests for these designations. For emergencies, short-term acute effects are the important parameter. Long-term health and environmental effects, such as groundwater pollution, cancer, and birth defects, depend on the situation. Days after the accident, even after all the information is collected, experts may disagree about the effects. If there is disagreement, reporters have to start asking detailed questions to pin down the disagreement.

The type of accident can give important clues to the kinds of effects to expect. In transportation accidents, the spill usually, though not always, stays close to the accident site. The toxic material may be highly concentrated, but is usually confined to a small area. The potential for environmental damage is severe, but the risk to human health is relatively low. Often there is an acute risk for those present and a chronic risk for those nearby. In the case of a factory fire involving chemicals, the toxic material is spread over a much larger area in a lower concentration, increasing the public health risk. Fumes from both chemical fires and spills may require evacuation of downwind residents.

Responders to a chemical emergency—and that includes journalists who wish to get close to it—often must wear protective clothing and use self-contained breathing apparatus. Equipment and training is to be provided by the employer. In most instances, a respirator, protective suit, gloves, boots and hood cost under $200. National distributors of these items are Mine Safety Appliance Equipment Co., ARAMSCO Safety Equipment Co., and Scott Air-Pack Company.

Decontamination takes place when the emergency is declared over. Tyvek plastic protectors worn over full-scale protective suits are washed down, scrubbed with a harsh soap, and covered with bleach before being given to the waste removal contractor for disposal. They are never to be mixed with regular garbage since they are considered to be hazardous waste. Showers can be set up in the field, and large waste contractors even have modular units containing showers which they truck to emergency sites. Waste water from the decontamination process is also removed by the contractor, but if injured personnel have to be treated at a hospital, the hospital must perform the decontamination. The chemical substance is usually so diluted by that time that it is safe to treat the contaminated water in the hospital's sewage system. Schools and other facilities with showers are sometimes used following chemical emergencies.

ⅢⅢ CORRECTING THE PROBLEM ⅢⅢ

There are three steps to any remedial action plan: containment, disposal, and follow-up environmental surveillance. Containment and disposal are often handled by private clean-up vendors licensed by the states and by the U.S. Environmental Protection Agency.

ⅢⅢⅢ **CONTAINMENT**

For land spills, contractors employ a method of diking, using earth, sand, or tarps made of plastic or other impervious material to cover sewer manholes and drains to prevent runoff. They may also use absorbent materials such as Dri-Rite, which resembles kitty litter, and absorbent pads or rolls of material that soak up certain organic matter such as gasoline and alcohols. During excavation, contaminated soil is put in reclaiming containers, such as drums.

For water spills, contractors employ floating booms made of material that absorbs chemicals but not water. Oil spill contractors are now using removable booms that attract the oil floating on the surface of the water. Booms are squeezed out using a wringer, and the oil is reclaimed. Contractors never rely just on a primary containment source. There is always a series of dikes or a row of booms. (See the brief on "Oil Spills in Marine Environments.")

When the materials to be cleaned up are corrosives or acids, it may be better to neutralize the substance, rendering it less hazardous, with lime or other buffering agents. However, it is always removed after it is safely neutralized.

Not all chemical fires are contained by extinguishing them. Some are allowed to burn because the hazardous chemical or by-product may be rendered safer by burning off. For example, emergency response personnel routinely allow pesticides to burn off unless the fire can be extinguished rapidly. Scientists claim that it is less risky to release burning pesticides into the atmosphere than to have contaminated water runoff. If a leaking tanker or sealed storage tank contains a flammable liquid or gas, and there is a threat of explosion, the most urgent task for fire fighters is to quench the heat and prevent a deadly BLEVE (boiling liquid expanding vapor explosion). To do this, they may use unmanned fire sprays to bathe the tank in cooling water until the threat has passed. Fire personnel then evacuate to safer positions. This is normally recommended when dealing with corrosive materials such as dimethyl-sulfate and nitrogen tetroxide and poisons such as arsine (arsenic gas).

ⅢⅢⅢ **DISPOSAL**

With landbound spills, material trapped by dikes is sucked into fireproof vacuum trucks and then deposited into containment tankers. Disposers must get temporary storage disposal licenses from the EPA to move the tankers and reclaiming drums that carry the excavated material to approved rendering facilities—facilities that break down and neutralize contaminated matter—or to chemical burial sites. Under the Resource Conservation and Recovery Act— passed in 1976 and amended in 1980 and 1984—the chemical waste must be manifested so that state and federal officials know the history of that waste from point of production to final disposal.

ⅢⅢ **ENVIRONMENTAL SURVEILLANCE**

Monitoring wells may be dug to assure there was no penetration or intrusion into the groundwater. Officials can require an analysis of potable water supplies; air monitoring; ground, soil and vegetation sampling; and, if necessary, medical and epidemiological surveillance of responders and the affected populace. Environmental surveillance is not always done. But it is not always needed either. However, if an emergency is big enough to deserve massive coverage when it occurs, it probably deserves follow-up by the government, and the reporter. The exception to this rule, of course, is the emergency that receives great attention because of what *might* happen—but is prevented from happening. Here government follow-up is unnecessary, except to determine how the accident happened and what could be changed to prevent further accidents.

ⅢⅢ **IMPORTANT POINTS FOR RESEARCHING A STORY** ⅢⅢ

ⅢⅢ Determine what quantity and form of material has been released into the environment and whether it is going into the surface water, groundwater, soil, or air. This will determine the route of human exposure.

ⅢⅢ Find out if the material is persistent in the environment and its other properties. For example, even though a volatile material may be confined to a small container, it may evaporate easily and spread over a large area.

ⅢⅢ Be sure to ask what quantities are considered dangerous, especially to specific groups like children, the elderly, and pregnant women.

|||||| Find out why the material is considered to be dangerous, whether effects are acute or chronic, and whether it reacts with air, water, or other chemicals found nearby. Determine what happens when these materials react and whether they are more dangerous or less dangerous after a reaction. For instance, a spill of methyl chloroform will evaporate harmlessly if flushed with water into the nearest stream, but may turn into a persistent contaminant of local well water if allowed to seep into the groundwater supply. Likewise, a spilled mercuric salt will not percolate deeply into most soils and can be confined in place if scooped up, but if flushed into surface water may make fish unacceptable for human consumption.

|||||| Learn the symptoms of exposure and determine if they can be differentiated from other symptoms, (e.g., a cold, the flu, or smoking).

|||||| **PITFALLS** ||||||

|||||| Chemical emergencies are tough to cover because they are difficult technical stories in the middle of crises. While covering crises is basic to a reporter's job, covering technical issues in the midst of crisis requires special skills and knowledge.

|||||| A common source of misinformation stems from asking the wrong person for technical information. People working to clean up an accident may not necessarily be qualified to discuss the health risks it poses. At the same time, people at the site of an emergency, may be too busy dealing with the emergency to give thorough answers, even if they have the technical background to provide them.

|||||| Reporters at the site of a chemical spill or factory fire run the risk of being forced to leave the scene by police because they are at risk. Every newspaper should consider investing in protective equipment and have suppliers in to train reporters in its use.

|||||| The chemical emergency is often better reported than the health risk. Exposure information may not be known accurately for several days. Follow-up stories on health risks

are extremely critical if a community is to be kept informed.

|||||| Remember, not all questions are best answered at the scene.
Many times the cause and effect of the accident cannot be
determined until after the dust has settled.

|||||| On significant stories, reporters should stay with the story—
not just in terms of who was to blame and who was indicted
or fined. Lessons for other facilities can be highlighted in
follow-up. When company x had a fire, authorities may
have determined that a leak in y was the problem. Has
company z—located five miles down the road—done anything about y, or are they waiting for a fire too?

|||||| Remember that keeping the reporter from getting close may
not be a cover-up. The risks involved often necessitate this.
Also, reporters at chemical emergencies sometimes assume that emergency responders know everything and,
therefore, that what they will not say is a cover-up of very
alarming information. Consider the possibility that they
simply may not know the answer to a question (yet).

|||||| In some situations—not doing anything (e.g., letting a fire
burn) is sometimes the right response.

|||||| If it is a big story, then the story is more than the emergency
itself. It also includes technical information on health risk
(or ecosystem risk), how an area is being decontaminated,
where the disposal site is located, follow-up surveillance,
assessment of responsibility, and lessons to be learned. It
is hard to imagine an emergency that deserves extensive
coverage when it happens and no follow-up coverage at
all. Yet, disposal, surveillance, and what went wrong are
often parts of the story that get less media attention than
they deserve.

|||||| SOURCES FOR JOURNALISTS ||||||

|||||| Emergency responders are good news sources. They may in-
clude state and local police, environmental agency emergency teams, and health departments, as well as fire
departments, first aid squads, and emergency management
officials. Police and fire departments are the best sources

for logistical information. They will know what is being done to contain the emergency, how traffic is being affected, whether there are injuries, and if there is need for an evacuation. For information on health effects, talk to health departments and environmental agency officials, since in most cases, other on-site responders have little training in this field.

IIIIII In the event of a large emergency (e.g., a factory fire involving chemicals), a command post may be set up. The command post is where sources gather and where decisions are made. There you may find company representatives and experts from industry and academia called in by responders. In the event of minor emergencies, a command post probably will not be established. Reporters should look for an on-scene coordinator, the person responsible for seeing that each group does its job and has the support it needs. Small accidents, such as a minor transportation spill, may not have coordinators, and reporters should direct their attention to the local fire or police chief or perhaps a health officer or emergency management coordinator. Expect that on-site experts may be busy managing the emergency and reporters may have trouble finding out the information.

IIIIII In the event of a transportation spill, find out what materials were spilled by asking officials about the manifest. The manifest can be followed like a trail of bread crumbs to the original source of the material. It documents every movement and change in material from origin to final resting place. Contact the Hazardous Materials Safety Office in the federal Department of Transportation (202-366-0656) for specifics about materials you identify. For complete information on placarding see the 1991 Title 49 CFR (Code of Federal Regulations), specifically, Title 100-177. Section 172.500 is the section that explains placarding.

IIIIII In any chemical emergency, an important source of information is the U.S. Public Health Service's Agency for Toxic Substances and Disease Registry, (202-472-7136).

IIIIII Two other sources of information are Chemtrec (899-424-9300) and Chemical Referral Service. To use the Chemical Referral Service call 800-262-8200 or 202-887-1315 in Washington, D.C. In Alaska and outside the continental United States, call collect. These services are operated by the Chemical Manufacturers Association and are designed to answer questions directly or connect reporters with manufacturer of the product involved. Chemtrec is also for emergency responders.

ⅢⅢ The Scientists' Institute for Public Information (SIPI) offers an information service that connects reporters with sources and names of experts on both sides of controversial issues. Its phone number is 800-223-1739.

ⅢⅢ Three important books for the reporter covering chemical emergencies are the NIOSH *Pocket Guide to Chemical Hazards:* 1980. Washington, D.C.; N.I. Sax. 1979. *Dangerous Properties of Industrial Materials.* New York: Von Nostrand Reinhold Company; and S. Budavari, ed. 1989. *The Merck Index.* Rahway, N.J.: Merck and Co., Inc.

ⅢⅢ Sets of chemical fact sheets are available from state departments of health or some universities. These may be worth the investment for the newspaper library.

ⅢⅢ For information specifically about oil spills, contact the Oil Spills National Response Center of the U.S. Coast Guard at 202-267-2188.

ⅢⅢ The Federal Emergency Management Agency (FEMA) is a federal agency chartered mainly to give advice to other agencies about emergency situations including chemical emergencies. Its number is 202-646-2500.

ⅢⅢ The Office of Science and Education at the U.S. Department of Agriculture (202-720-4751) has information about pesticide emergencies.

ⅢⅢ The videotape, *Covering an Environmental Accident,* is a half-hour analysis of how reporters and emergency response teams communicate during (and after) an accident. It is available through the Environmental Research and Communication Program at Rutgers University, New Brunswick, New Jersey; 908-932-8795.

ⅢⅢ See also the briefs on "Oil Spills in Marine Environments," "Incinerators," "Nuclear Power Plants (Commercial)," and "Hazardous Waste."

DIOXIN AND PCBs

During the last decade, dioxin and PCBs have been probably the most politically contentious substances. Scientists have strong and very different feelings about the danger of exposure to these chemicals.

|||||| IDENTIFYING THE PROBLEM ||||||

Dioxin and polychlorinated biphenyls (PCBs) are chemical compounds (often called cogeners or isomers) that have received considerable attention because of their potential hazard to humans.

|||||| DIOXIN

Dioxin is an umbrella name for a class of seventy-five chemical compounds that contain carbon, hydrogen, oxygen, and chlorine. Dioxins are part of the larger class of compounds known as polycyclic halogenated aromatics.

Dioxin is an unavoidable by-product in a variety of different processes including chemical manufacturing, incineration of

|||||| The original dioxin brief in the first volume of the *Handbook* was written by Peter C. Kahn, associate professor of biochemistry, Cook College, Rutgers University. Additional comments on this second edition were provided by Craig Nessel of Exxon Biomedical Sciences, Theodore Berger of Hoffmann–La Roche, and Ellen Silbergeld of the University of Maryland for the Environmental Defense Fund. ||||||

municipal garbage, refining some metals, burning leaded gas in automobiles, and the manufacture of paper products. It is produced in the manufacture of certain herbicides such as 2,4,5-T. It is also inadvertently formed in industrial processes involving the use of chlorine; one important example of such a process is the bleaching of paper. Dioxin can also be formed when organic wastes that contain chlorine are burned; the general mix of plastics found in municipal waste is likely to contain such organics.

Dioxin was first described in the petrochemical industry in Germany in 1957, although occupational health incidents involving dioxin have been recorded back to the 1930s. Dioxin is highly stable and insoluble in water. It adheres to clay and soot and dissolves in oil and organic solvents.

The toxicity of dioxin is species-specific. Although highly toxic to some small animals (e.g., guinea pigs), it is less toxic to others (e.g., mice), and it is much less toxic to larger animals. No human deaths resulting from dioxin exposure have been recorded.

Toxicity also depends on the kind of dioxin involved. The scientific community lists thirteen dioxins as being of concern to human health because they all lodge in organs and fatty tissue and accumulate with continued exposure. The dioxin probably most familiar is called 2,3,7,8-tetrachlorodibenzo-p-dioxin, often abbreviated 2,3,7,8-TCDD or more simply, TCDD. TCDD has been called "the most toxic synthetic substance known," a statement based on studies of certain species of experimental animals.

Dioxin first became the subject of a major public-health debate during the United States's military defoliation program using Agent Orange in Vietnam. Veterans who participated in this defoliation program have experienced a variety of health problems that might be related to dioxin exposure.

Agent Orange was a mixture of the two herbicides-2,4-D and 2,4,5-T. TCDD was produced as an unintentional by-product during the manufacture of 2,4,5-T. Depending on the batch, the TCDD level in 2,4,5-T ranged from a fraction of a part per million (ppm) to approximately 100 ppm. (The exposure to 2,4,5-T itself would typically be in parts per million or less, so the TCDD exposure would be in parts per million/parts per million.) Only an extraordinarily toxic substance such as TCDD would cause worry in such small quantities.

In 1983, TCDD-contaminated waste oil was accidentally sprayed on local roads in Times Beach, Missouri, to keep dust down. This forced several thousand residents to permanently flee their tainted community.

The chlorine and paper industries also became involved in the debate over dioxins—stemming from concern over the effluent from paper mills that use chlorine bleach. Outside research firms, acting at the behest of these industries, proposed a less conservative dioxin standard. Syntex Corp. (responsible for the Times Beach cleanup) noted the higher clean-up costs caused by the more stringent standards. These industries convened a key meeting of experts and published a "consensus" summary of their findings. Following this meeting, Dr. Vernon Houk, the scientist at the Centers for Disease Control and Prevention (CDC) who spearheaded the evacuation of Times Beach, supported industry on the proposed change. He was reported as stating that the evacuation of Times Beach was unnecessary since new evidence suggested dioxin was at worst a "weak carcinogen." However, other toxicologists have challenged this conclusion. The EPA considered a possible revision of the standard, but announced in 1992 that it would not make changes. Dioxin continues to be the subject of debate. Diamond Shamrock in the Ironbound section of Newark, New Jersey, was the site of another dioxin controversy. The factory manufactured and stored chlorinated phenols for years. Dioxins were found in the soil as a by-product of chemical manufacturing.

Dioxin has also been involved in disputes over local waste incineration. Concern centers on exposure from the breathing of, or skin contact with, the fumes and ash that result from the burning of municipal garbage, particularly if the garbage contains polyvinyl chloride or other organic substances containing chlorine.

As noted above, concerns with regard to dioxin have been raised in relation to the paper and chlorine industries. Bleached paper and cardboard food containers often contain trace amounts of dioxin which is produced when paper is bleached. Typical concentrations of dioxin in bleached paper products range from undetectable to about 10 parts per trillion. Fish found downstream of paper pulp mills have also been found with higher levels of dioxin as a result of contamination from discharge waters.

Symptoms of exposure to TCDD include chloracne, damage to

the central nervous system, liver damage, and immune system disorders. While chloracne is a consistent symptom of exposure to TCDD, other symptoms have been shown in only studies following high-level exposure. With the exception of chloracne, every one of the health effects described here has been the subject of considerable debate.

Chloracne is a severe skin condition. It appears days to weeks after the exposure and is similar in appearance to a severe case of adolescent acne, with blackheads and pimples, which develop when the sebaceous glands are blocked. The skin areas are densely packed with a virtual carpet of blackheads which, in medical terminology, are called comedones. Cysts and pustules frequently form also. The condition can permanently disfigure. Most cases disappear within one to two years of the last exposure to TCDD, but some have been known to persist for more than thirty years.

Exposure to TCDD has been associated with neurological problems or psychological disorders, or both. Neurological changes include pain and weakness in the lower extremities, sleep disturbances, and loss of vigor and drive. Those exposed may suffer psychologically as a result of central nervous system damage caused by the chemical or, indirectly, as a result of chloracne disfigurement and other debilitating symptoms.

Liver degeneration, including the development of "fatty liver," porphyria, and other disorders can occur following exposure to TCDD. Porphyria is a disorder in which the liver can no longer synthesize an essential blood component, leading to extreme sensitivity of the eyes and skin to light, memory loss, and other problems.

There is some evidence TCDD may cause a rare class of cancers known as soft tissue sarcomas. This class of cancers makes up approximately 1 percent of all cancers. These cancers have been studied on a very limited basis among farm workers handling agricultural chemicals that contain TCDD. Two well-constructed studies—one in Sweden and one in the United States—have also shown an association between exposure to agricultural chemicals containing dioxins and the development of non-Hodgkin's lymphoma and soft-tissue sarcoma. However, other studies have not shown an association between TCDD exposure and cancer incidence.

Recent studies of dioxin and immune suppression in mice suggest that dioxin's impact on the immune system, which occurs at extremely low doses, may be more important than cancer in determining dioxin's primary health risk.

TCDD is not alone in posing extreme hazards to human health. A recent study found an eightfold increase in non-Hodgkin's lymphomas among a group of Kansas wheat farmers who had frequent contact with 2,4-D. This chemical contains other forms of dioxin, but not TCDD. Similar results were obtained in a Swedish study of agricultural and forestry workers.

‖‖‖‖ **POLYCHLORINATED BIPHENYLS**

Polychlorinated biphenyls may also contain TCDD. PCBs belong to a class of compounds containing a variable number of chlorines. Toxicity varies with the degree of chlorination and the actual position of the chlorine atoms on the basic structure. Theoretically, more than two hundred different cogeners or forms of PCBs are possible.

Because of their low flammability, PCBs have been used for insulating and cooling electrical equipment, such as transformers. In such an application, the flow of PCBs to the environment is restricted. PCBs have also been used in plasticizers, in inks and dyes, in pesticide preparations, and in carbonless copy paper. When it was learned that PCBs persist in the environment, accumulate in the food chain, and pose a hazard to human health, manufacturers stopped the sales of products that might leak PCBs to the environment. However, until recently, PCBs have continued to be used in closed systems—such as electrical transformers.

PCBs are chemicals that are fairly resistant to degradation. This has resulted in the environmental persistence of the compounds, its ubiquitous distribution, and bioaccumulation in fish, birds, and mammals.

Reservoirs of PCBs persist in soil, sediment, water, waste-disposal sites, and existing electrical capacitors and transformers. As a result, PCBs can be taken up from the soil by organisms and transferred through the food chain. In addition, they can be accidentally leaked from electrical equipment. An incident in Binghamton, New York, resulted in the need to close an entire government building following the accidental leakage of PCBs from the cooling system. PCB concentrations are usually higher in urban and heavily industrialized areas, where there is greater use of capacitors and transformers, than in rural areas. PCBs can also escape to the atmosphere when they are improperly incinerated (that is, at temperatures insufficiently high to destroy them).

Fish-eating populations have high levels of PCBs. Surface waters are major environmental reservoirs for PCBs. However, PCBs predominantly settle to sediment or accumulate in biota (animal and plant life of a region). Ingestion of contaminated fish is believed to be a significant route of exposure to PCBs in humans.

Symptoms associated with PCB poisoning include chloracne, respiratory distress, and liver damage. Two episodes of human exposure, the Yusho and Yucheng incidents in Japan and Taiwan, respectively, have provided much of the information on human response to PCBs. Early symptoms in exposed individuals included chloracne; pigmentation of the skin and nails; swelling of the limbs; jaundice; and neurological effects, including numbness, headache, and dizziness. Furthermore, infants were born hyperpigmented, and some individuals suffered from chronically infected airways or an impaired immune system. However, no adequate studies have been conducted to determine whether chronic exposure to PCBs is associated with human carcinogenesis or adverse reproductive outcomes, and no chronic health effects have been causally associated with exposure. On the basis of animal tests, PCBs are classified as probable human carcinogens. NIOSH recognizes PCBs as an occupational carcinogens.

|||||| CORRECTING THE PROBLEM ||||||

|||||| DIOXIN

Currently all herbicidal products containing 2,4,5-T (and hence, dioxin) are banned by the federal government for most uses. Dioxin is also regulated under the Clean Water Act. One type of dioxin—2,3,7,8-tetrachlorodibenzo-p-dioxin—is listed as a "hazardous air pollutant" in the 1990 Clean Air Act, thereby requiring the EPA to establish emission standards. In 1989, the FDA ordered that manufacturers of milk cartons alter the bleaching process to greatly reduce dioxin levels in cardboard containers by 1992. Substitutes for the use of chlorine in the paper-bleaching process now exist.

The toxicity of dioxins depends upon their bioavailability— whether plants and animals can absorb the chemical from the environment. Although laboratories can extract virtually all the dioxin in environmental samples from soil, the chemical may be so tightly bound in nature to the soil that living systems or natural processes cannot absorb it. In this case, the dioxin is not bioavailable.

Whether dioxin and other pollutants in the soil are bioavailable appears to depend on the soil type and on the way dioxin was deposited in or on it. For example, the soil found at Times Beach was nonretentive. The dioxin found there migrated more easily from soil to hand to stomach to human cell than in soil samples taken at Diamond Shamrock. In Newark, the soil was retentive. Thus, the same amount and type of dioxin would be more danger- ous at Times Beach than in Newark.

At present, there is no inexpensive way to destroy dioxins in soil; disposal is only through containment, which is not a perma- nent solution to the problem. Research is needed to develop a commercial means to detoxify dioxins. Scientists working on this problem have noted that dioxins are more resistant to degradation than other organic chemicals. Therefore, they are a good prototype for environmental waste detoxification. However, some data sug- gest that dioxins will decompose if exposed to sunlight.

Municipal incineration of certain organic wastes that contain chlorine can produce dioxin as a by-product. However, not all dioxins produced are hazardous. Nevertheless, the bottom ash and fly ash from smokestacks with scrubbers that remove chlorine-containing compounds must be treated as hazardous waste. High-heat inciner- ation can be used to dispose of TCDD and other dioxins in liquid. The higher the temperatures, the greater the likelihood of breaking down dioxins. But this process is difficult and expensive. And there is controversy among experts over its effectiveness. Efforts are underway to develop incinerators in which the risk of dioxin exposure to humans is minimized. (See the brief on "Incinerators.")

PCBS

Beginning in the mid-1970s, EPA regulations have restricted the manufacture, import, export, transportation, and disposal of PCBs. PCBs are no longer commercially manufactured. Current law required that most (but not all) equipment that contained PCBs be retired by 1990. PCBs are listed as "hazardous air pollutants" in the 1990 Clean Air Act.

Because of some improper disposal of PCBs, Congress is attempting to propose methods to assure safe disposal of the remaining PCBs.

The preferred method of dealing with existing PCBs is high-temperature (2,000–3,000°F) incineration with excess oxygen. This can achieve virtually complete destruction. However, as noted above, even in high efficiency incinerators, some unwanted by-products may be produced, particularly dioxin.

|||||| IMPORTANT POINTS FOR RESEARCHING A STORY ||||||

|||||| Find out the types of dioxin or PCBs involved in your situation and confirm whether tests have been done to identify the type.

|||||| Determine the length and means of victims' exposure.

|||||| Since dioxins occur only as a by-product, check what other types of hazardous materials may be present in the situation. If dioxins are present, other hazardous chemicals are also likely to be present.

|||||| Find out who is responsible for putting the compounds at the contamination site, who will remove them, and how and where disposal will take place.

|||||| See also the brief on "Incinerators."

|||||| PITFALLS ||||||

|||||| Always be specific about which chemical compounds are involved in a situation. While 2,3,7,8-TCDD is the most toxic

of the cogeners, it is usually in much lower concentrations than other dioxin congeners. Remember, there are 75 different compounds called dioxin and another 200 possible PCBs. With PCBs, toxicity varies with the degree of chlorination and the actual position of the chlorine atoms on the basic structure.

⫿⫿⫿⫿ Dioxins are not manufactured products, they are by-products. They are not manufactured intentionally.

⫿⫿⫿⫿ Dioxin is often referred to as "the most toxic substance known to man." This needs several qualifiers. One needs to determine which dioxin is involved—TCDD is the worst. But TCDD is not the most toxic substance known to man. It is the most toxic *synthetic* substance known in its effects on some test animals. The bacterial toxin which produces botulism, for example, is more acutely toxic to humans than TCDD. Of course, dioxins are highly toxic—at least some of them for humans. Highly toxic does not necessarily mean that the effect is extremely bad, but rather that the amount of exposure needed to produce the effect is extremely small (one part per billion in Times Beach).

⫿⫿⫿⫿ So far, there is no standard for human tolerance of TCDD in the United States. At the request of the EPA, the CDC recommended a guideline for TCDD levels in soil of one part per billion in Times Beach, Missouri. This guideline has been criticized as being too cautious because of the exposure assumptions used in determining the value. Journalists should note that this figure should only be used when writing about the Times Beach case and similar residential exposures involving soils where dioxin is termed bioavailable. Although the CDC suggested that 1 ppb was the level at which to consider action to limit human exposure to contaminated soil, regulatory agencies have begun to accept this guideline as the standard for cleanup regardless of circumstances at a site.

⫿⫿⫿⫿ Agent Orange contains the dioxin TCDD as a contaminant, but Agent Orange itself is not a synonym for dioxin.

⫿⫿⫿⫿ Health professionals studying the medical problems of Vietnam veterans have claimed it is difficult to determine whether central nervous system and psychological disorders are related to TCDD exposure or Post-Traumatic Stress Disorder sometimes experienced by people who have endured life-threatening situations.

IIIIII SOURCES FOR JOURNALISTS IIIIII

IIIIII TCDD and other dioxins are top issues in stories dealing with chemical manufacturing and handling; incineration of municipal, hospital and hazardous wastes; emissions from motor vehicles that burn leaded gasoline; paper processing plants; the smelting and refining of metals; and Agent Orange. For information on dioxins and PCBs contact the Scientists' Institute for Public Information in New York to provide chemical experts. For other points of view, contact trade organizations such as the American Petroleum Institute (202-682-8000) and the Chemical Manufacturers Association (202-887-1100). In addition, the concern for TCDD and PCBs has resulted in inclusion of a chapter on these compounds in most toxicology and environmental health reference texts. State health and environmental regulatory agencies are usually helpful. For information on Agent Orange, check with the Agent Orange Commission set up in most states within the Department of Veterans' Affairs, as well as Vietnam veteran's groups. In New Jersey, the number of the Agent Orange Commission is 609-530-8162.

IIIIII World Health Organization. 1976. *Environmental Health Criteria No. 2: Polychlorinated Biphenyls and Triphenyls.* Geneva.

IIIIII American Medical Association. 1981. *The Health Effects of "Agent Orange" and Polychlorinated Dioxin Contaminants,* Chicago.

ELECTROMAGNETIC FIELDS

The risk from proximity to electromagnetic fields (EMFs) is uncertain. In view of the equivocal nature of the epidemiological findings (i.e., risk is small and not consistent), it is likely that the health effects produced by electromagnetic fields are small or nonexistent for each individual. However, even a small effect can be worth further investigation, from a public health standpoint, given that electricity is omnipresent. Nevertheless, we think everyone would agree that children are far more likely to die from electrical shock than from cancer induced by EMF exposure.

IIIII **IDENTIFYING THE PROBLEM** IIIII

There are three major types of radiation: nuclear radiation (high energy particles—alpha and beta particles—given off from the nuclei of certain types of atoms), cosmic radiation (high energy particles—cosmic rays—that come from the sun and other objects in outer space), and electromagnetic radiation (electromagnetic waves that travel through space). This brief focuses on electromagnetic radiation.

Electromagnetic waves of energy are similar to waves formed on the water's surface by a pebble that has been dropped into it. However, these waves differ in wavelength and frequency. The full

IIIII Comments on this brief were provided by Tom Ledoux, Allen Stern, and Deborah Wenke of the New Jersey Department of Environmental Protection and Energy and Betty K. Jensen of Public Service Electric and Gas Company. IIIII range of wavelengths and frequencies defines the electromagnetic spectrum.

Gamma rays and x-rays, followed by ultraviolet light, are at the extreme high frequency end of the spectrum—where wavelengths are shortest. Visible light, including sunlight, occupies the middle of the spectrum. Infrared light, microwaves, and radio waves are found at the low frequency (long wavelength) end of the spectrum. Finally, at extremely low frequencies (ELFs), are the electric and magnetic fields associated with 60 herz (Hz) electricity. All of these electromagnetic waves of energy represent forms of radiation since radiation is energy in motion.

Radiation is generally classified either as ionizing radiation or nonionizing radiation. Ionizing radiation carries enough energy so that when it passes through matter, it is capable of transferring large amounts of energy to individual atoms in the region through which it passes. It can knock electrons out of position or even free them from their atoms. The process by which an atom loses an electron is called ionization. Radiation without enough energy to ionize atoms is called nonionizing radiation.

Ionizing radiation has long been considered a hazard. [See also the briefs on "Radon (Indoor)" and "Nuclear Power Plants (Commercial)."] Some types of electromagnetic waves (gamma rays, x-rays) are examples of ionizing radiation. Recently, however, some scientists have begun to investigate the possible negative health effects of nonionizing radiation. Nonionizing radiation is given off by some types of electromagnetic waves including microwaves, radio waves, as well as the radiation given off by common appliances and power transmission lines.

Electromagnetic waves of energy are made up of electric and magnetic fields. These fields are the invisible lines of force that occur wherever electricity is being conducted. The electric power that is used in our homes, offices, and factories uses AC or alternating current: it alternates back and forth rather than flowing steadily in one direction. The power used in North America alternates back and forth 60 times each second. This is called 60 Hz power. (1 Hz = 1 cycle per second.)

Electromagnetic fields are around all large and small power lines, wiring, lighting, and electrical appliances. Electric fields are measured in units of volts per meter. When the field is strong, larger units of a thousand volts per meter or kilo volts per meter (kV/m) are used. Magnetic field intensity is commonly measured in gauss and tesla. Just as ounces and gallons are units for measuring liquids, gauss and tesla are units for measuring magnetic field intensity. The gauss is a relatively large unit so magnetic field intensity is reported in thousandths of a gauss or milligauss (mG). One tesla is equal to 10,000 gauss. Sixty hertz (60 Hz) magnetic fields are commonly reported in milligauss. Electric and magnetic fields can be measured using a field meter or calculated from their voltage and current. Levels of electric and magnetic fields are independent of each other, that is, high voltage does not necessarily indicate high magnetic field, and vice versa.

Fields weaken rapidly with distance from their source, falling off inversely with the square of distance from the source. While electric fields can be shielded by vegetation, buildings, fences, and other objects, magnetic fields readily penetrate almost anything, without losing strength, including the human body.

According to a report by Carnegie Mellon University on electric and magnetic fields from 60 Hz electric power, the electromagnetic fields with which most people come into contact are quite weak. Typically families using ordinary electrical appliances like lights and toasters in their homes are exposed to between .1 and 20 milligauss. However, some items in the home produce higher magnetic fields. The average magnetic field produced within the body by an electric shaver ranges from 100 mG to over 1,000 mG. Fields produced by an electric blanket range from 5 to 100 mG, those from a hair dryer can be as high as 400 mG, and those from a circulating pump in a fish tank can be over 1,000 mG.

The approximate strength of the average magnetic field generated within the body by power distribution lines on poles ranges from less than 1 mG to approximately 50 mG. Those generated by 500 kV transmission lines range from approximately 20 to 800 mG. The intensity, however, drops off quickly with distance from the source. So having a large power line down the street could be less of a threat than sleeping directly under an electric blanket.

Until recently, it was commonly thought that low-frequency fields had no effects on the human body because 60 Hz fields cannot break molecular or chemical bonds, unlike ionizing radiation such as x-rays. In addition, unlike microwaves, 60 Hz fields cannot produce significant heat in the body. Consequently, it was assumed that nonionizing radiation passed through living tissue with little or no effect.

However, within the last fifteen years, scientists have begun to raise concerns about possible health effects from exposure to low-frequency fields. Two major controversies involve the possible effects of electric power transmission lines and video display terminals (VDTs), or monitors, on health.

The evidence, as yet, is not conclusive. Cell studies have found effects at particular frequencies and field strengths (with uncertainty about their relationship to health). At the same time, epidemiological studies have sometimes found effects related to field strength, sometimes found effects assumed to be related to other aspects of wire configuration, and sometimes found no effects at all.

Some epidemiological studies of the effects of power transmission lines have found associations between some kinds of cancer and details of how the power lines were configured, rather than correlations simply with the strength of the magnetic field. However, most of these studies did not measure field exposure, and where field exposure was measured, the evidence was not conclusive. Some have reported statistical associations between increases in field exposure and increased cancer rates, while others showed no such association. What is most confusing is that effects are sometimes seen at lower field strengths rather than higher ones, making it difficult to interpret the data. One explanation of this phenomenon is that if tissues respond at all to extremely low frequency fields, they respond only to quite narrow bands of frequency and field strength.

VDTs, whether color or monochrome, produce both ionizing and nonionizing electromagnetic radiation. Their nonionizing electromagnetic radiation is in the form of weak, pulsed electric fields, which create very low frequency (VLF) and extremely low frequency (ELF) fields. The amount of ionizing radiation—the kind that contains sufficient energy to change or destroy the chemical bonds in living cells—is very small. It is blocked by the monitor's screen and case according to experts.

The radiation emitted from a monitor is not uniform: it is highest at the back and sides, and lowest at the front. The level of frontal radiation falls off rapidly at short distances from the monitor. Color monitors give off more radiation than monochrome monitors. The more powerful the monitor, the more radiation it emits.

No definitive conclusions have emerged about the long-term health implications of computer use. Some studies have suggested a link between low-frequency electromagnetic radiation and health problems. Other researchers dispute these findings or are skeptical of them because most studies of electromagnetic fields do not involve computers but, rather, are based on other devices that emit extremely low frequency magnetic fields of a similar type and level as that produced by VDTs.

Health concerns also have been raised about VDT use and miscarriage rates. While a study conducted by the National Institute for Occupational Safety and Health found that radiation emitted from VDTs did not increase the risk of spontaneous abortion or miscarriage, a 1992 study conducted by the Mount Sinai School of Medicine in New York reported an increased risk of miscarriage among VDT users.

Research has demonstrated more conclusively that extended sessions in front of a VDT can produce muscle and eyestrain, as well as problems caused by being seated in one position for too long. Carpal tunnel syndrome refers to nerve damage in the wrists due to improper flexing and extension while at the keyboard.

|||||| CORRECTING THE PROBLEM ||||||

As yet, no U.S. government agency has determined a maximum safe level for electromagnetic fields in milligauss. The International Radiation Protection Association has issued draft guidelines for the general public's exposure to power-frequency electric and magnetic fields. They call for a limit of 5 kV/m for continuous exposures to electric fields and 1 G (1,000 mG) for magnetic fields.

In 1989, the Office of Technology Assessment recommended a policy of "prudent avoidance" in dealing with electromagnetic fields in and around the home. This policy raises serious questions. It is unclear what constitutes prudence: Does it require moving because there is a power line down the street? expanding green belts or improving insulation around new lines? blocking the construction of new lines? Dr. M. Granger Morgan of Carnegie

Mellon University, who coined the phrase, notes in *Transmission and Distribution* (June 1991) that "the prudent thing to do is to try to keep people out of fields, when it can be done at modest costs; but not go off the deep end with expensive controls which may not be beneficial."

Six states (Florida, Minnesota, Montana, New Jersey, New York, and Oregon) have taken regulatory action to limit the intensity of the electric field on transmission line rights-of-way. New Jersey has voluntary guidelines. Regulations are proposed, but not promulgated. The proposed regulations include magnetic fields. Only New York and Florida have magnetic field regulations in place. Czechoslovakia, Germany, Japan, Poland, and the former Soviet Union have regulations governing electric fields. Sweden has magnetic field guidelines for facilities with "concentrated activities for children." Standards for power line electromagnetic fields have been developed primarily as an attempt to make sure new lines generate no higher fields than already existing ones. These standards tend to be set at very high levels and health concerns have been raised (albeit, with uncertain research support) about much lower levels. In fact, the standards in place would not affect most of the controversies that have threatened or stopped the construction of power lines all over the country.

In most states, public utility commissions (or their equivalents) have so far avoided the issue. It is generally possible to reduce electromagnetic fields by as much as one decides by making the transmission line higher, insulating wires more, establishing larger "green belts" between the right-of-way and people's homes, putting the wires underground, etc. However, all of these solutions are expensive, especially in the case of retrofitting existing lines. These costs then tend to be added to the cost of electricity and passed on to the consumer.

The irony is that utilities in most states have no right to make electricity more expensive for ratepayers everywhere in order to reduce electromagnetic fields in a particular neighborhood through which the transmission line passes or will pass. They are obligated to pick the least expensive route that satisfies all safety standards promulgated by the Public Utility Commission. Therefore, the commission has to set an electromagnetic field standard; the more conservative (cautious and protective of health) the standard is, the more costly electricity will be in the region. While this has traditionally been a utility decision, it more properly should be a public policy decision. Since the data are not definitive and the issue is an emotional one, public utility commissions tend to avoid setting a standard and prefer to let the individual utilities fight it out with the neighborhoods instead.

Sweden has established tight guidelines for very low frequency emissions from video display terminals. While compliance is voluntary, pressure from labor unions has made them, in effect, de facto standards for Scandinavia and much of Europe. In addition, Swedish guidelines now call for reduced extremely low-frequency emissions. In the absence of definitive research, Swedish guidelines are becoming the common reference point for computer monitors in the United States. American computer makers already offer low-radiation monitors for sale in Europe and several American computer makers sell low-radiation monitors in the United States.

While some computers are fitted with radiation shields or glare guards that fit over the screen of the monitor, these shields do not block magnetic fields. The best precaution against high levels of exposure is to sit at least an arm's length from the front of the monitor and at least three or four feet away from the sides and backs of monitors. Radiation from a monitor is not uniform: it is highest at the back and sides and lowest in the front. The same precautions apply to laser printers.

The city of San Francisco and Suffolk County in New York had regulations in place on VDT use. In both cases, the regulations were struck down by the courts. Regulations were proposed, but not passed, in New York and New Jersey.

〰 **PITFALLS** 〰

〰 We now know that nonionizing EMFs can affect cells—something previously considered impossible. However, the effects are peculiar (e.g., not always proportional to strength) and the health implications of these biological effects remain unclear.

〰 Epidemiological studies are inconclusive: some find a relationship to wire configuration and some show none; some show a relationship to field exposure, while others show none; and some find windows of health effects at particular field exposure levels. It is always possible that reported findings may be the result of data limitations or that the cancers may come from various other unknown causes (including smoking, occupational exposures, and socio-economic status). In addition, conclusions about the health impacts of VDT use have often been based upon studies of the health impacts of other similar devices that emit extremely low frequency magnetic fields of a similar type and level, but not VDTs. Resolution of these issues will require more and better data. In particular, studies of EMFs must measure fields accurately. In general, definitive conclusions can only be reached if consistent results are obtained from several well-done studies.

||||| No one has found a consistent dose-response relationship, (i.e., how much exposure to EMFs is too much). Factors such as sensitivity to specific frequencies, amplitudes, and orientations may play critical roles and may prove more important than classical measures such as duration and intensity of exposure. Furthermore, because of differences in size and body architecture, animals may not be as useful as models for human health effects as they are in tests of toxic chemicals. Complicating efforts to establish a consistent dose-response relationship is the finding that some experiments show no effect with a strong field, but when the field strength is slightly reduced the effect appears. Thus, it is possible that, unlike most pollutants, with EMF more may not be worse. Because of the uncertainty, no government agency has yet determined a maximum safe level for milligauss.

||||| While people can control their exposure to appliances (e.g., turn on the electric blanket an hour before bedtime, and turn it off before getting into bed), they cannot control the power line that runs outside their window. As a consequence, this generates much more outrage. But which generates the greater hazard? The reporter needs to consider the relative risk from appliances, household and building wiring, distribution lines, and huge main power transmission lines.

ⅢⅢ A power-line battle is a populist one with angry citizens raising the specter of cancer at public hearings. Rampant
citizen outrage is and should be a good story. If hundreds
of neighbors are angry and frightened, that is news whether they are right or not. But whether the risk is big or small
is also news—news that typically gets lost in the outrage
story. (See also the brief on "Cancer Cluster Claims.")

ⅢⅢ Currently, many local communities are resisting the location
of new power transmission lines, adopting a not-in-my-
backyard mentality. The NIMBY syndrome moves the problem around. It does not help resolve the larger question of
how much money should be spent protecting against a risk
that may be real—but small. (See also the brief on "Hazardous Waste.")

ⅢⅢ Reporters should not overlook the fact that people often have
other, solid objections to transmission lines and utility
easements. These range from purely aesthetic concerns to
the possible social impact of dividing once cohesive neighborhoods in two. Coupled with general outrage over rate
hikes imposed by electric companies, people can easily
rally around EMF concerns. At times, these unrelated forces
can be manipulated by those who would oppose the line
anyway. An activist journalist can bring such issues to the
forefront (for better or for worse) as illustrated by the
series of investigative reports in *The New Yorker* by environmental writer Paul Brodeur.

ⅢⅢ Since journalists use VDTs extensively, they are a labor-man-
agement issue in many newsrooms. Unions representing
journalists have been in conflict with management over the
issue. This makes coverage of the VDT issue sensitive. Be
sure to check the history of the issue in your own newsroom and consider making this a part of the story.

ⅢⅢ SOURCES FOR JOURNALISTS ⅢⅢ

ⅢⅢ In general, contact the U.S. Environmental Protection Agency
first, then the state agencies responsible for the environment and health.

⁞⁞⁞⁞⁞ During the 1980s, the Department of Energy's Office of Energy Storage and Distribution and the U.S. Navy were the main federal sources of research support for EMF studies.

⁞⁞⁞⁞⁞ Several states have been involved in EMF research including the New York State Department of Health and the Maryland Power Plant Siting Program. For several years, California has had a utility-funded, state-run EMF research program. California recently passed a bill requiring the state's utilities to fund a larger research program. This bill, however, was vetoed by the governor.

⁞⁞⁞⁞⁞ One can and should call the local electric utility company. Many companies will take electric and magnetic field measurements, discuss the issue, and provide broad-based literature on the subject.

⁞⁞⁞⁞⁞ The Electric Power Research Institute (EPRI) is the major utility industry research group. The EPRI is the single largest source of funding for EMF research in the world at present. The EPRI can be reached at 3412 Hillview Ave., P.O. Box 10412, Palo Alto, California 94303; 415-855-2411. The EPRI takes a moderate ("the problem may be serious, let's take a look at it") approach to EMF.

⁞⁞⁞⁞⁞ Abroad, research is being conducted in many locations, including the Swedish State Power Board and Sweden's National Institute of Occupational Health; Power Gen, National Power and Scottish Power, in the United Kingdom; and Ontario Hydro and Hydro Quebec, in Canada.

⁞⁞⁞⁞⁞ The Electromagnetic Energy Policy Alliance (EEPA), 1255 23 St. N.W., Suite 850, Washington, D.C. 20037; 202-452-1070. The EEPA takes a harder ("the problem is not a serious one") approach.

⁞⁞⁞⁞⁞ The Department of Engineering and Public Policy at Carnegie Mellon University, Pittsburgh, Pennsylvania 15213, issued a report on the subject entitled *Electric and Magnetic Fields from 60 Hertz Electric Power: What Do We Know about Possible Health Risks?*

⁞⁞⁞⁞⁞ The National Council on Radiation Protection and Measurements, 7910 Woodmont Avenue, Suite 800, Bethesda, Maryland; 301-657-2652.

ⅢⅢⅢ *Microwave News*, (P.O. Box 1799, Grand Central Station, New York, New York 10163; 212-517-2800) provides coverage of research involving electromagnetic fields.

ⅢⅢⅢ Women's Occupational Health Resource Center in New York (212-305-2500).

ⅢⅢⅢ Office Technology Education Project in Somerville, Massachusetts (617-776-2777).

ⅢⅢⅢ Center for Office Technology in Virginia (703-276-1174).

ⅢⅢⅢ Paul Brodeur. 1989. *Currents of Death*. New York: Simon and Schuster.

ⅢⅢⅢ U.S. Environmental Protection Agency, Office of Research and Development's External Review Draft document *Potential Carcinogenicity of Electromagnetic Fields* ([EPA/600/6-90/005B] and the statement prepared January 1992 by EPA's Scientific Advisory Board (Radiation Advisory Committee's Nonionizing Electric and Magnetic Fields Subcommittee) on the review draft entitled *An SAB Report: Potential Carcinogenicity of Electric and Magnetic Fields* (EPA-SAB-RAC-92-013). U.S. Environmental Protection Agency, Washington, D.C. 20460.

ENDANGERED SPECIES

There are many environmental problems that, like endangered species, are not directly health problems. The focus of this book is environmental/human *health*. The endangered species brief is an exception, one made because the death of some species may result in the loss of materials that could be used as the bases of medicines that could save lives. Hence, endangered species might well be related to human health.

IIIIII IDENTIFYING THE PROBLEM IIIIII

Endangered species are species of plants, insects, and animals that are in danger of extinction (dying off). Endangered species differ from threatened species. The latter are defined as not yet endangered, but as likely to become endangered in the future.

It has been hypothesized that past periods of mass extinction were caused by natural events—possibly sudden changes in climate, or the bombardment of earth by comets. Today, however, we are currently in the middle of a mass extinction caused by human activities. Compared with the dawn of the twentieth century, the beginning of the twenty-first century will be marked by the disappearance of one million species on the planet. Most of the

IIIIII Comments on this brief were provided by Jo Ann Frier-Murza of the Endangered and Non-Game Species Program of the New Jersey Department of Environmental Protection and Energy and by senior attorneys at the Environmental Law Institute. IIIIII disappearing species are not "charismatic megafauna" like the bald eagle or even the spotted owl; they are not even catalogued. Most of the species we are losing are plants and insects that have yet to be identified. This is not to say that they are not precious in some unknown way, only that they are, as yet, not beloved.

Man-made changes in the surrounding environment have resulted in the destruction of "critical habitat"—areas of land, water, and air needed by a species for survival. Critical habitats such as wetlands and forests are being destroyed to make room for human development. In the process, genuine economic concerns come up against endangered species problems. Sometimes, but not always, one or the other must lose. In the late 1960s, the Tennessee Valley Authority (TVA) proposed the Tellico Dam Project. The goal of the project was to flood a large valley and then create a lake for recreational purposes. The dam would be used to generate electricity, needed to encourage growth and development of the region. However, when it was discovered that the flooding would threaten the habitat of the snail darter, protected under the recently passed Endangered Species Act, the TVA was ordered to stop. The TVA fought back, and in 1979, a bill was passed exempting the Tellico Dam from compliance with the act. The dam was built, the valley flooded—and the habitat of the snail darter was destroyed. The species was transplanted to other, similar rivers where it was hoped it would be able to survive. However, no one knows what the long-term fate of the snail darter will be.

Agriculture, logging, and cattle ranching threaten to destroy both old-growth forests in the United States and rain forests of the southern hemisphere—perhaps the most important endangered species habitat. Although tropical forests cover only 7 percent of the earth's surface, over half of the world's species of plants and animals live in them. In the case of the spotted owl in northern California, the impact of preserving its habitat threatened the future of logging in the region along with thousands of jobs. Dilemmas such as these raise many questions: is protection of all endangered species an absolute good or does it depend on what species, what cost (in terms of money, lost jobs, etc.) and what chance of success?

Human activities have applied deadly pressure on other species in several other ways. The introduction of chemicals or artificially manufactured materials into an ecosystem (pollution) has posed a deadly threat to plants and animals, endangered or otherwise. The use of insecticides, which work their way up the food chain, has a far-reaching impact. For example, several bird species have become unable to reproduce because of DDT ingestion. Discarded plastic is another pollutant with very serious negative consequences for wildlife. Discarded plastic is commonly ingested by marine wildlife. Sometimes wildlife get entangled in it. Possible threats to plant and animal wildlife have come from the introduction of new species into their areas. This can lead to both the introduction of new diseases, which can be devastating to native species of plants and animals, and fierce competition for habitats. For example, the English sparrow was introduced into the United States in the 1800s. This produced problems for many native species of birds when the sparrows took over the nesting sites of other species.

Accidental kills (on roads and waterways) are another serious problem for species that live near large human populations. Examples include the Florida Key deer and the Florida panther—both threatened by the automobile. Other examples include the rattlesnakes, pine snakes, and corn snakes in New Jersey.

There are many reasons to be concerned about endangered species. For example, all plant and animal species play a part in the larger food chain. The loss of certain species (plants or animals), may have a negative impact on other species dependent upon them or a source of food. As their numbers dwindle, this can start a chain reaction, reaching upwards, and affecting many other species. It has also been argued that conditions that threaten certain species will eventually threaten human health—the "miner's canary" analogy. Finally, many believe that human beings have a moral responsibility to protect endangered and threatened species. We are the only species to possess consciousness and foresight; hence, we have the ability to foresee the consequences of current actions and to recognize both the sheer beauty of nature and the wastefulness of killing living things.

|||||| CORRECTING THE PROBLEM ||||||

In 1973 Congress passed the Endangered Species Act. It prohibits trade in species designated as endangered. The act gives the

Secretary of the Department of the Interior, acting through the U.S. Fish and Wildlife Service (FWS), broad powers to protect all forms of wildlife and plants in danger of extinction. The FWS is responsible for designating species as threatened or endangered. More importantly, it designates critical habitats for these species. The main threat to critical habitats is uncontrolled land or water development. No federal agency may engage in a project that threatens the critical habitat of an endangered species. The act also gives the Secretary of Commerce, acting through the National Marine Fisheries Service, the responsibility for protecting most marine life.

The Endangered Species Act and the Lacey Act (which forbids importing any animal taken illegally from a wild habitat in another country) commit the United States to an international treaty that regulates the sale and purchase of endangered wildlife. This treaty, called the Convention on International Trade in Endangered Species of Wild Fauna and Flora (CITES), was developed in 1975 by the International Union for the Conservation of Nature (IUCN). Today more than one hundred nations have signed the treaty. Unfortunately, enforcement of the CITES treaty is not uniform. Furthermore, any nation may make a "reservation" on a species, thereby exempting itself from the restrictions on that species.

The Endangered Species Act provides penalties for anyone who sells an endangered species or product made from the body of an endangered species, or who transports an endangered species product between states or countries. Exceptions to the act, however, can be granted. In addition, the act makes it illegal for an endangered species to be "killed, hunted, collected, harassed, harmed, pursued, shot, trapped, wounded, or captured."

While many assumed the Endangered Species Act would be weakened following the decision on the Tellico Dam Project over the snail darter, the act has withstood challenges. However, some think the recent dispute over the habitat of the spotted owl may backfire—generating the energy and fuel needed to weaken the act.

In addition to federal laws, many states, such as New Jersey, have laws that complement and enhance the Endangered Species Act. Furthermore, every state but Alabama and Arkansas has a Natural Heritage Program. Here botanists, zoologists, and ecologists compile existing data and take inventory to locate a state's rarest plants, animals, and natural communities. Using computers, information is then processed to identify which species are most in danger. The program provides states with current information about the needs of their endangered species.

The World Wildlife Fund (WWF) is a private U.S. organization working worldwide to protect endangered wildlife and wild lands. It has established a network of agents, called TRAFFIC, to support the CITES agreement by calling attention to violations of wildlife trade laws.

The Nature Conservancy is another organization concerned with the plight of endangered species. It takes a slightly different approach to conservation, focusing on preserving the diversity of living things. The organization obtains land (through either purchase or gifts) and sets it aside as wildlife preserves. It has obtained approximately 3.5 million acres in the United States. About 1.5 million of these acres are in a thousand Conservancy preserves, the largest private sanctuary system in the world. Thousands of acres more have been turned over to state and national parks and wildlife refuges.

In some cases, the situation for certain species is so perilous that only deliberate rescue efforts will save them from extinction. For example, the black-footed ferret lost its habitat as humans encroached on its territory. Once thought to be extinct, the ferret has been bred in zoos in an effort to save it from extinction. Recently the ferret has been re-released into the wild, demonstrating the success of this effort.

Some observers believe that someday zoos may become the last refuge for certain wild species teetering on the brink of extinction. However, the capacity of zoos is very limited. They would be capable of sustaining only a minuscule fraction of those species that would eventually become extinct if the habitats of the world are destroyed.

IIIIII PITFALLS IIIIII

IIIIII The issue of critical habitat is an example of how environmental concerns often run up against human welfare issues. It is important to remember, when looking at concerns expressed about endangered species, that proposals for correcting problems must not neglect the concerns of indigenous populations who reside or work within critical habitat areas. For example, blanket proposals for protecting the habitat of the spotted owl or preserving the rain forest sometimes fail to adequately address the concerns of the local population who have made a living from the forest all their lives. It is important to get both sides of this issue in a story.

|||||| While programs for captive breeding in zoos may be the only salvation for some endangered species, some conservationists argue that an endangered species has not been truly saved unless it continues to exist in the wild. Zoos are aware of this dilemma and many are attempting to re-release animals bred in captivity. The black-footed ferret is one success story. But to keep a species captive too long could result in its eventual domestication. Programs such as the Species Survival Program (SSP) are attempts to maintain the genetic diversity of captive species for the future when the species can be re-released into the wild. This program is promoted by the American Association of Zoological Parks and Aquariums, in Wheeling, West Virginia. In other words, check to determine exactly what is being proposed in an effort to save an endangered species.

|||||| Some conservationists have suggested that there is no point in wasting resources on species that have no chance of surviving even with their aid. Their reasoning is that if no effort to save the species can possibly be adequate, then the effort would best be applied to a species with a greater chance of survival. With limited resources for endangered species, the concept of triage—making the difficult choices between species as to which will survive and which will become extinct—is very timely. Investigate the criteria used in the triage of endangered species cases. Why is a particular species and its associated ecosystem deemed worthy of preservation?

|||||| Restoration ecology has developed in an attempt to protect endangered species and their critical habitats. Restoration

ecologists attempt to rebuild damaged ecosystems. For example, they attempt to relocate wetlands in more convenient locations in order to allow development of existing wetlands. However, ecosystems and the species that survive within are very complex. Expectations for restoration ecology must be realistic. Restoration and relocation of critical habitats cannot replace protecting the remaining unspoiled natural habitats. Furthermore, restoration ecology is a growing industry. As such, its success requires production of quick results. Some research suggests that the end product of restoration is often less than promised by developers. The reporter should try to report the overall preservation plan for an area rather than focus on a single species.

IIIIII Find out whether your state has other laws that complement and extend the Endangered Species Act.

IIIIII In some case (but certainly not all), the fight to protect an endangered species has served as a camouflage for antidevelopment efforts. When the Tellico Dam was proposed, activists rallied around the fate of the snail darter, less because it was a much-beloved species, but rather because they wanted to stop the dam. Often fights to protect threatened wildlife are characterized by a split within activist groups, those who are genuinely concerned with the fate of a particular species and those who use the controversy as a way to stop development. The controversy surrounding the building of the Point Pleasant Pump in Bucks County, Pennsylvania, in the late 1980s is a case in point. The pump was proposed as a method of channeling river water from the Delaware River to cool the Limerick nuclear power reactor, which was needed to allow greater development of the region. Activists joined in opposition to the pump for several reasons. Some wanted to protect the Delaware River and were afraid of what the drop in water levels would do to fish and other species living in the river. Others, were opposed to the further development of Bucks County. Still others were opposed to nuclear power plants. In covering such a story, it is important to uncover all rationales involved in endangered species controversies.

|||||| SOURCES FOR JOURNALISTS ||||||

|||||| Most states have an endangered and nongame species program. This program is usually located within the fish-and-game division of a state's environmental agency. However, in some states the program may be located within the state's recreational agency.

|||||| The U.S. Fish and Wildlife Service is located within the Department of Interior, 1849 C St., Washington, D.C. 20240; 202-208-5634. The FWS regularly publishes a list of threatened and endangered species. The list is entitled *Endangered and Threatened Wildlife and Plants*.

|||||| The Office of Protected Resources within the National Marine Fisheries Service is a part of the Department of Commerce. It is located at 1335 East-West Highway, Silver Spring, Maryland 20910; 301-427-2239.

|||||| The World Wildlife Fund, 1250 24th St. N.W., Washington, D.C. 20037; 202-293-4800. For information specifically about the TRAFFIC USA program, call 202-778-9699.

|||||| The International Union for the Conservation of Nature (IUCN), Avenue du Mont-Blanc, CH-1196 Gland, Switzerland. The IUCN publishes the *Red Data Book* a comprehensive listing of endangered and threatened species around the world. Each entry contains data about an endangered species, detailing its habitat, its lifestyle, and its degree of endangerment. It is available in most libraries.

|||||| The Nature Conservancy, 1815 N. Lynn St., Arlington, Virginia 22209; 703-841-5300.

|||||| The Environmental Defense Fund, 257 Park Avenue South, 16th Floor, New York, New York 10010; 212-505-2100.

|||||| The National Wildlife Federation puts out *The Conservation Directory*. The directory provides information on who is doing what in the area of endangered species. It provides an extensive list of agencies along with their telephone numbers and addresses. The directory can be obtained by calling 800-432-6564.

GREEN MARKETING

The briefs on "Green Marketing" and "Right-to-Know (SARA Title III)" are included in this volume because they represent non-technology–based solutions to reducing risk.

IIIIII **IDENTIFYING THE PROBLEM** IIIIII

Green marketing is an advertising approach that promotes environmental sensitivity to would-be buyers. In the 1990s, surveys have suggested that many shoppers would chose products labeled "environmentally friendly" over those that are not. In a 1992 Gallop poll, 65 percent of the people polled in the United States said they would be willing to pay higher prices so that industry could better protect the environment. According to a 1990 survey conducted for Gerstman and Meyers, a New York packaging design company, approximately 75 percent were willing to pay 5 percent more and approximately 45 percent were willing to pay 15 percent more. Faced with this trend, manufacturers of both consumer products and package designers are attempting to improve their image with people concerned about the environment.

"Green" products are being introduced at twenty times the rate of regular products according to one ad agency. In the 1990s, Cheerios are "packaged in recycled paperboard," McDonald's uses

IIIIII Comments on this brief were provided by Linda Curran of Amoco. IIIIII "global releaf" bags, diapers are "biodegradable," and US Sprint offers environmental dollars.

Common "green labels" include "environmentally friendly," "safe for the environment," "ozone-friendly," "recycled," "recyclable," "degradable," and "compostable."

Recently concerns have been raised about the use of green labeling. Some environmental groups and state attorneys general are concerned that a growing number of companies, in their attempt to take advantage of consumer interest in the environment, are making claims that do not stand up to examination. They argue that too many environmental claims are trivial, confusing, and often misleading. The public, too, has become skeptical of green claims. According to a recent poll taken in Princeton, New Jersey, 47 percent of consumers have come to dismiss green labels as gimmicks.

There are three ways a company can connect itself to the environment. The first involves promoting a product's environmental advantages. The second is proactive environmental image advertising unrelated to the company's essential activities. Examples of this are the commercials that point out how the company recycles its office paper and contributes money for wetland preservation. The third approach involves the company's claims of environmental responsibility in manufacturing. For example, they point out how they have been able to cut factory effluent by 70 percent. All three types need monitoring for accuracy and relevance, but slightly exaggerated claims are better than ignoring the environmental impact of production altogether.

A group of ten state attorneys general has offered recommendations for what it calls "responsible environmental advertising." This report, issued in 1990 and called *The Green Report*, evaluates ecological assertions. Statements such as "environmentally friendly" and "safe for the environment" have been criticized by *The Green Report* as too broad and vague. In many cases, *The Green Report* concludes that such assertions represent value judgments, and as such, fail to reflect the pros and cons of what is most important for the environment. That is, important ecological questions are left unanswered: whether ease of disposal is more important than toxic pollution generated during manufacturing, or whether cutting down trees to make paper is worse than oil spills associated with the production of plastics.

The Green Report advises manufacturers to make environmental claims as specific as possible and to provide accompanying justifications. For example, the vague claim "better for the environment" can be better justified by the addition of the phrase "less packaging to throw away."

In 1992, the Federal Trade Commission (FTC) issued its own guidelines for environmental marketing. They are entitled *Summary FTC Environmental Marketing Guidelines* (*Federal Register*, vol. no. 157, Thursday, August 13, 1992, 16 CFR Part 260).

Other problems have arisen in the use of green labeling. Often a manufacturer labels a product "environmentally friendly" when one ingredient has been removed from it. This has been the case with aerosol cans. The removal of hydrofluorocarbons from aerosol cans has led some manufacturers to label the product "ozone friendly." However, as long as the product contains other ozone-threatening ingredients, such as methyl chloroform, the claim can be misleading. It should be noted, however, that methyl chloroform is a lot less damaging to the ozone layer than are CFCs. Furthermore, some companies, in an attempt to eliminate environmentally damaging ingredients, substitute new ingredients that are harmful in another way. They simply shift the nature of the problem, not eliminate it. For example, in aerosols, volatile organic compounds (VOCs) have been substituted for chlorofluorocarbons. Some scientists believe that VOCs contribute to the formation of harmful low-level smog and could add to the danger of global warming. Other scientists are less certain of the role of VOCs in causing ground-level ozone.

Another problem can arise when the public is environmentally ill-informed. The question then becomes whether or not companies pander to public perception of what is environmentally sound and thus market products based on that perception? Problems often need to be attacked from more than one perspective. The Mobil trash bag is a good example. People demanded a biodegradable plastic bag. Mobil knew that very little degrades in a well-designed sanitary landfill and that one does not necessarily want things to degrade in a sanitary landfill since doing so may then give off effluent that can cause smells and leaching into the groundwater. Ideal garbage is inert, that is, the opposite of biodegradable. Mobil also believed that the environmentally best way to handle a used plastic bag is probably to incinerate it and capture the energy.

However, incineration and siting of a plastics-to-energy incinerator is very problematic for the public. Mobil had a choice—to either attempt to convince the public otherwise or pander to public demand. Mobil chose to follow consumer demand. Unlike McDonald's which quietly switched from polystyrene to cardboard in its packaging, Mobil chose to boast about its choice—a decision that, with hindsight, proved foolish when its claims were proven environmentally irrelevant. The problem is that green marketing is typically aimed at the public's environmental concerns. If these concerns are oversimplified, the marketing also is going to be oversimplified, and vulnerable to charges of misleading the public. "Misfollowing" the public might be a more accurate charge.

It should be noted, however, that some environmentalists have argued that efforts to promote legitimately benign products as environmentally safe is acceptable, so long as it gets companies to "think green."

Some companies have always had environmentally friendly products. But only since the 1990s has it made any sense to promote them as such. Others do not want to rush into green marketing. Promoting environmental claims that are subsequently questioned can hurt business, as was illustrated in the case of Mobil's trash bags.

Several commonly used terms are problematic. "Recycled" is a common green label used in packaging. By itself, it provides no information on what percentage of a product or package is made of recycled material, and currently there is no standard. There also is no standard definition of the term. Some consumers assume it refers to the re-use of materials used by consumers, reducing the drain on natural resources. However, for some manufacturers, it refers to the re-use of scraps from their own manufacturing process. While this is a good thing to do, it has been done by companies for years, and, therefore, does not solve any current environmental problems. Recycling "post-consumer waste" is newer and harder to do, not intrinsically better.

"Recyclable" is a hotly contested term. Almost anything can be recycled with enough effort and money. What makes something truly "recyclable" is whether it is economically worth recycling. Manufacturers claim that use of the term raises the consumer's consciousness. Environmentalists, however, argue that use of the term is misleading, particularly in areas where there are no convenient recycling plants. Here all products, whether they are or are not recyclable, end up in a landfill or incinerator.

It is also debatable whether reusing something in a degraded form is recycling. The purest sort of recycling uses a glass bottle as a bottle again. Grinding it up into "glasphalt" is better than throwing it away, but it is not pure recycling. The American public puts more emphasis on recycling than a complete "life-cycle analysis" might suggest. Cans and bottles are easily recyclable (and often recycled), whereas the individual-serving little juice boxes, for example, are more difficult to recycle. But these little juice boxes use much less material in the first place (a juice box crumples down to about as much waste as the cap from the bottle, which is not recycled). In addition, juice boxes do not need refrigeration, which eliminates concern with CFCs from refrigerated trucks on the highway. Calculating which is ultimately better for the environment—a 6-ounce juice box or a 6-ounce bottle—is very difficult. But calculating which is better in the minds of a society concerned with recycling is easy—many primary schools forbid kids to bring juice boxes to school.

The benefits from products that are "degradable" and "biodegradable" is another controversial area. Environmental groups argue that there is no evidence that degradability offers any advantage if a product is disposed in a landfill, where all waste decays very slowly. Several states have brought legal action against companies that made degradability claims for plastic trash bags and disposable diapers. In fact degradable garbage can be *more* harmful than inert garbage. If the landfill leaks, it is the degraded garbage that presents a problem.

The claim of "compostable" is problematic as well. Composting refers to the biological decay of organic materials. The problem arises from the fact that even though many products can be composted, there are very few plants available in the United States that engage in composting municipal solid waste.

It is true that green marketing can distort, mislead, and trivialize environmental issues. It has even been referred to as "eco-pornography." However, an important point, too often ignored, is that green marketing is, at the same time, a very good sign. Producers and advertisers develop products geared toward what it is they think people care about. The increasing frequency of green marketing serves as a barometer of public concern for the environment. A society in which companies are jockeying for environmental product loyalty is better served than one in which companies are ignoring the issue—unless, of course, green marketing produces such public complacency that it prohibits the development of more far-reaching, long-term solutions to environmental crises.

|||||| CORRECTING THE PROBLEM ||||||

There are several possible ways of correcting the problem. One approach focuses on educating the buying public. Another aims at greater regulation of claims.

Because green labeling is perceived as a marketing issue, the Federal Trade Commission has been asked by both manufacturers and the packaging industry to issue a nationwide rule regulating environmental claims. The FTC has formed a task force to deal with environmental claims.

In an attempt to educate the public, several countries, including Germany, Canada, Japan, the European Communities and the Nordic Council have developed a program of "green seals." This label can only be applied to products meeting certain criteria (e.g., emphasis on recycling, reducing pollution) in defined product categories. The U.S. Environmental Protection Agency considered proposed legislation to set up a quasi-governmental reviewing board that could issue a seal of approval. However, based on problems other countries were having, the EPA dropped the idea. In the absence of leadership at the federal level, several states and regional groups have developed their own state green labels. There are also private national environmental certification (green seal) programs.

Some industries have developed an ethical code that forbids environmental/health/safety appeals. Pesticide manufacturers, for example, consider themselves ethically obliged not to market their products as less environmentally risky than the competition. However, this diminishes the incentive to develop an environmentally better product, and it prohibits consumers from finding out when such a product has been developed.

||||| **PITFALLS** |||||

||||| Environmental marketing is complex. First there is the issue of whether a product does what it claims to do. Then the question is, even if it does what it claims, does it actually do any good. Finally comes the question of whether debatable product claims are guilty of misleading the public or just deferring to public concerns and convictions that may themselves be debatable.

||||| It is hard to find products that are completely good for the environment. For example, the mining of the metals used in making a water-saving showerhead adds significantly to its environmental price tag. In analyzing the environmental impact of any product, it is important to consider its entire life-cycle. Looking at only part of the story can lead to real distortions, as in the case of recycling bottles versus juice boxes discussed above.

||||| When considering a company's green products, it is probably wise to also consider its record of compliance with other environmental programs (e.g., water, air, and land quality).

||||| Journalists should be skeptical of both industry *and* environmental activist claims. Too often only industry claims are scrutinized. For example, the notion that paper recycling saves trees is as foolish as the notion that degradable trash bags improve landfills. The trees that are made into paper are a crop, planted to be harvested. When paper recycling decreases the demand for trees, fewer trees are planted. The result may be a natural ecosystem left to the forces of succession, or, it may be a new housing development. Paper recycling, though a good idea, no more saves trees than a boycott on eating asparagus would save asparagus plants. Take seriously the goal of helping the public develop a deeper, more complex understanding of environmental impacts. All sides are now looking for ways to stake out

environmental claims. While that is certainly good, we need to assess these claims—not just punish industry for daring to make any.

||||||| **SOURCES FOR JOURNALISTS** |||||||

||||||| The U.S. Environmental Protection Agency has launched a major research project to determine how to evaluate products as "environmentally preferable." For more information on this call the Pollution Prevention Program of the EPA at 202-260-5733.

||||||| Another source of information is Green Cross of Scientific Certification Systems (510-832-1415) a California-based organization paid by manufacturers to substantiate environmental claims. Green Seal (202-331-7337) is an independent Washington-based group that makes its own environmental evaluation of claims.

||||||| For a copy of *The Green Report*, contact the attorney general's office in Minnesota.

||||||| The *Summary FTC Environmental Marketing Guidelines,* issued by the Federal Trade Commission, can be found in the *Federal Register,* 57, no. 157, Thursday, August 13, 1992. You can obtain a copy by calling the FTC at 202-326-2222.

GREENHOUSE EFFECT

Many people feel passionately about global warming. The extreme positions (we cannot afford to stop economic growth, and we must reduce population growth and economic development based on resource extraction) leave most Americans with nothing concrete to do but worry. Journalists could make the issue more concrete by emphasizing, in their reporting, energy efficiency and conservation practices in which individuals can engage.

IIIIII **IDENTIFYING THE PROBLEM** IIIIII

The "greenhouse effect," or global warming, is the behavior of the earth's atmosphere that causes heat from the sun to be trapped near the earth's surface. It can be compared to the mechanism by which a greenhouse can maintain warm temperatures in the cold winter. The earth's atmosphere acts much like the glass of a greenhouse. The glass allows the sun's radiant energy to penetrate and warm the inside, but slows the escape of the heat. Similarly, the earth's atmosphere allows sunlight that reaches it to pass through and heat the earth's surface. The earth sends the heat energy, called infrared radiation, back into the atmosphere. Some

IIIIII Comments on this brief were provided by Barbara Litt of the New Jersey Department of Environmental Protection and Energy, Brian Flannery of Exxon Research and Engineering Company, Paul Zakriski of BF Goodrich, and Leonard Lapatnick of Public Service Electric and Gas Company. IIIIII of the energy escapes into space but some is trapped by the atmosphere. It is this natural greenhouse effect that makes life possible on earth. Without the atmosphere, the average surface temperature of the earth would be approximately 59 Fahrenheit degrees (33 Celsius degrees) lower than it is today.

Many scientists fear that the buildup of greenhouse gases caused by human activities may give us too much of a good thing. Increased amounts of the natural greenhouse gases, as well as man-made greenhouse gases, are being sent into the atmosphere. As these gases build up in the atmosphere, they can trap heat, thus raising the earth's average temperature. The National Academy of Sciences (NAS) has observed that there has been a measurable increase in the earth's temperature over the past one hundred years. However, it is not possible to tell whether the temperature increase is due to the growing concentrations of greenhouse gases or to natural fluctuations in the earth's temperature. Furthermore, the increase has not been uniform. Some parts of the globe have been cooled and others have stayed the same. Many scientists now believe that the temperature increase (0.3-0.6 C) is due to the greenhouse effect and that continued production of greenhouse gases will increase the earth's temperature even more. Many others remain skeptical.

Most scientists agree that increased concentrations of greenhouse gases will raise the earth's average temperature. Nevertheless, opinions among responsible scientists range from fears of doomsday to beliefs that there is no problem. And while many leading scientists are convinced that the enhanced greenhouse effect will result in significant future climate change, they acknowledge that there is considerable uncertainty about the magnitude, timing, and distribution of the possible effects. Even if large climatic changes do occur over the next century, it will probably take a decade or more before it is possible to confirm this, given the large natural variability in temperatures.

Models have been developed to forecast the impact of global warming, but they are highly uncertain as to the magnitude, timing, and regional distribution of climate change. Some scientists suggest that these models will lack predictive capability for at least another ten to twenty years. In addition to the limitations in the models, it is hard to project the impact of global warming because of the lack of understanding of the responses of stressed ecosystems.

A warmer world will probably mean a rise in sea level caused by thermal expansion of the oceans and the melting of glaciers and land ice sheets. Areas most at risk from rising sea level include low-lying islands and coastal regions, especially densely populated fertile river deltas. Studies done by the United National Environment Program have identified the ten most vulnerable countries as Bangladesh, Egypt, the Gambia, Indonesia, the Maldives, Mozambique, Pakistan, Senegal, Surinam, and Thailand. Most studies suggest that cities can be protected from rising sea levels. But protection of large coastal areas and ecosystems is more difficult.

Previous climate changes have had far-reaching effects on the nature and distribution of natural vegetation. A changing environment is likely to affect agriculture in a variety of ways. It is possible that some agriculturally productive areas might become deserts, while other areas that were previously unable to support crops might become agriculturally capable. Global warming, therefore, will have some winners—presumably countries like Canada and Siberia, along with the losers.

Long-term deviations in temperatures could require the use of different planting techniques or the planting of different crops. Studies by the Intergovernmental Panel on Climate Change (IPCC)— an organization set up under the auspices of the United Nations Environment Program and the World Meteorological Organization—suggest that agricultural needs can be met through the twenty-first century even if global warming occurs.

Natural ecosystems could suffer a loss of species diversity. Whether species become extinct would depend on the speed and severity of the climate change, as well as the species' ability to adapt to change.

Other possible changes have been suggested. Change in climate could produce modifications in the occurrence of diseases and pests. Changes in ocean currents could alter fish populations. Variations in rainfall could affect river flow and groundwater storage, with important consequences for irrigation, water resources, and navigation.

The earth's infrared radiation does not pass freely into space because certain gases in the atmosphere absorb it. They send the infrared radiation back toward earth, adding to the warming of the surface. Natural greenhouse gases include water vapor, carbon dioxide, methane, and ozone. (See the brief on "Ozone.")

Water vapor is by far the most important natural greenhouse gas in the atmosphere. Of the people-made greenhouse gases, the most important are carbon dioxide, methane, nitrous oxide, and the halocarbons, of which the chlorofluorocarbons (CFCs) are the most significant. Ozone in the lower atmosphere, whose concentration is affected by people's activities, is also an important greenhouse gas. Apart from CFCs, these gases also occur naturally. Water vapor is intimately involved in the greenhouse question because its concentration is linked with those of other gases through a "feedback mechanism." Warming brought about by other greenhouse gases increases evaporation and allows the atmosphere to hold more water vapor, thus, in turn, enhancing the warming.

Carbon dioxide flows in a natural cycle. It is exchanged naturally between huge reservoirs of carbon in the atmosphere, the oceans, and the living world. Biological processes on land contribute 110,000 million tons of carbon as carbon dioxide to the atmosphere each year. This is largely balanced by the annual uptake of carbon during photosynthesis. The oceans are also believed to emit and absorb similar amounts. Human activities add 5,700 million tons to the atmosphere through the burning of fossil fuels (coal, oil, and gas), plus between 600–2,500 million tons through land-use changes, mainly the loss of tropical forests. Carbon dioxide levels began to increase in the nineteenth century with the industrial revolution and increasing deforestation.

To produce equivalent amounts of energy, coal gives off more carbon dioxide than gasoline, which in turn gives off more carbon dioxide than natural gas. Cars, space heaters, and power plants are common sources of carbon dioxide. The destruction of tropical and temperate rain forests continues to release still more carbon dioxide. Based on current global trends (assuming continued growth of 1 to 2 percent a year in the production and use of fossil fuels), carbon dioxide concentrations will double preindustrial levels by about the year 2065. The atmospheric lifetime of carbon dioxide is uncertain, but is between 50–200 years.

Methane gas is another greenhouse gas that is being added to the atmosphere in greater amounts. Methane gas is given off by decaying animal waste, ruminant animals (cows, sheep, goats, camels, and buffaloes), and rice paddies. Methane levels have been increasing since the beginning of the nineteenth century, with a more rapid rise in the last few decades of about 1 percent a year. This is partly because changing agricultural practices, waste disposal (landfills give off methane gas), and mining produce significant amounts of methane. Another possible source is termite populations, which thrive in areas where vast tropical forests have been burned. In addition, human processes which remove methane from the atmosphere can be impaired by other emissions, principally carbon monoxide. Recent measurements show that the rate of growth of methane has decreased, but, as yet, there is no explanation of why the rate has slowed.

Natural vegetation gives off large quantities of nitrous oxide, but the increase in the concentration of this gas (about .3 percent a year) is thought to come mainly from agriculture and mass burning.

Atmospheric ozone exists mainly in the high upper atmosphere, in the stratospheric ozone layer. Stratospheric ozone plays a crucial role since it absorbs most solar ultraviolet radiation, preventing it from reaching the earth's surface where it is harmful to life. Ozone also exists in the lower atmosphere, or troposphere. In the troposphere, ozone plays a significant role both as a greenhouse gas and as a pollutant. (See the brief on "Ozone.")

CFCs are people-made compounds containing chlorine, fluorine, and carbon. They are nontoxic and inert, which makes them useful as aerosol propellants and as refrigerants and insulators. CFCs in the troposphere act as powerful greenhouse gases because they absorb infrared radiation in a region of the spectrum where there is little absorption by other gases. CFCs have a lifetime of around one hundred years in the atmosphere. Emission rates exceed the slow atmospheric decay rate, so CFC levels are increasing by about 4 to 5 percent every year.

The greenhouse effect is a complex problem. It is a long-term problem in several ways. First, it will take a long time to predict the problem with any degree of certainty. Second, it will take a long time to see the effects. And third, once realized, it will take a long time to reverse. These characteristics, taken together, make deciding what to do difficult. An even more difficult problem is deciding whether we can afford to wait until we know with certainty.

In addition, both the existence of, and solutions to, the problem are rife with uncertainty. For example, for many years to come, it will not be possible to determine by direct observation whether global warming is occurring because the earth's climate naturally fluctuates, and the climate has a delayed response to increases in concentrations of greenhouse gases.

There are so many factors contributing to the greenhouse effect that no single solution will be effective. If the problem is as serious as many scientists fear, each factor that causes some of the problem will need to be addressed. Although scientists cannot say for certain that global warming is occurring, the consequences, if it is occurring, may be so serious that it must be taken seriously.

While much attention has been directed toward consideration of the likelihood and possible impact of global warming, other related issues surrounding global warming have received less attention. For example, how much sense does it make to act before we have clear answers to the questions of likelihood and impact? Exactly how much worse will things be if we wait until we know more? And how long will that take? The problem may be very serious, but it is slow-moving, and some scientists have suggested that we may be able to afford to study the problem for ten more years before we begin costly efforts to solve it. Another issue involves the types of solutions that would make the most sense now. Considerations here involve what can be done that is not too expensive, that is likely to help, and least likely to cause unexpected problems.

‖‖‖‖ CORRECTING THE PROBLEM ‖‖‖‖

In 1988, nations around the world established the ongoing Intergovernmental Panel on Climate Change for scientific and technical assessment of the climate issue. The IPCC was established to conduct technical assessments of scientific information on climate change, the potential impact of climate change, and possible response strategies. Today, over one hundred countries participate in, or actively support, the IPCC. The IPCC is scheduled to complete a second assessment report in 1995, in which economic issues are to be addressed. The IPCC's first assessment, in 1990, provided primary input for negotiation of the Climate Convention.

Between 1991 and 1992, nations of the world negotiated a Framework Convention on Climate Change, which was open for signature by heads of state at the United Nations Conference on Environment and Development, held in Rio de Janeiro in 1992. The convention was ratified by enough countries to enter into force in 1993. While the convention does not call for explicit limits on greenhouse-gas emissions, it does require developed countries to adopt policies to limit future emissions and to provide new and additional financial aid to developing countries. It also requires detailed national reports of programs to respond to climate change, emissions inventories, and projections of future emissions. The convention established an ongoing Conference of Parties which will be the primary legal forum for future international actions to address climate change.

To reduce the possibility of climate change, many believe it is now necessary to restrict emissions of the principal greenhouse gases. How much reduction will be necessary and at what cost is at issue. The IPCC estimates that reductions of more than 60 percent in people-made emissions of long-lived greenhouse gases are required to stabilize atmospheric concentrations at current levels. The Bush administration, in 1992, said future carbon dioxide emissions could be cut by 11 percent from original projections by the year 2000, without significant strains on the economy. But this falls short of stabilizing emissions at 1990 levels, which many scientists consider a minimum starting point. Scientists say the trick, for the long run, is to cut emissions by 20 to 40 percent so that existing concentrations of the gas in the atmosphere do not increase markedly. Industry studies estimate that U.S. utilities will spend as much as $24 billion a year by 2005 on programs aimed at conservation and developing new energy sources if carbon dioxide emissions have to be cut by 20 percent or more. On the other hand, a Natural Resource Defense Council study by Lashof suggests the economy could save as much as $2.3 trillion over the next forty years if aggressive conservation and fuel-switching programs are adopted to stabilize greenhouse emissions.

While individuals and nations can take steps to reduce the threat of future climate changes, the problem is obviously global in scope and impact. Proposals to stabilize and reduce emissions will be costly and require changes in lifestyle. Measures that have been proposed include:

ⅢⅢ promoting greater energy conservation and efficiency;

ⅢⅢ phasing out production and consumption of CFCs;

ⅢⅢ switching fuels to lower emissions of carbon dioxide per unit of delivered energy;

ⅢⅢ increasing the use of nuclear power and developing renewable energy sources;

ⅢⅢ transferring aid and technology to developing countries where emissions of greenhouse gases are expected to rise;

ⅢⅢ limiting and taxing emissions;

ⅢⅢ halting the destruction of rain forests and starting a program of reforestation; and

ⅢⅢ changing agricultural practices to reduce methane and nitrous oxide emissions.

While everyone agrees that energy efficiency improvements are an avenue society should pursue as a response to climate change, there is great debate over how much can be achieved through efficiency and what it will cost. Some economists put the annual cost to the United States at more than $100 billion a year, while others argue there actually will be savings as the average citizen and factories alike learn to use energy more wisely.

ⅢⅢ PITFALLS ⅢⅢ

ⅢⅢ Among outstanding scientists, especially in the United States, there is a very wide range of opinion about the "science" of global change. Avoid taking a single point of view.

ⅢⅢ Avoid focusing solely on technical solutions without acknowledging that many are untried. They too may cause climatic or other problems.

ⅢⅢ Be sure to distinguish between stratospheric and ground-level ozone. In the troposphere, ozone causes adverse health effects in both plants and animals. In the upper troposphere and lower stratosphere, it acts as a greenhouse gas. In the stratosphere, it prevents harmful ultraviolet radiation from reaching the earth's surface. (See the brief on "Ozone.")

|||||| Try to understand the economic and social aspects of proposals to reduce the threat of climate change, especially proposals in the international arena.

|||||| The public is often confused about warming versus thinning. Carbon dioxide and methane are heat-trapping gases that cause *warming*. Chlorofluorocarbons, widely used as refrigerants, contribute to global warming as well. CFCs are also the sole agent of the *thinning* of the ozone layer. (See the brief on "Ozone.")

|||||| The tough question is not necessarily whether or not the greenhouse effect is real, but what to do when you do not know if it is real: wait or act. Certainly this depends on the environmental and economic costs of acting if it turns out to be unreal, and the environmental cost of waiting if it turns out to be real.

|||||| SOURCES FOR JOURNALISTS ||||||

|||||| The United Nations Environment Program is a source of information on global warming. The program is located within the Industry and Environment Office, 39-43 Quai Andre Citroen, 75739 Paris, Cedex 15, France. The phone number is 33 (1) 40 58 88 50.

|||||| The U.S. Environmental Protection Agency has an Office of Climate Change that will provide information on the greenhouse effect and rain forest deforestation. Its number in Washington, D.C. is 202-260-8825.

|||||| The National Oceanic and Atmospheric Administration is located within the Department of Commerce. Its Public Affairs Office in Washington, D.C. is 202-377-8090; its Education Office is 202-606-4380.

|||||| University departments such as Earth Sciences, Environmental Sciences, Meteorology, Agronomy and Geophysics.

|||||| The Environmental Defense Fund provides information on global warming. It is located at 257 Park Avenue South, New York, New York 10010; 212-505-2100.

||||| Greenpeace, 1611 Connecticut Ave. NW, Washington, D.C. 20009; 202-462-1177.
||||| Natural Resource Defense Council, 122 E. 42 St., New York, New York 10168; 212-949-0049.
||||| The Worldwatch Institute, 1776 Massachusetts Ave., N.W., Washington, D.C. 20036; 202-452-1999.
||||| Intergovernmental Panel on Climate Change. 1990. *Scientific Assessment of Climate Change*, Summary and Report, World Meteorological Organization, United Nations Environment Program. Cambridge, Mass.: Cambridge University Press.
||||| U.S. Congress, Office of Technology Assessment. Feb. 1991. *Changing by Degrees: Steps to Reduce Greenhouse Gases*, OTA-O-482. Washington, D.C.: U.S. Government Printing Office.
||||| U.S. Environmental Protection Agency, *EPA Journal*, 16, no. 2, March/April 1990.

HAZARDOUS WASTE

More controversy surrounds the issue of the impact of hazardous-waste sites than almost any other kind of environmental activity. Every Superfund site has a health assessment made by the Agency for Toxic Substances and Disease Registry (ATSDR) in Atlanta—an unprecedented requirement. Many millions of dollars have been spent on these assessments. The results, even if making very conservative assumptions, show little impact compared to other environmental and occupational health problems presented in this volume. New and well-managed hazardous-waste sites should reduce public exposures and worker risk.

IIIII IDENTIFYING THE PROBLEM IIIII

The Resource Conservation and Recovery Act (RCRA), enacted in 1976, requires that hazardous waste be controlled from the time it is produced to its final disposal—from cradle to grave. RCRA defines a hazardous waste as one that may cause, or significantly contribute to, illness or death, or that may substantially threaten human health or the environment when it is not properly controlled. A waste can be hazardous for a number of

IIIII This brief is based on an earlier version by Frank J. Popper, Department of Urban Studies and Community Health, Rutgers University, in the first edition of the *Handbook*. Additional comments were provided by Ellissa Parker of the Environmental Law Institute, Ron Burstein of National Starch and Chemical Company, David Boltz and Thomas Weidner of Bethlehem Steel Corporation, L. S. Bernstein of Mobil Oil Corporation, and Robert Lewis of Exxon Engineering. IIIII reasons. It can be toxic, ignitable, corrosive, or dangerously reactive. A hazardous waste can be a solid, liquid, sludge, or gas.

There are numerous sources of hazardous waste, including industrial plants, military arsenals, hospitals and laboratories, gasoline stations, and power plants. All produce waste that can be hazardous and in need of careful management. Management of hazardous waste involves transportation, treatment and storage, disposal—and, of course, efforts to reduce the amount of hazardous waste to be managed through source reduction and recycling. At issue each step of the way is the population's (both workers' and communities') potential exposure to hazardous substances that may pose serious health risks.

Three major concerns surrounding the issue of hazardous waste are the cleanup of the thousands of previously contaminated sites, the regulation and management of active sites, and the siting of new hazardous-waste facilities.

|||||| **CLEANUP OF ABANDONED HAZARDOUS-WASTE SITES**

Abandoned contaminated properties containing hazardous waste exist across the United States. Hazardous waste is produced in every state, but it tends to be concentrated in major industrialized regions, since industry is its major producer. During the late 1970s and into the 1980s, a wide variety of programs were put into place to regulate the cleanup of abandoned hazardous-waste sites. Prior to the enactment of legislation, most hazardous waste was disposed using methods that did not protect human health or the environment. The most common method was to pour liquids, sludge, and slurries into "surface impoundments"—that is, pits or areas encircled by dikes. The impoundment usually lacked any liner to prevent seepage into the ground. Generally there was little or no treatment to reduce the hazards. Some waste was dumped into landfills. These landfills were not specially designed for hazardous waste and have tended to leak (though typically not as badly as the impoundments).

Though some hazardous-waste sites clearly present serious hazards, the riskiness of most is debated, and most experts judge that many are simply unlikely to threaten public health. In the EPA's

BLOOM COUNTY   by Berke Breathed

massive study of public versus expert assessments of risk, hazardous-waste cleanup was one that the public considered enormously more risky than the experts do.

Substantially reducing the risk (to health and the environment) of dangerous sites is usually expensive. Typically, it has been done by containment and monitoring rather than cleanup. It is often impossible, and almost always expensive, to reduce the risk to almost nothing; we do not know, for example, how to clean soil down to the last molecule of contaminant. Policies and politics that force cleanup (especially "total" cleanup) increase the cost much more than they increase the measurable benefits.

Hazardous-waste cleanup justifiably generates an enormous amount of fear and anger (outrage). Even if a site poses little threat to health and the environment, it is still a major threat to the value of one's home and the quality of one's life; the stigma of living near a Superfund site is real, whether or not the hazard is real. People feel betrayed, misled, mistreated, and ignored. The laborious, bureaucratic and legalistic cleanup process only exacerbates these feelings. Since the law does not provide for compensation (much less reparations), the only avenue for these feelings is the demand for total cleanup.

Cleanup efforts generally can be divided into programs organized under the EPA, programs operated by the U.S. Department of Defense (DOD) and the Department of Energy (DOE), and other federal, state, and private programs.

The EPA is directly responsible for, or indirectly involved in, the cleanup of hazardous waste at both private and government sites, (including DOD and DOE installations) that are on the National

Priorities List (NPL)—a list of more than twelve hundred sites scheduled for cleanup. The EPA is only marginally involved in the tens of thousands of sites that do not make the NPL. Cleanup of NPL sites is regulated under the Comprehensive Environmental Response, Compensation, and Liability Act (CERCLA), which is the Superfund law. Under CERCLA, the EPA administers a Superfund program to identify the legacy of hazardous-waste disposal, determine responsible parties, and finance the cleanup of sites where responsible parties are unable to do so. The Superfund is a trust fund that was established from revenue drawn from taxes on oil and other specific compounds for the purpose of cleaning up hazardous sites. Wherever responsible parties—current or former site owners, or operators, or generators of hazardous waste—could be found, they were to be held financially responsible for site cleanup.

The EPA established a formal process to choose NPL sites. First, staff do a preliminary in-house assessment to determine if field investigations are needed. Then data obtained for sites requiring field investigations are entered into the Hazard Ranking System (HRS). Sites are ranked on consideration of five pathways: ground water, surface water, air, fire and explosion, and direct contact. Integrated into the equation is consideration of waste characteristics, waste quantities, releases, and proximity to people. Sites are then assigned a single site score. Sites with a score greater than 28.5 are placed on the NPL. In 1990, the EPA reported that actions had been initiated at over two thousand sites, cleanup was in progress at four hundred NPL sites, and cleanup had been completed at sixty-three NPL sites.

When the Superfund was first established as a $1.6 billion program, many people hoped it would solve a serious national problem. With time, the magnitude and intricacies of the mandate became clearer. In 1986, the Superfund Amendments and Reauthorization Act (SARA) was passed, and the fund was increased by $8.5 billion. [See the brief on "Right-to-Know (SARA Title III)."] In 1990, the program was again reauthorized through September 1994, and $5.1 billion was added to the Superfund.

In 1991, the EPA reported 33,834 potential sites through its Comprehensive Environmental Response, Compensation, and Liability Information System (CERCLIS), with 1,236 sites on the NPL. Of the original 33,000-plus sites, over 19,000 were eliminated after a preliminary screening by the EPA. Nevertheless, it is anticipated that the number of NPL sites identified will continue to increase over time to between 2,100 and 6,000 sites. The University of Tennessee estimated that remediation of 3,000 NPL sites will consume approximately $151 billion during the period 1990–2020—an average cost of between $5–15 million per site. The most hazardous and expensive sites are controlled by the DOE. Estimates of the cleanup of some of these sites are considerably in excess of $1 billion if, in fact, they can be cleaned up at all.

Cleanup of hazardous waste has proceeded at a slow pace. The process has been slowed by legal battles and bureaucratic bungles, including investigations by other government agencies that concluded the program was poorly managed and ineffective. Regulatory and administrative changes over the years have served to slow the process and make it significantly more costly. For example, since the 1986 reauthorization of SARA, the ATSDR is required to provide a second opinion on health criteria applied to sites. Containment at sites or removal and transport to permitted landfills is no longer acceptable. Congress now requires permanent on-site remedies that reduce the volume, toxicity, or mobility of hazardous substances. Capping, removal, and transport is allowed only as a last resort. Even the definition of a clean site has proven to be problematic. The EPA policy allows regional offices to establish levels of acceptable risk on a region-by-region basis. Therefore, while residual cancer risks of 1 in 10,000 might be permitted at some sites, others have decided to define the level of acceptable risk more stringently at 1 in 100 million.

The DOD and the DOE are responsible for the cleanup of sites that they and/or their contractors have contaminated. However, under SARA, the EPA can place these sites on the NPL list as well. In 1991, the DOD reported over seventeen hundred potential sites, and the DOE identified close to four thousand sites. As with the Superfund program, the projected and actual costs for remediation of DOD and DOE sites have increased rapidly. Cleanup costs for many of these sites often exceed costs for the typical Superfund site since they often involve the cleanup of land contaminated with both radioactive and chemical wastes. In 1991, the DOD estimated its total cleanup costs at $24.5 billion. Predictions place total DOD costs between $18 and $70 billion. Comparative estimates for the DOE sites range from $92 to $360 billion.

The Department of the Interior's (DOI) Bureau of Land Management remediates waste generated at mines, oil and gas exploration sites, and landfills located on DOI land. Hazardous waste resulting from research activities and operations undertaken by federal governmental agencies such as the Department of Agriculture and Health and Human Services is another set of federal liabilities.

States, too, have important hazardous-waste cleanup mandates. According to the Superfund legislation, states with sites on the NPL must pay 10 percent of the capital cost of site cleanup as well as all future operating and maintenance costs. States are also responsible for sites not on the NPL. Non-NPL sites far outnumber NPL sites. There is considerable variation among states in the level of development of their programs for hazardous-waste cleanup.

|||||| **REGULATION AND MANAGEMENT OF ACTIVE SITES**

In the United States, over 260 million tons of hazardous waste is produced each year. The proper handling of this waste at active sites is a critical health and environmental issue. The Resource Conservation and Recovery Act mandated the development of regulations governing the proper handling, transportation, storage, treatment, and disposal of hazardous wastes. The regulations set standards for the following: identification and listing of these hazardous waste; requirements for generators and transporters of the hazardous waste; standards for active hazardous-waste treatment, storage, and disposal (TSD) facilities; and permit requirements for TSD facilities.

The intent of the law is to develop a broad-based, comprehensive regulatory program that properly tracks the movement of hazardous waste currently being produced from the point of generation through its ultimate disposal. Individual states are encouraged to develop their own programs. Under the provisions of RCRA, the states are allowed to assume primary authority to regulate hazardous-waste management within their jurisdiction provided they adopt regulations equivalent to, or more stringent than, the federal requirements. Federal funds are allocated to states, in the form of grants, to be used for the development of such programs.

In November 1984, Congress passed the Hazardous and Solid Waste Act (HSWA) to RCRA to upgrade the existing federal hazardous-waste regulatory program. HSWA contains many technical requirements for hazardous-waste management and includes specific timetables for their implementation. States, such as New Jersey, that had been authorized by the EPA to run their own program, in lieu of the federal program, are mandated to revise their regulations to include the new RCRA provisions.

The University of Tennessee estimates the cost of cleaning up functioning sites at between $150 and $423 billion during the period 1990–2020.

|||||| **SITING HAZARDOUS-WASTE FACILITIES**

The proposed siting of a hazardous-waste facility invariably causes controversy, pitting the developer of the facility—a waste disposal company, manufacturer, or public agency—against the facility's neighbors-to-be. Although a few very small hazardous-waste sites have been approved in the United States in the past decade, no new large-scale, free-standing hazardous-waste facilities have been sited anywhere in the nation since 1980. Hundreds, however, have been proposed. All have either failed to gain the necessary approvals or, in a few cases, been delayed. As the United States increases its production of hazardous wastes and implements laws to close inadequate, unsafe facilities, new and stronger pressure to find sites is emerging.

Many states, especially those in the industrial Northeast and Midwest, have boards and agencies whose specific duty is to find sites for hazardous-waste facilities. These agencies, traditionally, establish need, criteria, and procedures, and, in time, select a number of possible sites with the advice of siting consultants. These consultants are then paid to do preliminary environmental impact studies before winnowing down the number of potential sites. Most sites are ruled out at this level for environmental reasons; they may be too close to an important wetland or forest; they may sit atop a large supply of groundwater that provides well water to residential areas; or they may be too close to a school or hospital.

Usually, as the siting authority gets closer to finding an acceptable site, political and legal action begins at the targeted site. People tend to ignore the process until their neighborhood is targeted. Court suits are often filed to block the process.

There are many different types of hazardous waste ranging from electroplating wastewater treatment sludge, lead, chromium, electric steel furnace sludge, and petroleum refinery wastes to common hazardous household products. (See the list of hazardous household products on page 44.) Another environmental hazard of increasing concern is nuclear waste, including waste from commercial and military reactors, output from hospitals and university laboratories, and radioisotopes from industry. [See the brief on "Nuclear Power Plants (Commercial)."] Different types of hazardous waste require different types of processing with variation in the levels of risk entailed and the siting issues they raise.

Some hazardous-waste facilities are simply add-ons to existing sites. The developing agency may want to change the technology used at the facility from storage to incineration. In the case of a new site application, the developing agency may come up with an innovative scheme to chemically treat hazardous wastes. Reporters must familiarize themselves with the specific site technologies involved, learning what types of waste will be processed, the amount to be processed, and the source of the waste.

||||||| CORRECTING THE PROBLEM |||||||

The realities of extremely high costs and a program that may take decades to complete are now being weighed against the desire to sanitize every contaminated site. To speed up the process, the EPA recently proposed shifting to standardized clean-up plans for different types of sites and switching EPA personnel from nonsite activities to site cleanup. Other changes being considered include exempting some wastes from strict disposal requirements; replacing enforcement actions against polluters with negotiations; encouraging the use of innovative technologies by exempting companies that use new clean-up techniques from the strict legal liabilities contained in federal toxic-waste laws; and allowing companies that conduct toxic-waste cleanups to pile contaminated soil and other debris at the site without having to gain special permits.

The cleanup of hazardous-waste sites will involve innovative technologies that, in many cases, are still in the development stage. In the meantime, given the enormous costs of remediation, there is need for a better system to choose among priority sites and to determine the degree to which these sites can be cleaned and made accessible to the public in the future.

To control hazardous-waste generation and prevent future damage to the environment, waste minimization efforts are being encouraged. There are two basic methods of waste minimization: source reduction and recycling. Source reduction is achieved through activity that lessens or eliminates the generation of hazardous waste within a process. It includes the improved operation and maintenance of production equipment, material substitution, and the reformulation of products, production process redesign and modernization, and waste-stream segregation. Recycling is defined by the EPA as either the substitution of a waste material for a commercial product or use of a waste as an ingredient in an industrial process to make a product (use or reuse), or reclamation of a material in pure or reusable form from a hazardous waste.

Because of the low cost of land disposal and underground injection (where former oil wells or underground caverns are used to hold waste), only a small percentage of the waste being generated is disposed with state-of-the-art technology. Greater use of waste minimization methods will require incentives for industry.

With regard to the siting of future facilities, interest in development of an alternative siting process has increased in recent years as state after state has failed to site new facilities. Increasingly states are seeking another approach to the problem. One possible alternative—a voluntary approach—attempts to lighten the technical standard. Rather than searching for the "best" place for a facility, the state will just distinguish between acceptable and unacceptable sites. Once acceptable sites have been identified, communities would be offered the opportunity either to rule themselves out immediately or to explore the possible benefits to the community, with the option of rejecting the proposal later if they do not like what they learn. If a community becomes seriously interested, a contract is negotiated that covers compensation, mitigation, stipulated penalties in the event of accidents, and community oversight, so the community does not have to rely on the developer or the regulatory agency. As yet, such an approach does not have a track record for siting, but it is widely thought to be more promising than the old "decide-announce-defend" method.

Many think that the failure to find sites has, so far, done more good than harm. In the years during which developers were insisting on the desperate need for hazardous-waste facilities, and we failed to get any, enormous progress was made in source reduction, recycling, and facility design. Today, developers are proposing to build fewer and better facilities than they said were needed a decade ago. Eventually, however, the improvements will have reached their limit, and the case for building a facility *now* will be much stronger. Many think that time has already come. But it is important to remember that many thought it had come a decade ago. If they had had their way, we would now have less source reduction, facilities that are less safe and less efficient, and more sites then needed.

|||||| IMPORTANT POINTS FOR RESEARCHING A STORY ||||||

|||||| When assessing the environmental impact of a site (abandoned, active, or potential), be sure to find out what were, are, or will be the facility's effects on public health. In particular, inquire about its impact on water quality (both drinking water and groundwater), air quality, and surrounding vegetation and wildlife.

|||||| Be sure to look carefully at the suggested economic impact of any site (abandoned, active, or proposed). The site may decrease the value of some nearby businesses while causing that of others to soar (e.g., trucking and hauling firms). Residential property values are usually affected negatively.

|||||| See the briefs on "Landfills," "Right-to-Know (SARA title III)," and "Chemical Emergencies."

‖‖‖‖ **SITING A NEW FACILITY**

‖‖‖‖ Determine how many workers the proposed facility intends to hire and how much the facility may contribute to local tax revenues—this number is called a ratable. In some instances, the developing agency may offer, or be required, to compensate local businesses and neighbors for the negative economic impact of the facility on their property. Compensation is in the form of complex, legal agreements which should be scrutinized.

‖‖‖‖ Determine how the facility will be screened from public view and whether truck traffic into the site will be heavy. Many groups that oppose hazardous-waste sites do so on grounds that waste-carrying trucks will travel through heavily residential areas, thereby threatening (and irritating) large numbers of families. There also may be noise factors associated with a facility. Hours of operation and effects of this noise must be determined.

‖‖‖‖ Find out who will regulate the proposed facility once it is in place and what standards regulators will use to protect workers and the community. Some regulatory agencies have a history of improper or poor monitoring. If there are violations once the facility is in place, determine what the enforcement tools and penalties are to be. Know how the developing agency, the local government, and other regulating agencies will respond in the event of an emergency at the facility. In case the emergency-response plan calls for assistance from local fire and rescue squads, determine whether these groups have the capacity to handle an environmental emergency. At times, local emergency-response groups are unaware that their participation has been specified in emergency-response plans.

‖‖‖‖ Take the time to check the developer's record operating a landfill or hazardous-waste facility. Developers of hazardous-waste facilities may come from other states or distant parts of your state. Investigating the record of the facility's technology may also be useful. Traveling to a similar waste facility, even if it means significant travel expense, is often helpful in explaining the technology to readers. Before a specific site is picked, some reporters journey to alternate sites out of their coverage area, interviewing local officials and neighbors.

ⅲ **CLEANUP**

ⅲ Find out who will be conducting the cleanup and how their clean-up activities will be regulated. Check the track record of the agency conducting the cleanup.

ⅲ Include the perspectives offered by both the affected community and the industry, as well as those of state government. Discuss both estimated levels of risk and the costs of cleanup with less directly affected parties. For example, several court decisions have forced banks and other lending institutions with a financial interest in contaminated properties to participate in sharing the costs of cleanup with owners, operators, and waste haulers. This has presented a real problem in view of the savings and loan crisis. It has been estimated that 1 percent, or 400 of 40,000 properties held by failed savings and loan institutions in the United States may have some form of environmental contamination in need of cleanup.

ⅲ **PITFALLS** ⅲ

ⅲ Not every hazardous-waste site poses a public health threat. It is important to determine if actual exposure has occurred and if it is still occurring.

ⅲ Keep in mind that cleanup of hazardous waste has become big business, with a strong lobbying effort of its own. In fact, some members of the military establishment view cleanup as the new military mission.

ⅲ Keep in mind that opinions in siting controversies are fluid. It is impossible to predict whether a state environmental agency will be for or against a specific site, even though it may have been the top priority selection of that state's siting commission. Group positions can change with the political winds. For example, a private environmental coalition may initially oppose siting in a given region on any grounds, but may later regard that site as acceptable if subject to strict regulations. Local politicians sometimes support a proposed site, then get attacked by constituents who don't and quickly withdraw their support.

|||||| "Hazardous waste" is a legal term. "Hazardous" does not mean the same thing as "toxic" or "dangerous." Some materials that are dangerous are not legally defined as hazardous waste and vice versa. The ash from incineration, for example, is not defined as a hazardous waste, thereby making incineration a feasible technology.

|||||| Especially in the earlier years, getting sites onto the national priority list was very hotly contended. Some states (New Jersey, for example) fought hard to get many sites onto the list in order to qualify for financial help in their cleanup; other states (Louisiana, for example) did not try hard. Therefore, whether a site is on the NPL is not necessarily a good measure of the level of risk it presents.

|||||| Over time, the measures to improve the design and operation of hazardous-waste facilities makes those of today superior to those built in the past. As a result, Superfund sites are usually primitive (often relying only on impoundments, even without liners) compared to sites operating under RCRA. Furthermore, current sites are primitive compared with new ones being proposed in the midst of siting battles. This does not mean that new or newer facilities are guaranteed not to become the future's Superfund sites. Only that they have a better chance of working well.

|||||| Among the many debated issues covered in this handbook, Superfund cleanups and hazardous-waste facility siting are probably among the hottest. Outrage is often very extreme—and amply justified, in many cases, by the ways communities have been treated in the past. The hazard, on the other hand, is only sometimes substantial, often modest, and sometimes small. Society, and therefore journalism, needs to make an effort to distinguish between remedying a serious hazard and atoning for a serious

outrage. We can spend great amounts of money on hazard reduction at places in which the hazard does not justify the expenditure and still leave people as outraged as they were in the beginning of the process. People living near Superfund sites certainly deserve good treatment, an apology for past bad treatment, and compensation for what they have endured. However, cleaning up the last molecule of the problem is often not a good way of meeting these needs and rights, and seldom does anything whatever for health or the environment.

ⅢⅢ SOURCES FOR JOURNALISTS ⅢⅢ

ⅢⅢ In a siting case, the developing agency and the neighbors are the primary sources. Most groups battling siting of a hazardous-waste facility will elect a chairperson who acts as the group's spokesperson and is usually available to the press. The group's attorneys are accessible to discuss legal procedures pertaining to the case. Often an environmental group may get involved on an ad hoc basis. Also involved in the siting are the local government, its planning and zoning board, and health and environmental boards. Local governments in neighboring communities may want to be involved, especially if incineration is being considered or if the proposed site straddles the border between communities. Information can also be obtained from manufacturers who are not developers of the proposed hazardous-waste site, but who need to use the facility to dispose of their manufacturing waste.

ⅢⅢ State environmental agencies usually have some sort of hazardous-waste program. In some states, the department of health may have a toxic substances control program.

ⅢⅢ The EPA has an Office of Solid Waste and Emergency Response (202-260-4610) as well as a Hazardous Site Control Division (703-308-8313). The EPA regional office can also be a good contact. (See appendix for a complete list of EPA regional offices.)

ⅢⅢ The DOE has an Office of Environmental Restoration and Waste

Management (202-586-7745). It handles questions on hazardous wastes.

|||||| For industry's side, check with Waste Management Inc., in Oak Brook, Illinois (708-572-8800).

|||||| The Chemical Manufacturers Association's Communications Department (202-887-1211) handles questions on cleanup of hazardous waste.

|||||| The Environmental Hazards Management Institute is a private firm that provides information on hazardous waste. It is located at 10 Newmarket Rd., P.O. Box 932, Durham, New Hampshire 03824; 603-868-1496.

|||||| Another source of information is the National Solid Waste Management Association. It is located at 1730 Rhode Island Ave. N.W., Suite 1000, Washington, D.C. 20036; 202-659-4613.

|||||| The Hazardous Substance Management Research Center (201-596-3233), based at the New Jersey Institute of Technology, conducts research directed toward development of systems/options that would allow industry to effectively manage hazardous waste materials created in production processes.

|||||| The Environmental Law Institute's annual analysis of state Superfund programs is a useful document for information on individual state programs. It is located at 1616 P. St. N.W., Washington D.C. 20036; 202-328-5150.

|||||| National Research Council. 1994. *Ranking Haszardous Waste Sites for Remedial Action*. Washington, D.C.: National Academy Press. This book is a recent report that describes the process of prioritizing our efforts to manage active and abandoned hazardous-waste sites.

INCINERATORS

U.S. Environmental Protection Agency scientists estimate that forty cancers annually result from the products of all municipal solid-waste disposal sites, which include landfilling, sludge, and waste incineration. Municipal solid-waste incinerators should not be a major public health threat if properly operated (controlled for air emissions and proper disposal of incinerator ash). The big concern is the possibility that routine malfunctions will release toxins into the atmosphere. It should be noted, however, that many believe the risk to be negligible. However, municipal incinerators can reduce property values.

||||| IDENTIFYING THE PROBLEM |||||

Incineration is the high-temperature combustion—that is, oxidation—of organic compounds containing carbon and hydrogen to form carbon dioxide and water. Carbon and hydrogen are present in most burnable matter as are trace quantities of substances such as sulfur, chlorine, and metals, which form by-products of incineration. Some of these by-products, like dioxin, chromium, and mercury, are potentially harmful.

||||| This brief was written by Richard S. Magee, executive director of the Hazardous Substances Management Research Center and professor of mechanical engineering, New Jersey Institute of Technology. Additional comments were provided by Harold Englund of Air and Waste Management Association, Nancy Blatt of the Water Environment Federation, and senior attorneys for the Environmental Law Institute. |||||

The process of incineration takes place in an engineered device in which time, temperature, and mixing can be controlled. Incineration processes, incinerator designs, and temperature levels differ according to the type and quantity of material being burned. Facilities are designed with multiple trains (separate systems). This allows a facility to keep one system in operation while another is being repaired or reconditioned.

Incineration can reduce the total volume of municipal solid waste by about 90 percent and the weight by 70–80 percent. Landfills are then used to dispose of the remaining material. They are also used for materials that cannot go into incinerators, such as bulky items like refrigerators.

Incineration processes can be used to dispose of medical waste, hazardous waste, and municipal solid waste, but our focus here is on incineration of municipal solid waste. Municipal solid waste is sorted for large objects, and in some facilities, for metals and glass. In general, there is no further processing of the waste. Only in certain types of facilities (e.g., refuse-derived fuel [RDF]) facilities), is the organic material burned after conversion to small, uniformly sized particles.

Incineration has many benefits. It converts most of the waste into water and carbon dioxide, thus reducing its weight and volume enormously, and thereby saving landfill space. In the process, it produces heat which can be used as resource recovery in which the gases generated in the burning process are used to produce steam which can be used directly or to power electric generators. In 1990, 16 percent (or 28.6 million tons) of the solid waste in the United States was incinerated at 128 waste-to-energy plants. While reducing the volume of the incoming garbage by up to 90 percent, these plants provided electricity to 1.1 million homes. Incineration offers cities that have these facilities an important alternative for dealing with the problem of too much waste and too few (safe) places in which to dispose of it.

There are two potential environmental and/or health problems with incineration: toxic emissions during the process and what is left over following combustion.

Emissions can include both what was incinerated and what was produced during the process of burning, some of which is potentially hazardous. Emissions from municipal solid-waste incinera-

tors include trace organics, heavy metals, dioxin, and particulate matter. Hundreds of discarded items that can go into incinerators contain heavy metals, such as lead, mercury, chromium, and cadmium. Some of these metals are released into the air by burning. (See the brief on "Toxic Metals.")

In addition to heavy-metal emissions, the incineration process often results in the release of dioxin, the name for a family of seventy-five chemical compounds, some of which have been shown to be highly toxic to animals. The EPA is currently reevaluating the risk of dioxin exposure because of evidence that it may be considerably overstated. Efforts continue to develop and operate incinerators where the risk of dioxin exposure to humans is minimized. (See the brief on "Dioxin and PCBs.")

Incinerators produce two kinds of ash: "fly ash," which is a particulate matter emissions (it goes up the stack,) and "bottom ash," that part which falls to the bottom, following burning. Bottom ash is created because municipal waste contains approximately 25 percent noncombustibles. While less voluminous, bottom ash may be more hazardous than the initial waste since it concentrates the heavy metals into a smaller volume. Bottom ash must be disposed of properly, or processed and recycled into usable materials such as building or road paving substances. Emission of fly ash is strictly regulated by most states.

Incineration must be considered against the other options: source reduction, recycling, and landfilling. Most agree that the first two options are preferable, to the extent possible. However, there is always going to be waste that cannot be recycled, and, arguably, incineration is one way of coping with much of it.

Other objections to incineration have been raised. One nontechnical objection is to their voracious nature: they run well (both environmentally and economically) only when they are kept running continuously. Therefore, they require a steady supply of waste. Building an incinerator may serve as a disincentive to reduce the waste stream. Another concern is that incinerators tend to be large, coping with the waste from many communities. This raises issues of fairness; the risk from the incinerator, large or small, is concentrated in the immediate neighborhood, while the waste being incinerated comes from a much wider (and perhaps much richer) area. There are also annoyance issues—odors, trucks, noise—which are similarly unfairly concentrated in the immediate vicinity of the facility. Finally, some waste-disposal facilities— including incinerators—have not been well run. Many people fear that the designed performance of an incinerator will not be achieved in practice. However, it should be noted that all incinerators have mechanisms to cut off the waste feed and turn on auxiliary burners when burning temperatures drop below permitted levels. This is true whether or not the material being incinerated is hazardous.

||||||| CORRECTING THE PROBLEM |||||||

Scrubbers are a filtering mechanism that remove acids and parti-cles from incinerator emissions. Scrubbers can be wet or dry. Wet scrubbing systems concentrate the pollutants in a scrubbing liquor. The removal of pollutants (such as heavy metals like cadmium) from the liquors is then accomplished using precipitants (e.g., trimercapto triazine or sodium sulfide). Dry or semi-dry scrubbing systems result in larger amounts of heavy-metal contaminated filter dust. Dry scrubbing systems are usually operated at gas temperatures of 265–285°F. At these temperatures, mercury is only partially removed. While mercury emissions are a concern, new approaches, such as granulated activated carbon (GAC) injection have been successful in reducing them and may be required in the future. The solid residue from the scrubbers has to go to a landfill where it has the potential of creating leachate that has to be managed. A baghouse is a another piece of pollution control equipment that is often used after, or in addition to, scrubbers. It acts like a series of vacuum cleaners with different filter bags.

Efforts to control the amount of inappropriate (hazardous) waste in various products are important. Manufacturers can work to reduce the content of toxins and harsh chemicals in their products. For example, if paper was not bleached with chlorine and, if inks did not contain heavy metals, incineration of these products would pose fewer problems. Also important are program efforts to reduce the overall amount of solid waste that needs disposal through recycling efforts and reductions in packaging. Popular concern has generated new interest in this option. The EPA has set a national goal of recycling 25 percent of the waste stream with 20 percent of the remaining waste to be handled by incineration and 55 percent by landfilling. (See the brief on "Recycling.")

Regulation of incinerators to ensure that they perform to minimize the impact on human health and the environment is also important. While municipal incinerators were not controlled under the 1970 Clean Air Act, 1990 amendments to the act now control them in varying degrees.

|||||| IMPORTANT POINTS FOR RESEARCHING A STORY ||||||

|||||| Learn what type of incinerator is involved and find out how you can be assured that it will comply with your state's incinerator emission standards and how the ash will be disposed. Officials should be asked why this particular system was chosen. Occasionally, other waste disposal systems were considered and rejected.

|||||| Determine whether an incentive, if any, is being offered to the residents of the community hosting the incinerator.

Communities can be offered many types of benefits: a tax ratable; reduced disposal fees; and/or additional revenue for every ton of waste accepted from another community. These are the trade-offs for allowing an unwanted facility.

|||||| Find out how much it will cost to burn a load of trash. Because of the technology, incinerators can cost more than landfills in the short-run.

|||||| PITFALLS ||||||

|||||| Reporters sometimes only consider the costs and not the benefits when writing about incineration. There may be nowhere else for a municipality, especially an urban one, to turn after its landfills have reached their capacity and are being closed. In addition, many of these landfills have endangered groundwater and air quality. If you are going to report the downside of incineration, report the downside of alternatives as well.

|||||| It is important that the public be involved in the siting process at the decision-making phase. This often has not been the case. Incinerator fights are often fights over process and control—the communities right to control theirs own fate, to decide whether to accept an incinerator and, if so, to be able to oversee the design and management.

|||||| Incinerators in the 1990s are large, complex, high-technology operations. They are not the small, simple, apartment house incinerators of years past.

|||||| Find out where the ash from the incinerator will go. Often there is a good story if, for example, it is going into reconstructing a road or building a reef.

|||||| SOURCES FOR JOURNALISTS ||||||

|||||| Many local or county governments maintain their own solid-waste management bodies.

|||||| The American Society of Mechanical Engineers in New York (212-705-7722) has committees on incineration, solid waste, and dioxin issues.

ⅢⅢ The American Chemical Society in Washington, D.C. (202-872-4400) is a good source of information.
ⅢⅢ The Air and Waste Management Association in Pittsburgh, Pennsylvania; 412-232-3414.
ⅢⅢ The National Solid Waste Management Association in Washington, D.C.; 202-659-4613.
ⅢⅢ Greenpeace is a leading anti-incineration group. It has offices in Washington, D.C. (202-462-1177) and New York City (212-941-0994).

LANDFILLS

Scientists estimate that hazardous waste, contaminated sludge, and refuse, through their contamination of the water supply and air, are probably responsible for 50–150 cancers a year. Perhaps the biggest health effect associated with solid waste management is ergonomic injuries sustained by sanitation workers. Active landfills can cause property devaluation because of odors, unsightly appearance, wind-blown litter and dust, and contamination of local water supplies.

⫼ IDENTIFYING THE PROBLEM ⫼

A sanitary landfill is an area in which refuse is deposited, spread, and covered with a layer of soil. The site must be environmentally sound, with provisions for collecting leachate and venting methane gas. Leachate is polluted water that percolates through the layers of refuse. Methane is a combustible gas created when anaerobic bacteria (bacteria operating without oxygen) activate decomposition.

In the United States, thousands of sanitary landfills were built around World War II. Prior to that, refuse was simply dumped in designated areas or burned in the open.

Today, landfill space is disappearing. Existing landfills are

⫼ This brief is based on information provided by Frank Flower of the Cooperative Extension Service of Cook College, Rutgers University. Additional comments were provided by senior attorneys of the Environmental Law Institute. ⫼

either filling or closing because of environmental problems. There is great difficulty in siting new landfills because of citizen opposition and public insistence on new environmental safeguards and buffer zones, which help to reduce noise, dust, odor, and unsightliness. The costs of solid-waste disposal have skyrocketed as a result of landfill unavailability, which serves to justify higher prices and increases in transportation costs. There is a growing sense that we no longer can afford to throw away so much of what is potentially reusable. Above all, there is a litany of environmental and quality-of-life problems associated with most older landfills. Fears persist with new landfills being proposed, despite promises of improvements. These include fear of declining property values, groundwater and air contamination, unsightliness, and transportation problems involving the multitude of garbage trucks required by such undertakings.

The U.S. Environmental Protection Agency lists landfilling as its least desirable option. The EPA's preference is for waste prevention or reduction, followed by recycling and composting, and incineration and other waste treatments. Nonetheless, landfilling remains the most common form of waste disposal in most states. According to a survey reported in *Biocycle* (April 1991), Louisiana, South and North Dakota, Wisconsin, and Wyoming landfill approximately 97 percent or more of their waste. Delaware utilizes landfilling less than all other states (relying more heavily on incineration and recycling).

As landfill space has disappeared, a vast network of interstate transfer of solid wastes has formed. Many communities ship their solid waste across state boundaries, often to a number of states, for landfilling or incineration. Shipping waste is unpopular, but it is often less expensive than building a new facility (estimated at $90 million for 100 acres to be used for 20 years). Trash from New York and New Jersey travels the farthest, and to more locations, than garbage from other states.

In 1988, some 5,500 landfills were in operation, handling close to 80 percent of all solid waste in the United States. It is estimated that by the year 2009, 80 percent of these landfills will be full.

On the average, solid waste deposited at sanitary landfills, by weight, consists of about 40 percent paper, 5–10 percent metals,

5–10 percent glass, 10–20 percent vegetative matter, such as grass clippings, 10–20 percent food waste and 10–20 percent other wastes, such as plastics, rubber, textiles, wood, and stone.

Wastes that pose a risk to human health are often deposited at sanitary landfills. These wastes, which are hazardous from a technical substantive standpoint (e.g., household cleaners, motor oil, and paints) can be disposed of legally in sanitary landfills, and, therefore, are not considered legally, hazardous waste. While small quantities of these materials do not pose environmental hazards, large amounts do and should be disposed in other ways, such as recycling; incineration; physical, chemical or biological treatment; or entombment. This brief is *not* about legally defined hazardous waste. See the "Hazardous Waste" brief for a discussion of disposal issues surrounding this type of waste.

〽 CORRECTING THE PROBLEM 〽

What to do with the methane gas vented from sanitary landfills has long been a question confronting sanitary engineers. Because it is so combustible, it can be recovered as a fuel, and this is being done in many parts of the country, under resource recovery programs.

When a landfill reaches capacity, the area may be recoverable as a green space if it is covered properly with a cap of clay or similar material and other environmental safeguards are installed. Safeguards are necessary because the land is not stable. A landfill properly sealed can be developed as a commercial site. However, putting parks or homes atop landfills is discouraged. While landfills may have excluded legally hazardous wastes, other potentially risky things have been legally dumped in them. There is the potential for methane gas to build up. Proper venting operations must be in place. In Madison, Wisconsin, for example, a park built without proper ventilation exploded. And there is always the potential for gases to permeate the cap and filter through cracks into basements.

Landfills have long been the accepted means of getting rid of trash. However, landfills do not have infinite capacity and scientists and engineers are working on alternatives for refuse disposal.

Possible alternatives include:

|||||| reducing the amount of waste generated by making longer lived, better quality products with improved package designs to create less waste;

|||||| recycling and reprocessing glass, paper, metal, and plastic;

|||||| composting organic matter such as leaves, animal manure, grass clippings, and food waste; and

|||||| high-temperature burning, called incineration, with recovery of heat energy for use in heating/cooling, manufacturing processes, power generation, and such.

|||||| IMPORTANT POINTS FOR RESEARCHING A STORY ||||||

|||||| A CLOSED LANDFILL

|||||| Find out the quantity and quality of contained refuse (household, small business, demolition, ash, etc.), the amount of compaction and cover that was used, and the environmental integrity and sensitivity of the site.

|||||| Determine if provisions were made to prevent illegal disposal of hazardous substances.

|||||| Check to see if all necessary official permits and approvals were obtained.

|||||| Find out what environmental safeguards were used when the landfill was operating.

|||||| Determine if ground and surface water are being monitored after the closing.

|||||| Learn about the venting operations at the site.

|||||| AN ESTABLISHED OPERATIONAL LANDFILL

|||||| Find out how close it is to being full and whether it will be expanded. If the landfill is to be closed—as more and more are—learn the deadline by which closure must take place, and find out how closure is to be accomplished.

‖‖‖ **A PROPOSED LANDFILL**

‖‖‖ Find out the proposed size and capacity of the facility, the number of truckloads of trash to be accepted daily, and how trucks will enter the site.

‖‖‖ Find out if the community will be involved in planning and oversight and whether it will benefit economically from the landfill.

‖‖‖ Find out what types of waste will be allowed (household, small business, demolition, ash, etc.) and if all necessary official permits and approvals have been obtained. Remember that all states have their own requirements in addition to federal requirements.

‖‖‖ Find out what environmental safeguards are planned. Determine whether the site is over an aquifer, water recharge area, or other fragile water sources from maps and how these will be protected. Consider how the impact on ground and surface water will be monitored, and review plans for treatment and disposal of leachate. Find out what measures will be implemented to control vectors (rodents, insects, birds, etc.) and whether buffers between the public and the active landfill are adequate

‖‖‖ See also the brief on "Hazardous Waste." Many of the siting issues are the same.

‖‖‖ **PITFALLS** ‖‖‖

‖‖‖ Do not characterize every landfill as a dump. Familiarize yourself with the particular site and the specific problems that have occurred, or could occur, for example, road congestion, noise, or odors.

‖‖‖ When covering a public hearing on a landfill issue, try to present as many facts as possible as well as the highly charged emotional reactions of speakers.

‖‖‖ Although landfills appear to be simple to report on, this is not always the case. Landfills differ from one another in many respects—quantity and quality of contained refuse; amount of compaction and cover; environmental integrity; degree of leachate generation and treatment; environmental sensitivity of surrounding areas; degree of landfill gas collection and recovery. All of these factors must be taken into consideration when evaluating a landfill.

ⅢⅢⅢ Remember that landfills must always be used for the disposal of materials that cannot be recycled or burned. Since sanitary landfills are needed, the key issues are: 1. whether demand has been reduced appropriately by source reduction, recycling, and incineration; 2. whether the facility is sited and managed properly, to reduce both environmental and quality-of-life effects; and 3. whether the neighborhood has been consulted properly, so its interests are protected rather than sacrificed to the interests of the larger community.

ⅢⅢⅢ There is an important distinction between solid-waste disposal and hazardous-waste disposal. Solid-waste disposal does not include the disposal of materials legally defined as hazardous. However, some solid waste that winds up in sanitary landfills may be hazardous, or debatably hazardous (e.g., household cleaning products, paints, etc.). The legal category "hazardous waste" only applies to materials that cannot be legally put into sanitary landfills and must be disposed in special hazardous-waste facilities. (See the brief on "Hazardous Waste.")

ⅢⅢⅢ Biodegradability is often used by both journalists and citizens as a symbol of environmental safety. However, the risks arising from use of landfills comes from degradation of various sorts. For example, organic waste biodegrades and gives off methane, or newspaper ink degrades and winds up in leachate. The safest material in a landfill is often that which will not degrade, for example, most plastics. While it certainly wastes materials and space to fill landfills with plastics, it does not endanger anybody. Since much that we throw away does biodegrade, landfills must be designed to minimize degradation (as well as control the outcomes of it). If the landfill is working correctly, not much air or water are able to reach what is buried, so it does not

degrade. Therefore, claims that materials like plastic garbage bags) are biodegradable are usually misleading. While
the bag is likely to biodegrade in your backyard, it probably will not do so while buried in the landfill.

⁣⁣⁣⁣⁣ **SOURCES FOR JOURNALISTS** ⁣⁣⁣⁣⁣

⁣⁣⁣⁣⁣ Landfills are usually regulated by their individual states. State
environmental agencies and local solid waste management
bodies are good places to start. Others sources include the
EPA, sanitary engineering departments at universities, and
environmental advocacy groups. Another source is the
Scientists' Institute for Public Information in New York
(212-661-9110).

LEAKING UNDERGROUND STORAGE TANKS

Leaking underground storage tanks (LUST) contribute to ground and surface water contamination, and worker exposure while cleaning and repairing tanks. There are no reasonable estimates of health effects, though they probably are small, less than one cancer per year. Their economic impact, however, is considerable. It may cost thousands of dollars to replace a homeowner's well and millions to obtain a new municipal potable water supply. A recent study estimated the cost of remediation of the existing underground storage tanks at $60 billion.

IIIIII IDENTIFYING THE PROBLEM IIIIII

Underground storage tanks that leak pose an unseen threat to the nation's groundwater. A u.s. Environmental Protection Agency random survey of several thousand of the nation's underground motor fuel tanks showed leakage in one in every three tanks tested. A report issued by the EPA in 1986 indicated that as many as 300,000 underground gasoline storage tanks were leaking petroleum products into the soil. Another EPA document identified

IIIIII   This brief is based on information supplied by Thomas Taccone of the Hazardous Waste Programs Branch, U.S. Environmental Protection Agency, Region II, New York, New York. Additional comments were provided by senior attorneys of the Environmental Law Institute.   IIIIII more than 10,000 incidents of leaking underground gasoline storage tanks reported to state governments. It takes a daily leak of only a single gallon of gasoline, for example, to contaminate millions of gallons of water. In a number of towns, drinking water supplies have been rendered unusable because of these leaks.

Underground storage tanks are used to store fuel products and chemicals, among other substances. When they develop a leak, they can contaminate both the soil and groundwater supply. Once in the soil, they can run off into lakes and streams and serve as a source of surface water contamination. While people worry about the health impact of these leaking tanks, there are little data on health effects because of the difficulty in linking health outcomes with leaks.

There are between one and two million underground storage tanks nationwide that fall under federal jurisdiction. Since 1988, the EPA has enforced new regulations under the Hazardous and Solid Waste Amendments of 1984, which were designed to protect groundwater from tanks leaking regulated substances such as gasoline and chemicals. However, except for notification requirements, individual states rather than the EPA are the primary enforcers. Hazardous "substance" tanks (including oil tanks) are regulated by the 1984 legislation, hazardous "waste" tanks are regulated by RCRA. To qualify as an underground storage tank, 10 percent or more of the tank's total volume must be under the surface of the ground or grade. Tanks must be made of steel or other nonearthen material. However, there are exceptions under the amendments of 1984, including farm or residential tanks storing less than 1,100 gallons of motor fuel for noncommercial use; tanks for heating oil consumed on the premises; septic tanks; pipeline facilities regulated under other acts; storm or wastewater collection systems; process tanks and connected lines and traps relating to gasoline or oil production; and storage tanks in an underground structure such as a basement. These exceptions are often regulated by states or municipalities.

From 1985–1986, the EPA, in conjunction with state environmental agencies across the United States, collected information on location, age, size, use, and type of regulated underground storage tanks and whether or not they were in active use. All owners of tanks were required to respond by May 8, 1986. By the end of 1987, the EPA had completed a special survey of all other underground storage tanks, including farm and heating oil tanks, which are excluded from EPA regulations but now recognized as potential environmental threats. These tank registries, to be kept up by the individual states, help determine the impact of tanks on the environment and may lead, for example, to the elimination of the exemption for farm and heating oil tanks.

‖‖‖ **CORRECTING THE PROBLEM** ‖‖‖

The EPA has made a commitment to beefing up underground tank regulations. Beginning in 1985, there were interim rules for newly installed tanks, and by February 1988, the EPA instituted new regulations, including separate requirements for petroleum tanks and for tanks used to store the 698 identified hazardous substances. The agency also produced a manual covering installation, reporting of leaks, and liability.

Under new regulations, owners must prevent releases caused by corrosion or structural failure during the life of the tank. Tanks must be coated or have an electrical current passed through them so corrosion cannot take place. The material used for the tank and tank liner must be compatible with the substance the tank is intended to store.

States' programs must be at least as stringent as the new federal program and can be more restrictive than EPA guidelines.

In conjunction with the Superfund reauthorization, the federal government allocated $500 million for the cleanup of leaking underground storage tanks. Primary responsibility, however, is being left to states and local government. But there is a "catch 22" for states that may need the funding the most: If a state does not launch a program because it lacks the funds, it may be ineligible to receive federal funds. This could lead to delays in locating contamination, causing both the extent of the contamination and ultimate clean-up costs to grow.

Wherever possible, storage tanks should be located aboveground. However, above ground tanks are thought to be unattractive and space-consuming. They often reduce property values and are usually opposed by everyone—facility owner and neighbor's alike—despite the fact that they better protect against spills. In some cases, local fire regulations forbid above-ground storage.

If underground tanks are used, they should be placed within an additional barrier or vault so that any leaking substance is trapped within. Monitoring devices attached at the time of installation will indicate if there is any leakage.

Leak detection technologies are available. They include use of devices to monitor vapors that drift up through the soil, groundwater monitoring wells near the tank, and a method where pressurized air is forced into a soap-coated tank, showing leakage in the form of bubbles at fissures or cracks.

▏▏▏▏ IMPORTANT POINTS FOR RESEARCHING A STORY ▏▏▏▏

▏▏▏▏ Find out the type of substance that has leaked, the volume, the capacity of the tank, and of what material the tank is made.

▏▏▏▏ Find out whether the tank has a leak detection system and/or corrosion prevention, as required by law.

▏▏▏▏ Find out what steps have been taken to stop the leak and clean up the spill. Reporters should know who is responsible for the leak cleanup. Check ownership of the tank, and find out the name of the manufacturer in case of lawsuits. Soon after a spill is discovered, the agency responsible for cleanup may drill monitoring wells to find out what path the leak is taking. Reporters should learn the results of the monitoring-well testing.

▏▏▏▏ Check with the state's tank registry to see whether the tank has been identified and properly registered.

▏▏▏▏ Determine which bodies of surface water are nearby that might be contaminated by a tank leak. Find out how close the nearest residences are and whether they, too, might be affected. You may want to call in a geologist—most state environmental agencies have one on staff—to check the subterranean rock layers to learn whether they promote or impede the flow of underground pollutants. Find out if neighbors use well water or if they draw their water from local surface water, since the major threat to people is through drinking water. If neighbors use piped-in municipal water, the threat is minimal.

⦀ Determine the cost to the town and to each taxpayer of installing a new water supply service if LUSTs are not controlled.

⦀ PITFALLS ⦀

⦀ Not every underground tank contains hazardous material. Know the contents before you describe them in a story.

⦀ Make sure you know the distinction among toxic, hazardous, and poisonous substances. Hazardous materials are usually corrosive, reactive, or flammable. Toxicity is also one of the tests for a hazardous substance or waste. Some toxic substances like arsenic, strychnine, and cyanide are poisonous, even in small doses, but not all toxics are poisonous.

⦀ SOURCES FOR JOURNALISTS ⦀

⦀ Consult the national survey of underground motor fuel storage tanks done by the EPA's Office of Pesticides and Toxic Substances. Its phone number in Washington D.C. is 202-260-7505. Within state environmental agencies, there usually is an office or division in charge of underground storage tanks. They keep the EPA registry current. Reporters can check the document for location and condition of tanks. An additional source is the local health department. Service stations, chemical companies, petroleum refineries, metal processing companies, vehicle leasing firms, lithography and printing businesses, and municipal maintenance garages are sites where underground tanks are prevalent.

⦀ See the briefs on "Recycling," "Incinerators," and "Water Pollution."

NUCLEAR POWER PLANTS (COMMERCIAL)

The volcanic eruption of Mount St. Helens released much more radioactivity into the atmosphere than the accident at Three Mile Island (TMI). When operated properly, nuclear powered reactors do not significantly contribute to health risk. The big risk issue is the impact of the low probability—but high consequence—accident. Such was the case in the full-scale meltdown of Chernobyl. However, in the United States, no reactors have a design similar to that of Chernobyl. Mining risks and waste disposal (beginning and end points in the fuel cycle) are also legitimate issues.

IIIII **IDENTIFYING THE PROBLEM** IIIII

C urrently there are 108 commercial nuclear power plants in the United States. Nuclear reactors provide abundant energy with distinct environmental advantages. Nuclear power plants produce less pollution (and thus do not contribute to global warming and acid rain) than conventional power plants. They are, therefore, to be preferred—if they can prove themselves safe and economically feasible. So far, these have been big "ifs." Chernobyl,

IIIIII This brief is based on an earlier version by Liz Fuerst, Department of Journalism and Mass Media, Rutgers University in the first edition of the *Handbook*. Additional comments were provided by Theodore Berger of Hoffmann–La Roche. IIIIII and to a lesser extent, TMI, have left unresolved concerns in the minds of some experts and many citizens: cost overruns and problems with nuclear reliability (both exacerbated by safety concerns) have made nuclear reactors a financial disaster for many utilities. No new reactors have been ordered in the United States in more than a decade. Many previously ordered have been canceled (some of these after completion). And many now in operation will exhaust their operational lives soon and come up for renewal.

The nuclear industry is currently confronted by major issues, including whether or not to commission and build a new generation of reactors; whether to extend the life of today's aging reactors; what to do with the large number of reactors that will become unusable over the next couple of decades; and how to dispose of the nuclear waste currently being generated.

Nuclear power plants have become expensive to build. More than one hundred of the new plants under construction in the 1970s and 1980s were abandoned because of their cost. In addition to increased general construction costs, safety demands and the process of public involvement have added significantly to the costs. Antinuclear activist groups support the public process because of its importance in assuring that safety issues are made public. Activists have raised issues the Nuclear Regulatory Commission (NRC) started out dismissing, but ended up endorsing (e.g., carefully prepared evacuation plans). Antinuclear groups have used the public process to force delays and design changes, not to make reactors safer, but to effectively make them prohibitively expensive to build. Consequently, these groups pursue costly delays and design changes even when no significant gains in safety result. To the extent that the NRC is tough on safety issues, opponents see this, in large part, as having been forced upon the agency as a result of public involvement in the process.

The industry, with the support of the Bush administration, attempted to streamline the licensing process in order to control costs, while trying to keep the NRC tough on safety. Proponents argue that the process adds to delays enormously and, therefore, cost, without adding much to safety. The battle is really between an industry that has often ignored real issues until forced to confront them and a movement that has often pretended issues were serious when they were not, simply to slow down the process and increase the cost.

The fundamental logic of nuclear power was that once built, nuclear plants would generate energy "too cheap to meter." However, the operating costs of nuclear plants have become too high to compete against a rising tide of cheap surplus electricity generated by using natural gas and, to a lesser extent, oil. In addition, overall demand for power has been driven down by the recession and by conservation measures. Of course, this trend could be reversed. Some experts believe that as the economy turns around, the demand for power will rise, and, hence, so will its price. Furthermore, recent and proposed legislative developments may spur growth of the nuclear industry. Requirements of the Clean Air Act will raise the cost of coal-fired power and could make nuclear power competitive once again. In addition, the possibility of a carbon tax in the next few years (a measure being considered as a means to stave off global warming) could add to the momentum.

The age of nuclear power plants has become another important issue in generating higher costs. Over time, costly equipment must be replaced, and the safety of older equipment is questioned. For example, it has been projected that over the next few years, as many as ten utilities will need to replace steam generators that have shown a tendency to rust and crack. In addition, the condition of reactor vessels—the great steel pots that hold the fuel—has raised concerns. Radiation has made the vessels brittle as a result of years of bombardment by neutrons. The question is precisely when the brittleness becomes a safety hazard.

Problems such as these raise serious concerns about recommissioning older plants, many of which have licenses coming up for renewal. Recommission through licensing extension is an important part of the industry's survival plan. Plants are generally granted standard forty-year operating licenses. A plant, nearing the expiration of this license, and in need of a major investment, has to face the economics of amortizing the expenses over the few remaining years of operation. The NRC has established a policy for granting license extensions, but no plant has applied for one yet and no one is sure how easy it will be to get one.

Yankee Rowe in Massachusetts, the nation's oldest operating power reactor, closed in 1992. It was intended to be the test case for proving that nuclear power plants could operate safely beyond the standard forty-year operating license. The company made the decision to shutdown because the plant was too small and too old to justify the investment needed to keep it in service. Since 1957, sixteen plants have been retired for similar reasons. While many utilities still hope to run their plants longer than forty years, no one has approached that goal. With Yankee Rowe's retirement, another plant—Monticello, owned by Northern States Power Company— will furnish the first demonstration of relicensing procedures.

In addition to economic concerns, recurring scandals (e.g., drug use by guards, operators sleeping on shifts, and faked documentation of safety checks performed) have plagued the industry. Strong arguments can be made for nuclear reactors *if* they are run safely. But given the magnitude of a possible accident, the tolerance for scandal is appropriately lower. "Safe" has to mean a virtual guarantee that an accident will not occur. The question is whether such a guarantee is possible?

Disposal of nuclear waste from commercial reactors poses another serious dilemma. Radioactive waste must be isolated for ten thousand years before all the radioactive elements decay to background levels. Some of the wastes will keep their potency for hundreds of thousands of years. While many scientists believe feasible technical solutions for storage exist, others disagree. As in battles waged over siting and licensing reactors, the battle to manage radioactive waste has served to pit those who want to "solve" the problem without confronting some of the real issues, against those determined to prove it unsolvable. As they battle one another, the waste piles up (in essence, a victory for the activists).

Disposal of dangerous radioactive wastes remains the responsibility of the U.S. Department of Energy (DOE). The DOE wants to encase tons of spent uranium pellets, heavy metals, and other high-tech materials in a glass-like substance to prevent their mixing with water, then entomb them in catacombs burrowed into rock formations deep inside the earth.

The first permanent site for waste from five decades of atomic bomb production is awaiting opening in the New Mexico badlands. This project, called the Waste Isolation Pilot Project (WIPP), will be the final resting place for military wastes. It will cost $1 billion to carve out of salt beds. The WIPP may or may not ever open. Meanwhile, no final resting place has been approved for tons of commercial nuclear waste, now stockpiling at reactor sites around the country. Tests are being done at Nevada's Yucca Mountain,

"Remember when they used to send us poverty programs! . . . "

Doug Marlette
The Charlotte Observer
King Features Syndicate

where cooled lava formations are twelve times denser than concrete. However, there is stiff opposition to even beginning site characterization.

Responsibility for low-level radioactive waste is in the hands of the states, which are having just as much trouble in siting facilities.

‖‖‖‖ CORRECTING THE PROBLEM ‖‖‖‖

Reports by commissions both in the United States and abroad conclude that most nuclear accidents are caused by human error. After TMI, U.S. plants were forced to install improved warning systems and have plant operators undergo rigorous training. Control room operators at commercial nuclear reactors have become arguably the most extensively trained blue-collar workers in America. However, licensed operators are not the only source of concern. While licensed operators were the cause of 20 percent of mishaps reported by plants in 1987, errors by all other personnel represented 54.4 percent of mishaps in the same year.

The NRC makes regular, unannounced inspections of all plants and has the power to order changes in nuclear power plant design and operating procedures. It also regularly identifies what it considers to be the "best" and "worst" plants. There is wide divergence between the best and the worst reactors in terms of down time, violations, safety problems, and so forth.

Records from the NRC show that commercial plants are experiencing fewer unplanned shutdowns (as well as fewer accidents and incidents). The number of unplanned shutdowns dropped from an average of 7.4 per plant in 1980 to 1.6 per plant in 1990. This could be the result of either better operation or less conservative safety precautions.

The Bush administration began an aggressive nuclear program within the Department of Energy aimed at designing a standard type of reactor that would be almost immune to meltdown. The nuclear industry describes the new designs as "inherently safe" or as demonstrating "passive" safety features, which do not involve failure-prone mechanical systems or human actions. One design would deliver emergency cooling water to the reactor without the use of pumps; instead, the water would be forced in by the pressure of gas stored in the tanks. But the system is not perfectly passive since sensors must determine that the water is needed, and send a signal to mechanical valves.

Some of the proposed new designs do not have surrounding containment buildings. Others rely so heavily on built-in safety features that the control rooms and human operators would not be considered as having safety-related functions. Thus, they would be subject to far less regulatory scrutiny. A study commissioned by the Union of Concerned Scientists (an antinuclear group) questioned the "inherent safety" of the new designs.

A nuclear accident is a high-magnitude, low-probability accident. Most of the regulatory focus has been on reducing probability, and most of the political focus has been on debating probability.

However, more attention to magnitude is needed. Stockpiling potassium iodide (while not an antidote, when taken internally, it prevents radioactive iodine from lodging in the thyroid gland) is a way of taking magnitude/mitigation seriously. So is evacuation planning, which is often very poor, and which figured importantly in many of the key nuclear controversies since TMI (e.g., Seabrook near Boston and the LILCO plant on Long Island). Pronuclear forces do not want to pay much attention to magnitude because they do not want to acknowledge the possibility of a nuclear accident; antinuclear forces do not want to pay much attention to magnitude because they do not want to acknowledge that a nuclear accident might not be catastrophic. As a result, potassium iodide is not stockpiled, and evacuation plans remain deficient. Insurance is another problem that gets at magnitude. The Price-Anderson Act puts a limit on utility companies' liability for an accident; without that law, nuclear plants would probably be uninsurable, and, therefore, would not be built. In other words, the magnitude of a possible nuclear accident has a ceiling from the utility's financial perspective but not from the community's health perspective.

⦚⦚⦚⦚ IMPORTANT POINTS FOR RESEARCHING A STORY ⦚⦚⦚⦚

⦚⦚⦚⦚ Read all NRC documentation relating to safety at a specific plant. This agency sometimes seems inaccessible. Like the nuclear industry itself, the NRC has a peculiar combination of formal openness with stylistic unresponsiveness. Often experts at both the NRC and the companies involved can be hard to understand, impatient with journalists' questions, over-technical, and not proactive about getting out the information. Partly this is because the industry, having had such a hard time over the past few decades, has become defensive, partly because of the NRC's heritage. The NRC grew out of the old Atomic Energy Commission (AEC) which was charged with both promoting nuclear development and regulating the industry. Today the DOE has assumed responsibility for development. But some of the

NRC's top management still reflects old AEC attitudes. Nevertheless, all of this coexists with a legal/formal openness to documents that is unparalleled.

ⅢⅢ If there has been litigation resulting from attempts of a power company to locate a nuclear plant in an area, track down that litigation and read transcripts filed in offices of the local court clerk. Sometimes state environmental agencies have come out in opposition to the very plant approved by another state commission.

ⅢⅢ **PITFALLS** ⅢⅢ

ⅢⅢ In case of a major nuclear accident, try to get to the plant, but be prepared to be stopped and evacuated. You may miss the drama of the story if you try to cover it from the newsroom. If the situation is under control, there will undoubtedly be briefings by the power company and NRC staff monitoring the situation. State police and government emergency management teams responsible for evacuation and crowd control are usually not well equipped to answer what, why, or how questions. Try to pinpoint the cause of the accident. But remember, the causes of an accident often are not identified for days after the occurrence. Be careful not to jump to conclusions and not to accept opinions as facts.

ⅢⅢ In the case of a major nuclear accident, there may be mass evacuations in the area of the plant. These can be ordered by state government, possibly by the governor. Coverage of the evacuation effort is a big part of the story. Health professionals should be consulted to get the full scope of the medical impact. This is especially important after the evacuees return to the area. Remember, the statements of health professionals should be given the same scrutiny as those of all other people. Many are unqualified to answer questions about the health effects of radioactive materials. Try to deal with health professionals trained in this field.

ⅢⅢ With very small "incidents," the twin risks are that they will be under-covered because nothing serious really happened or over-covered as though something serious really did happen. The real story in a minor incident is what might have happened or what almost happened (if anything)—that is, whether the incident is the tip of an iceberg of potential troubles or a routine wrinkle in a complex technology that will inevitably have wrinkles. This is an important story and one that is difficult to cover fairly. On one hand, accidents happen with all technologies, and nuclear reactors have a much better safety record (in the United States) than the oil or coal industries. On the other hand, a nuclear accident could be devastating. Once again, the core issue is the low-probability, high-magnitude accident. And the only way to cover this is in terms of what might happen or (when there is a small incident) what might have happened. How close was the incident to becoming a major accident? What else would have had to go wrong to turn a minor incident into a major accident? How "in depth" is the plant's defense? Reporters should not let anyone talk them out of asking these questions on the grounds that they are hypothetical. "What if" *is* the story.

ⅢⅢ When referring to the most widely discussed nuclear accidents of the past—Chernobyl and TMI—it is important to emphasize the differences in the nature of these events and their outcome. The accident at Chernobyl (April 1986) represents the only full-scale meltdown of a graphite core in a nuclear energy station. The event left thirty-one dead and three hundred hospitalized, released radioactive material over parts of the former Soviet Union, Eastern Europe, Scandinavia, and, later, Western Europe. It also will lead to an undetermined number of future cancer deaths over a wide area. The accident at TMI near Harrisburg, Pennsylvania (March 1979), involved the loss of coolant to one of two nuclear reactors, which resulted in the overheating of radioactive fuel, and a partial meltdown. Radioactive material was released into the atmosphere, but there were no deaths as a result of the accident and epidemiological studies conducted on the population living in the vicinity of TMI indicated no significant health effects from the radioactive release.

ⅢⅢ Some of the operating nuclear reactors in Russia, the Commonwealth of Independent States, and Eastern Europe are considered unsafe by many—and getting worse with age and with political changes that have led many nuclear experts to leave for other countries and have cut budgets for those left behind. These facilities are really accidents waiting to happen. Nuclear authorities in the United States (in both industry and the NRC) have been pushing for measures to shut down the worst of these plants and to obtain aid for some of the others. Another Chernobyl would further dim the hopes for a next generation of U.S. plants. Journalists should be prepared, in the event these accidents do happen, not just to discuss, what went wrong, but what the radiation risk is in the United States (extremely slim for any conceivable accident overseas) and the enormous differences between the safety standards for reactors in the United States and in Eastern Europe.

IIIIII Another lesson in coverage learned from TMI involves the important distinction to be made between screw-up and cover-up. The former refers to mistakes made in understanding exactly what was happening and failures to control the technology. The latter refers to concerns that the public was not being told what really was happening. At TMI, reporters suspected the NRC of lying when it was more a case of fumbling as they tried to comprehend what was happening. And, most importantly, do not confuse either problem with the level of risk involved.

IIIIII Be sure to have outside experts to call upon for enlightenment. They can be very useful in explaining, not necessarily what is happening, but rather what it means and what questions should be asked of people at the site. The best reporters at TMI were getting questions, and background for questions, from their own experts.

IIIIII SOURCES FOR JOURNALISTS IIIIII

IIIIII The public affairs office of the NRC in Bethesda, Maryland (301-492-0240) is a good place to start an investigation of a plant. Public relations personnel for the power company that runs the plant may provide some information. In addition, every nuclear plant maintains a public document room. Here microfiche reports on plant operation are available to the public. The NRC in Washington, D.C., has a public document room as well. Perhaps more than any other industry, the nuclear industry has to make its problems public; the challenge to the journalist is to figure out what to ask for and what it all means.

|||||| Environmental regulatory agencies of state governments maintain liaison with the nuclear power plant industry and may serve as sources of information. In addition, experts on nuclear power and radiation can be found at most universities. Medical staff at hospitals in the vicinity of power plants are another source. They have been specifically trained to address problems that might occur.

|||||| The state public utilities commission or public service commission has to approve every plant, nuclear or not. They are an excellent source of information. The Safe Energy Communication Council in Washington D.C. (202-483-8491), is another source. It is devoted to helping reporters and editorial writers get the antinuclear side of issues. The Union of Concerned Scientists in Washington, D.C., is another good source for the antinuclear position. Its number is 202-332-0900. When covering nuclear plant construction or renewal of licensing, get in touch with citizen activist groups that deal with the environment. Nuclear experts tend to be pronuclear. To some extent, this is true in all fields, but it is more so in the nuclear arena than in other environmental areas. Universities have environmental science and environmental studies departments that maintain experts with widely divergent levels of support/opposition for the industries that create environmental problems. But nuclear experts are found mostly in nuclear engineering departments and have much closer ties to the industry. Medical schools are a better place to look for people with antinuclear expertise.

OCCUPATIONAL EXPOSURE TO TOXIC CHEMICALS

Along with indoor radon, occupational exposures to toxic chemicals are the major public health risks discussed in the *Handbook*. Estimates range widely on the percentage of cancers caused by occupational exposures but most range from 2–10 percent (9,000–44,000 cases in the United States annually).

IIIII IDENTIFYING THE PROBLEM IIIII

The workplace has traditionally been, and remains, a dangerous place because of the presence of hazardous substances. Many of the hazardous agents found in the workplace are toxic chemicals. The degree of hazard depends upon the dose, duration, and circumstance of exposure. Physical agents such as heat, noise, and vibration; psychosocial factors like stress; and biological agents such as bacteria and viruses are also commonly encountered. However, they are not discussed in this brief.

Potentially hazardous conditions are recognized and corrected as the result of a variety of precipitating events. For example, many are identified by the employer. Employers will hire on-staff

IIIII This brief was written by Michael Gochfeld, Department of Environmental and Community Medicine of the University of Medicine and Dentistry of New Jersey–Robert Wood Johnson Medical School. Additional comments were provided by James Kearney of Bristol-Myers Squibb Company, Theodore Berger of Hoffmann–LaRoche, and Paul Zakrisky of BF Goodrich. IIIII industrial hygienists who are specialists in occupational safety and health, or retain them as consultants. Workers are another source of hazard identification. In some cases, the worker, recognizing a hazard, will take steps to correct it. This can be accomplished by notifying the employer, a plant health and safety committee, a union, a local or state health agency, an attorney, or the Occupational Safety and Health Administration (OSHA) district office. Workers have the right to request a health hazard evaluation from the National Institute for Occupational Safety and Health (NIOSH), another agency that studies workplace health and safety issues nationwide. Complaints by workers are another potential source of identification.

Federal law assigns the responsibility for recognizing and controlling hazards to the employer. Public agencies respond only when this private responsibility has not been fulfilled.

The opportunity for recognizing workplace hazards has been enhanced, in recent years, by passage of the Federal Hazard Communication Regulation, administered by OSHA. This covers all employers and employees in the manufacturing sector. Some states have their own legislation, known as worker and community right-to-know laws. Both require a certain amount of labeling and hazard disclosure and entitle employees to specific information regarding substances in the workplace. Under these laws, employers must reduce damaging exposures to toxic chemicals to permissible levels. Some workplaces are periodically monitored by industrial hygienists employed by local, state, or federal agencies to make sure potential exposures have been controlled. Periodic monitoring is spotty, however. Due to staffing limitations, it usually requires a complaint or an accident to trigger a government review.

Although hazards exist in the workplace, they rarely come to the attention of the journalist unless there is an unusual precipitating event—a fire, a leak, or a cluster of illnesses.

|||||| CORRECTING THE PROBLEM ||||||

Traditional procedures for controlling a hazard, once it is recognized, include substitution, engineering controls, personal protection, and administrative controls.

‖‖‖‖ **SUBSTITUTION**

Often, a less toxic chemical or less hazardous process can be substituted for the one in current use, without great expense. Sometimes substitution has turned out to be very profitable for the company, while in other cases, it is simply not feasible. But a company should always examine it as the first choice for hazard control.

‖‖‖‖ **ENGINEERING CONTROLS**

At times it is possible to isolate a process or chemical so that even though it remains toxic, either no one is exposed to it, or the exposure is minimal. No exposure equals no risk. In many cases this is difficult to achieve without ceasing to use the compound entirely. Companies can modify existing ventilation systems to reduce airborne exposure to toxic chemicals. Increasing general ventilation dilutes toxic chemicals; installing local ventilation, such as laboratory hoods, removes the toxic substance from the air.

‖‖‖‖ **PERSONAL PROTECTION**

A variety of clothing, including goggles, face masks, helmets, and respirators is on the market. The safety industry manufactures several different types of respirators for varying degrees of risk, including dust masks, canister respirators (minigas masks with filter and chemical neutralizing substance), and air-supplied respirators, which use air hoses or a self-contained breathing apparatus carried in a metal tank on the user's back. The Occupational Safety and Health Act (OSHA)of 1970 requires that personal respirators must be coupled with ventilation and other engineering controls. However, OSHA allows use of respiratory protection alone on a temporary basis while engineering controls are being developed.

‖‖‖‖ **ADMINISTRATIVE CONTROLS**

These include worker education, labeling, rotating workers, reducing overtime, and other procedures that do not directly address the issue of exposure.

Air sampling must be done to determine the quantity of specific chemicals in the workplace. Periodic medical evaluations of exposed workers, known as medical surveillance, are required in some, but not all, cases. These are adjunct programs that assist in hazard recognition and control.

ⅡⅡⅡ IMPORTANT POINTS FOR RESEARCHING A STORY ⅡⅡⅡ

ⅡⅡⅡ Finding out information about occupational health can be difficult. Unlike infectious diseases or cancer, there is no registry of occupational illness and only a few states make occupational diseases reportable the way they do infectious diseases. Just a fraction of worker compensation benefits are paid for disease (most payments are for traumatic injury), so court records are sparse. New Jersey leads the nation in that 7 percent of its worker compensation benefits cover disease, but that is mostly hearing loss. Employers are required by state labor departments and OSHA to keep a log of significant diseases and accidents, but these estimates are low at best.

ⅡⅡⅡ Find out what the chemical hazard is and its toxicity relative to some well-known toxins such as ethanol (drinking alcohol) and benzene. You must be careful, however, in comparing carcinogens with noncarcinogens. Even comparisons between carcinogens can be tricky.

ⅡⅡⅡ Determine how the hazard was discovered and by whom. There may be malfunctions in a manufacturing plant that brought the hazardous exposure to light. Or, perhaps a plant is aging. Human error is another factor to consider.

ⅡⅡⅡ Investigate the extent and duration of the exposure and how many people are known to have been exposed, or could be exposed. There may be a particular group of workers at high risk from past exposure. Efforts should be made to locate those workers or their families and interview them.

ⅡⅡⅡ Learn what kinds of health effects have been identified. They could be diseases linked to a particular hazard, such as leukemia to benzene exposure, or there could be general symptoms that are attributable to many different types of chemical hazards that might be present. (See the brief on "Benzene.")

|||||| Find out who is responsible for controlling the hazard, how the hazard will be controlled, and what the timetable is. Reporters should know who is responsible for investigating the hazard—even local health departments involved in the case should not be ignored. Public officials may know what is the health risk to workers and, possibly, even to the community.

|||||| See also the briefs on "Asbestos," "Benzene," "Dioxin and PCBs," "Pesticides," "Radon (Indoor)," and "Right-to-Know (SARA Title III").

|||||| **PITFALLS** ||||||

|||||| Reporters may misunderstand the urgency or "imminence" of the hazard. Correction may have to be done immediately or, as in the case of chronic hazards, it may be achieved over a longer period of time in order to prevent irreversible disease or disability.

|||||| There are always questions about the severity of the hazard. Reporters need to know just how toxic the material is. Low toxicity usually means low risk, but with extended exposure, the risk increases. High toxicity at low or very short exposure may also result in low risk.

|||||| Reporters must learn the precise size and nature of the workforce exposed. An office workforce may react loudly to a mild change in air quality that might go unnoticed by a factory workforce because their expectations are different. Better educated workers and workers who are more secure in their jobs are more likely to raise concerns about workplace hazards. Reporters should be aware that "undocumented workers" like migrant farm workers often will not raise questions about even severe hazards.

|||||| Don't overestimate or underestimate the strength of the scientific data. Scientists may not be firm with toxicity data or they may be unsure of causal relations. Reporters should make every effort to find out whether symptoms reported

by an affected group match symptoms regularly associated with a specific type of hazardous agent.

IIIIII Employers and, even, public agencies charged with doing an investigation of chemical hazards may assign a low priority to the project if the hazard is not imminent, the risk is low, the workforce is not very vocal, or the scientific data are shaky. In a society in which only a tiny budget supports occupational health and safety action on the state and federal levels, not all situations identified as hazardous are able to be addressed. This may turn out to be frustrating and a source of hostility for a particular workforce who may seek an independent hazard investigation. Workers may turn to lawyers, journalists, physicians, or union leadership for help. Recognition of many significant hazards has been accomplished in this fashion. But there is a danger that vocal and well-organized workers will achieve public and regulatory attention for a small occupational risk while much larger occupational risks go uncorrected because affected workers may be less skillful at mobilizing attention.

IIIIII Occupational risk gets less media and public (and regulatory) attention than environmental risks. Reporters should be alert to this tendency to dismiss as "the price of a good job and a good economy" a hazard that would be the material of editorial crusades if its victims were neighbors rather than workers. At the same time, reporters should be aware that a literally risk-free job environment is impossible.

IIIIII The dominant occupational risks are nonchemical: falls, vehicle crashes, and other types of industrial accidents. Toxic chemicals are, on the one hand, more insidious than accidents; their effects can take decades to show up, and they can be too easily ignored. On the other hand, once toxic chemicals in the workplace become an issue, the issue can generate a lot more outrage and public regulatory response than more conventional occupational risks—even though the latter may represent the greater hazard to workers.

IIIIII The role of workers in the reporting of occupational exposures to toxic chemicals can vary. Traditionally, workers have paid little attention to these issues, preferring to bargain on bread-and-butter issues instead. Many unions and many nonunionized workers still take this position. Getting employees to take precautions seriously and wear protective gear is a major issue in most hazardous workplaces. On the other hand, some unions (e.g., the Oil, Chemical, and Atomic Workers Union) have made toxic exposures a major bargaining and organizing issue. In other words, reporters cannot always measure the seriousness of the hazard by the seriousness with which employees are taking it.

||||||| SOURCES FOR JOURNALISTS |||||||

|||||| The Occupational Safety and Health Administration and the National Institute for Occupational Safety and Health are excellent sources of information. The number for OSHA is 202-219-6091. The number for NIOSH is 202-690-7134.

|||||| In most states, health or environmental agencies have a right-to-know coordinator who may be able to provide information about the properties of hazardous substances.

|||||| In some cases, management of the plant at which there is exposure can be approached, although officials may be reluctant to talk because of pending litigation or uncertainty.

|||||| To get information about chemicals in the workplace, contact Chemtrec (800-424-9300) or the Chemical Referral Service in Washington, D.C. (800-262-8200 or 202-887-1315); in Alaska or outside the continental U.S., call 202-887-1315 collect. These services are operated by the Chemical Manufacturers Association. They will answer questions directly or connect reporters with the manufacturer of the product involved.

|||||| The American Chemical Society provides information. Its number in Washington is 202-872-4600.

|||||| The Scientists' Institute for Public Information is another service that connects reporters with sources and names of experts on both sides of controversial issues. Its number is 800-223-1730.

|||||| Two key books for the reporter are the NIOSH's *Pocket Guide to*

Chemical Hazards and *Dangerous Properties of Industrial Materials*. They can be obtained by calling 202-690-7134.

IIIIII In some states sets of chemical fact sheets and many other data bases are available on CD-ROM. These may be worth the investment for the newspaper's library. For example, in New Jersey, chemical fact sheets can be obtained on CD-ROM from SilverPlatter, Inc.

OIL SPILLS IN MARINE ENVIRONMENTS

The health effects of oil spills are not considered to be significant except, perhaps, to clean-up workers. Environmental effects depend on many local factors including the type of material spilled. However, they are worse in estuaries. Although the actual impact may not be severe, the visual images associated with spills have caused enormous political pressure to reduce the number of spills and make responsible parties liable for cleanup and damages.

|||||| IDENTIFYING THE PROBLEM ||||||

The world needs energy. Approximately 3 billion metric tons of oil are produced annually. Enormous volumes of this petroleum are transported and handled by the petroleum industry every day. According to the National Academy of Sciences (NAS), approximately 3.2 million metric tons annually (mta) enter the world's oceans.

While much attention has been focused on accidental spills, oil enters the sea from *many* sources including tanker and other transportation operations (1.1 million mta), municipal and industrial wastewater discharges and urban and river runoffs (1 million mta),

|||||| Comments on this brief were provided by Paul Hague of the New Jersey Department of Environmental Protection and Energy, Leonard Bernstein of Mobil Oil Corporation, and R. R. Lessard of Exxon Research and Engineering Company. ||||||

tanker accidents (.4 million mta), atmospheric fallout from trace amounts of petroleum, which evaporates (.30 million mta), natural seeps (.25 million mta), refinery wastewater (.1 million mta), and offshore oil production (.05 million mta).

Routine releases of oil into the ocean when tankers clean out their holds between cargoes have decreased from 1.3 million metric tons annually in 1975 to .7 million mta in 1985. Ballast water from crude-oil tanks containing trace amounts of residual hydrocarbons continue to be discharged. Discharge standards typically set limits of 10–15 parts per million of oil in water discharged by tankers. Exploration and production platforms face similar limits for the water they discharge. In addition, the petroleum industry has instituted many practices, such as segregating ballast, to minimize the amount of oil discharged as a result of routine operations.

A comparison of estimates by the NAS for sources of oil in the marine environment in 1975 and 1985 shows that all categories of inputs of oil into the sea, except spills, decreased by about 50 percent. According to the NAS, part of the reduction may be due to efforts to reduce oil pollution, such as international efforts to reduce tanker operational discharges. Part of the reduction may be due to refinements in estimating techniques. The increase for spills reflects the influence of major incidents such as the loss of the 220,000 deadweight-ton tanker *Amoco Cadiz*. In recent years, industry statistics indicate that accidental spills from tankers have declined.

The state of Alaska has estimated that a catastrophic spill similar in magnitude to the *Exxon Valdez* spill in Prince William Sound is likely to occur on the average of once every 13 years, or about once every 11,600 transits, under the circumstances that existed prior to the spill. Improvements that have been made, and additional improvements that are possible, can substantially lower this average recurrence.

Many people wrongly assume that oil spills cause long-term damage to ocean ecosystems. Even for catastrophic spills, oil is present in the water column at high levels for only a short time. Spilled oil generally stays in the marine and coastal environment less than a decade—often much less. The major ecological impact comes at the time of the spill or within the first few months after it. Beyond a few months, most oil is reduced to tarry residues or is chemically detectable in sediments and resident organisms. The short-term impact on marine animal life is dramatic, but recovery of species populations in almost every case studied has been swift. The National Academy of Sciences concluded that there has been no evident irrevocable damage to marine resources on a broad oceanic scale, by either chronic inputs or occasional major spills.

Nature is very accommodating. It has been able to assimilate steady doses of oil for millions of years without serious permanent damage. When oil seeps or spills occur, natural organisms and natural chemical processes act to decompose it. When petroleum enters the ocean, it immediately begins to undergo a series of weathering and biological processes that distribute the material in the environment and alter its physical and chemical nature. The ultimate result of these processes is the complete removal of essentially all traces of the original crude oil and the geochemical recycling of the carbon. The time involved in this chemical recycling process can range from a matter of minutes and hours for the removal of some components of crude oil to a few years for other components.

It is difficult to predict accurately the severity of the ecological impact of an oil spill. Many factors determine this, including the location of the spill and its natural environmental stresses, the type of oil involved, whether the oil is fresh or weathered oil, and the damages caused during cleanup.

The climate conditions and location of the spill area influence its ecological impact. In general, biological damage from spills in coastal or estuarine environments is much more severe than from spills in the open ocean. There are, generally, more diverse habitats and numbers of organisms in the near-shore areas and sensitive juvenile stages of species are more likely to be present. The effects of spills in a cold marine environment might be more severe and long-lasting than those of a spill in a more temperate area.

Location is important because different organisms react differently to oil pollution. What kills one species may have little or no effect on another. Furthermore, spills in low-energy marshy areas have longer lasting effects than spills in high-energy rocky coastlines.

Offshore spills can involve both crude oil and refined products. Generally, refined products, such as fuel oil or gasoline, have greater concentrations of toxic components than crude oil, and spills of refined products would likely have a greater ecological impact. On the other hand, because lighter refined oil is more volatile than crude oil, the impact of the spill will be of shorter duration and the likelihood of shoreline damage will be smaller. The lighter and more soluble compounds, which are the more toxic, are removed and degraded early in the weathering process. It follows that the longer a spill is exposed and weathered before it enters a sensitive area, the fewer harmful compounds it will contain.

Using the wrong method to clean an oil spill can increase rather than diminish the impact of oil pollution. For spills at sea, mechanical methods are considered the least damaging to the environment. These include the use of booms and skimmers or the spreading and retrieval of absorbent material. The use of dispersants has been shown to be helpful in some cases and harmful in others. Its usefulness depends, in large part, on the toxicity of the dispersed oil and the nature of the particular organisms one is protecting. The National Research Council's Committee on Effectiveness of Oil Spill Dispersants concluded that dispersants should definitely be included in the options considered for a first response.

On shore, the cleanup of oil-fouled marsh areas may actually prolong, rather than shorten, the recovery period. While scrubbing rocky coastlines with hot water is done to restore their beauty, it can destroy surviving organisms along the shoreline. One approach to cleanup that is less environmentally damaging than scrubbing shorelines is natural bioremediation—a process that involves providing nutrients to damaged areas. This technique, however, can take longer than scrubbing.

While oil breaks down in the environment over time, in the short term, spills can damage both the environment and health. Some of the oil evaporates into the air. Once in the air, oil reacts with oxygen in the presence of sunlight to form new materials, including carbon dioxide, several irritating combinations of sulfur and oxygen, and various kinds of acids. Scientists disagree about the dangers to plants and animals posed by the acids that thus form.

The contamination of beaches is the most visible effect of an oil spill. As oil reaches the shoreline it can temporarily, but severely, damage marine environments and important recreation sites.

However, as noted above, they do recover. Dead birds found on beaches are often the most obvious victims of oil spills.

In some cases, oil spills can also kill less visible animal species in far greater numbers. Fish have a sensitivity that allows them to swim away from oil. However, their eggs can be destroyed by spills. Other victims include shellfish and marine mammals, such as otters and seals who ingest petroleum products at the shoreline. The *Exxon Valdez* spill may be the only spill in history in which land mammals, such as deer and bear, were also killed.

Concerns have been raised about the poisoning of the food chain. When an oil spill occurs, the petroleum coats, or is absorbed by, countless numbers of phytoplankton. Zooplankton ingest this oil when they eat the tiny plants. However, most oil consumed by zooplankton is excreted as fecal pellets. There is very little bioaccumulation. Both animals and plants are able to clear their tissues by releasing the accumulated petroleum back into the water. Metabolic degradation and/or the clearing of petroleum from the tissues back to the water tends to balance uptake, without significant bioaccumulation in the tissue. There is no evidence that shellfish are oiled through the food chain. In situations in which shellfish are oiled, it is by direct coating with oil or through uptake of particulate oil through their filter mechanism.

Even with the most rapid response and the best available control technology, many spills have a significant environmental impact on shorelines. These shorelines include estuarine, ocean, and inland areas with considerable recreational, aesthetic, or commercial value. Wetlands are especially vulnerable, because once oil enters, natural flushing is slow. There is little that can be done to clean them. However, no wetland area has been permanently destroyed by an oil spill. With time, all have recovered. Techniques have been developed for speeding up this recovery, but some scientists argue that natural processes are sufficient.

Oil spills pose several concerns with regard to human health. The volatile components of crude and refined oils, such as benzene, are toxic to humans. However, the only proven health effects from oils spills are short-term acute toxicity symptoms in clean-up workers. (See the briefs on "Benzene" and "Occupational Exposure to Toxic Chemicals.") People may ingest small amounts of oil by eating contaminated animals, especially shellfish, which can accumulate oil in their systems. However, taste tests have shown that people can detect very small amounts of oil in shellfish and refuse to eat it. To date, scientists are uncertain of the physical effects of ingesting small amounts of petroleum.

IIIIII CORRECTING THE PROBLEM IIIIII

The release of oil is regulated under the Comprehensive Environmental Response, Compensation, and Liability Act (CERCLA). Spills are initially reported to the National Response Center, the Environmental Protection Agency, or the U.S. Coast Guard for response decisions.

Federal responsibilities for regulating oil spills are divided between the EPA and the Coast Guard. The law gives the EPA power to regulate spills occurring on land and in rivers. The Coast Guard has the power to regulate oil transportation and spillage in coastal waters and the Great Lakes.

The Emergency Response Notification System (ERNS) is a national computer database and retrieval system used to document and verify incident notification information as reported to the National Response Center, the EPA, and the U.S. Coast Guard. In 1989, 16,414 oil spill notifications were received. ERNS data show that the largest number of notifications regarding oil involved releases in quantities less than 1,000 gallons. Notifications regarding releases in quantities greater than 100,000 gallons represented an average of 0.7 percent of annual figures.

Since 1973, the EPA has required preparation of a spill prevention and control countermeasure (SPCC) plan by the owner/operator of any facility that could reasonably be expected to spill oil into U.S. waters. The Marine Spill Response Corporation has been set up by the petroleum industry and is funded at a level of more than three-quarters of a billion dollars annually. Its purpose is to ensure that an adequate response to marine oil spills is available in all U.S. waters. Similar efforts exist in other parts of the world.

Following the *Exxon Valdez* spill, the House and Senate passed the Oil Pollution Act of 1990 that made the immediate costs of pollution cleanup and damages the responsibility of the oil-handling industry (although ultimately they would be borne by consumers). The legislation offers financial protection to a number of industries and businesses affected by a spill. The legislation also addresses prevention through technology and operational requirements. Provisions include the establishment of an oil spill research and development program, tanker operation and design regulations, alcohol and drug abuse rules, access to the National Drivers Registry, and requirements for double hulls. Taxing provisions to establish a $1 billion compensatory fund were passed as part of the reconciliation act.

Many large oil tankers currently in use are old and in need of repair. However, even new tankers are not spill-proof. Nearly all oil tankers now in use have single-bottom designs (a single sheet of metal separates the oil from the ocean water). The Oil Pollution Act of 1990 requires full double hulls for all newly constructed tankers entering U.S. waters. Existing tankers that enter U.S. waters will be required to install double hulls on a phased schedule which begins in 1995. Of course, building double-hull ships is expensive. Conoco (Du Pont) has pledged—and advertised extensively to the clapping of seals—that it will build only double-hulled tankers in the future.

Over the years, concern over spills has encouraged the development of numerous devices used to prevent spills, including x-ray machines capable of searching the inside of pipelines for cracks, electronic scanners and sensors designed to detect spills, better alarm systems and automatic shutdown valves, and oil rig blowout preventers.

ⅢⅢ PITFALLS ⅢⅢ

ⅢⅢ Providing balance in coverage of oil spills is critical. Understandably, the media tend to present oil spills as catastrophic occurrences. Coverage tends to focus on the more emotional aspects of damage to the local environment, and irreparable harm is often claimed. However, it is also important to convey the fact that oil is a natural substance, and that natural processes, over time, will do much to remove it. The EPA's Science Advisory Board rates oil spills as a low-risk issue.

ⅢⅢ The damage caused by oil at sea is much smaller than the damage caused by oil that reaches shorelines. Although human intervention can help to make a shoreline look clean, it has rarely been very effective in removing oil, and improper clean-up methods can be detrimental to the ecological restoration of the area. Dispersants are useful in that they keep oil from accumulating on the shore. The EPA permits the use of only nontoxic dispersants. Use of dispersants is often opposed by those who want the oil removed, not dispersed, and who do not understand the value of dispersants in keeping the oil away from land.

IIIIII Be sensitive to important differences when covering spills. Unlike beaches, marshes and muddy swamp areas have no wave action to move the oil out to sea. Oil becomes trapped by plants and their root systems. Consequently, after a spill, concentrations of oil in marshes can be much higher than levels found on beaches. On wetlands, oil decomposes very slowly and remains in the environment for a longer period of time.

IIIIII Know the type of oil involved in a spill. Generally, refined products, such as fuel oil and gasoline, have greater concentrations of toxic components than crude oil. But this factor is balanced to some degree by the fact that they evaporate more quickly. In general, spills of refined products have less impact on the environment than spills of crude oil.

IIIIII Despite the use of modern techniques, most recovery operations have been unsuccessful. This is because many oil spills are in remote areas or far out at sea. For spills in more accessible areas, it is possible to recover more of the oil. However, in many cases, the best methods are still very inadequate. Consequently, prevention remains paramount.

IIIIII SOURCES FOR JOURNALISTS IIIIII

IIIIII Contact the state environmental agency for resource people within the state.

IIIIII The Oil Spill Office of the Environmental Protection Agency provides general information on oil spills. Its number in Washington, D.C. is 202-260-2180.

⊪⊪⊪ The Emergency Response Notification System is a national computer database and retrieval system used to store information on notifications of releases of oil and hazardous substances reported to the National Response Center, the EPA, and the U.S. Coast Guard. ERNS provides a direct source of data on the number and size of oil notifications received by region. ERNS is located within the EPA's Office of Solid Waste and Emergency Response in Washington, D.C. (202-260-2342).

⊪⊪⊪ The Risk Reduction Engineering Laboratory in Cincinnati, Ohio, (513-569-7418) conducts research on oil spills. It is a part of the Office of Research and Development at the EPA.

⊪⊪⊪ The Oil Spills National Response Branch of the U.S. Coast Guard in Washington, D.C. provides information on polluting incidents in and around U.S. waters. Its number in Washington, D.C. is 202-267-2188.

⊪⊪⊪ The Environmental Research Laboratory in Narragansett, Rhode Island, (401-782-3000) is engaged in research on better ways of responding to oil emergencies.

⊪⊪⊪ Joanna Burger's edited volume, *Before and After an Oil Spill: The Arthur Kill* serves as a useful resource for information on the effects of oil spills on humans and the environment. The volume was published in 1994 by Rutgers University Press, New Brunswick, New Jersey.

OZONE

Ozone thinning in the upper atmosphere could lead to thousands of additional skin cancers, including dangerous melanomas, over the next several decades. On the other hand, too much ozone in the lower atmosphere is a signature of smog, which is associated with respiratory irritation and acute respiratory distress for those with cardiopulmonary problems. Ozone clearly is the most complex environmental problem discussed in this volume.

IIIII IDENTIFYING THE PROBLEM IIIII

Ozone is an allotrope of ordinary oxygen. That is, it is composed of the same kinds of atoms as ordinary oxygen, but a molecule of ozone (its smallest identifiable unit) contains three atoms while that of ordinary oxygen contains only two atoms. This structural difference leads to a difference in chemical reactivity, the tendency to combine or otherwise interact with other substances. Ozone is much more reactive than (ordinary) oxygen and is called a strong oxidizing agent. Ozone can have beneficial or harmful effects in the atmosphere, depending upon its location.

IIIII Comments on this brief were provided by Jed Waldman of the University of Medicine and Dentistry of New Jersey–Robert Wood Johnson Medical School, Leonard Lapatnick of Public Service Electric and Gas Company, and Robert Farrauto of the Engelhard Corporation. IIIII

In the troposphere—that part of the atmosphere within about five miles of the earth's surface—ozone poses a health risk to humans and animals, severely affects plant growth, and can have deleterious effects on art work, buildings, etc. In the stratosphere, or upper atmosphere, ozone protects the earth from exposure to the sun's harmful ultraviolet radiation by absorbing that radiation. Thus, there are two different ozone problems, too much ozone down in the troposphere and too little ozone up in the stratosphere. We will discuss both problems in this brief.

ⅢⅢ **TROPOSPHERIC OR LOWER OZONE: A HEALTH HAZARD**

Harmful ozone forms close to earth in the troposphere. This happens when sunlight strikes nitrogen oxides and hydrocarbons, and other volatile organic compounds (VOCs) that come from a variety of industries, motor vehicle exhausts, and consumer products. The nitrogen oxides and hydrocarbons (precursor emissions) "cook" in the sun. The reaction that takes place produces ozone, the main ingredient in what is commonly known as smog.

Motor vehicles are the most significant source of nitrogen oxides. Other sources are industries and power plants.

In most parts of the nation, smog is at its worst during the summer. The increase in sunshine occurs in the presence of warm, stagnant air that hovers over metropolitan areas. Mountainous terrains can help to trap smog for days at a time in valley regions. Sunny areas like the southeastern and southwestern United States may have smog problems at any time of the year.

Ozone pollution adversely affects the health of far more people than other types of air pollution. Most smog problems occur in urban areas with large populations. However, smog can spread hundreds of miles from a large urban center to the surrounding countryside, as it does in the eastern United States and southern California.

High levels of ozone pollution can trigger respiratory problems. There is also some research that shows that long-term exposure to even relatively low-level ozone pollution may cause deterioration in lung function. Furthermore, several laboratory studies have shown that the immune system is affected by ozone, with animals exposed to even relatively low ozone levels becoming more susceptible to respiratory disease. Those most in danger from smog are the elderly, infants, pregnant women, those who work or exercise outdoors, and victims of chronic lung and heart disease.

The U.S. Environmental Protection Agency is charged with enforcing National Ambient Air Quality Standards (NAAQS). An area exceeds established limits if the ozone reading is over 0.12 ppm (parts per million) for more than one hour per day, a concentration of 0.25 ppm triggers a warning, and 0.35 ppm or more for 4 hours is considered an emergency condition. For tailpipe emissions from passenger cars, the limits are expressed in grams per mile (g/m).

‖‖‖ **STRATOSPHERIC OR UPPER OZONE: GLOBAL PROTECTION**

This very same material—ozone—which is harmful to people when it is present at ground level is, at the same time, essential for life. A protective ozone layer is formed more than 10 miles above the earth's surface. In the stratosphere, oxygen absorbs solar energy, which causes a photochemical reaction that produces ozone in the stratosphere.

In the stratosphere, ozone is a benefit to the environment because it is a very efficient shield that blocks ultraviolet (UV) radiation from reaching the ground. This is good because people, plants, and animals can be harmed by the sun's UV radiation. But even stratospheric ozone is not all good. Besides blocking UV, the good effect, stratospheric ozone partly determines stratospheric temperatures and acts as a greenhouse gas, contributing to global warming. (See the brief on the "Greenhouse Effect.")

Ozone is constantly being produced and destroyed in the stratosphere by the action of the sun on oxygen. In addition to natural destruction mechanisms, ozone is also being destroyed by chemical reactions involving such gases as nitrogen, hydrogen, and chlorine. In the past, ozone in the stratosphere maintained a dynamic equilibrium. The production and loss of ozone were balanced. This kept a stable layer around the planet.

Researchers have now identified a "hole" in the ozone layer over the South Pole. Scientists attribute this hole to the damaging effects of chlorine and bromine on the ozone layer from long-lived gases such as chlorofluorocarbons (CFCs) and halons. CFCs are released into the atmosphere, where they accumulate, by a variety of human activities. The major sources of CFCs include refrigerators, air conditioners, and the manufacture of foam packaging, as well as certain cleaning solvents.

CFCs are generally very stable. They are capable of lasting from eighty to hundreds of years. Eventually, they slowly drift up into the stratosphere. Here ultraviolet radiation is more intense, and the CFCs are ripped apart and broken down. The fragments that are produced then react with ozone in a chain reaction. Each CFC molecule that drifts up into the stratosphere is capable of destroying thousands of ozone molecules. After destroying one ozone molecule, it is regenerated and goes on to destroy thousands more.

Global destruction of ozone in the stratosphere could create serious problems for human health. Recent observations show an increase in ultraviolet light reaching the northern hemisphere. Some research suggests that a 1 percent loss in stratospheric ozone results in a 2 percent increase in ultraviolet radiation on the ground, however, this ratio has not been confirmed to date. The increase in radiation reaching the earth's surface can cause a variety of human health problems. These include damage to the immune system and a higher incidence of skin cancers, as well as certain eye disorders such as cataracts, retinal damage, and corneal tumors. Both CFCs and ozone are greenhouse gases that play a part in the gradual warming of the earth due to an enhanced greenhouse effect. But the real issue with CFCs is UV and the need to protect the stratospheric ozone layer, regardless of the greenhouse effect.

||||||| CORRECTING THE PROBLEM |||||||

||||||| LOWER OZONE

Strategies for reducing ozone pollution chiefly target controlling VOC and nitrous oxide emissions from mobile sources (cars and trucks) and stationary sources (industries and energy-producing facilities). Under the Clean Air Act, each state is required to submit a plan to control air pollutants and identify geographic areas that exceed health standards for ozone. The EPA must approve the plan or help a state set up a plan that would meet its approval. Each state must then apply the rules and regulations to attain the standards and prevent industries within its borders from polluting the air of other states. Interstate pollution is difficult to prevent because the precursors of smog can be transported very long distances. The EPA is authorized to impose severe economic sanctions on cities or areas within states that do not comply. These penalties include banning construction and withholding federal funds for highway construction and water projects. While the regulations exist, postponements, exceptions, and long-term tolerance of noncompliance are the way of life. It is virtually inconceivable that either Congress or the EPA would force places like Los Angeles to a virtual standstill in order to achieve acceptable ozone levels.

The 1990 amendments to the Clean Air Act imposed even tighter restrictions on the pollution that causes urban smog and stricter regulations on automobile exhausts starting in the 1994 model year.

|||||| **UPPER OZONE**

In the late 1970s, CFCs were eliminated from aerosol cans. Global producers of CFCs (Du Pont, Allied Signal, ICI, and Pennwalt) initially resisted early evidence of the connection between CFCs and ozone because of weaknesses in the data. As it turns out, waiting made the problem much worse. Today, the fight is over how quickly to make the phaseout. As the evidence mounts, timetables to eliminate CFC production keep getting more stringent. In 1989, more than fifty countries representing two-thirds of the world's users of CFCs agreed to reduce CFC use by 50 percent by 1999 and to ban imports of bulk CFCs and products containing CFCs. The 1990 amendments to the Clean Air Act established a timetable for an end to the production of chemicals that destroy the ozone layer in the upper atmosphere. In 1992, the parties to the Montreal Protocol agreed to further accelerate the phaseout of the production of CFCs, halon, carbon tetrachloride, and methyl chloroform. For example, CFC production will be phased out by the end of 1995.

All CFCs manufactured to date will eventually escape and make their way into the stratosphere. But once produced, it is better to use them than to dispose of them. Throwing out a CFC-using appliance is, therefore, much less environmentally sound than keeping it in good repair, or, if it is unrepairable, recovering and recycling its CFCs for another use. The key with CFCs is to stop producing them. However, there is no reason to stop using and reusing those already produced, so long as emissions during service and reuse are minimized.

Manufacturers of CFCs have developed substitute products and user industries have developed new technologies for refrigeration and mobile air conditioners. Some companies have eliminated or reduced the amount of foam used in food packaging. One substitute, hydrochlorofluorocarbons (HCFCs), are much better in ozone terms than CFCs, but they are not perfect since they breakdown in the stratosphere in a manner similar to CFCs. Although the United Nation parties have condoned the use of HCFCs, a battle looms over whether they are an appropriate transition technology or a greater trap, to be avoided at all costs.

‖‖‖‖ **PITFALLS** ‖‖‖‖

‖‖‖‖ The two ozone problems, ground-level pollution, or smog, and depletion of the beneficial ozone layer in the stratosphere, are very different. The production of ozone at ground-level causes smog, a health hazard, while ozone in the stratosphere plays a beneficial role for the environment. In both cases, ozone is the same molecule. Production of ground - level ozone and destruction of upper ozone have common ties in that they both are related to air pollutants that come from industry, transportation, and other human activities.

‖‖‖‖ Overall, reporters should avoid oversimplifying complex air pollution problems. While urging public cooperation, they should not promise immediate resolution if only civic-minded Americans would drive less and stop using CFC-containing products. Even then, it is very difficult to control ground-level ozone because naturally produced hydrocarbons, formed by trees and other plants, in the presence of nitrogen oxides and sunlight also produce harmful ozone. Even lightning produces ozone. New research suggests that natural hydrocarbon emission may play a much larger role in the production of harmful ozone than originally thought. Ronald Reagan was mocked for claiming that trees cause pollution. The real point is that trees, together with certain kinds of pollution, cause smog.

ⅢⅢ In reporting on the problem of "bad" ozone, it is important to make clear the role of lifestyle versus industry in generating ozone. Cars are responsible for much more of the ozone problem than are power plants and manufacturing effluents. However, the most progress in reducing the problem has been made in efforts directed toward automobiles. And for the future, it is likely that more progress will occur on the automobile front.

ⅢⅢ The worst smog problems (episodes) are caused by weather. They are not due to increases in traffic or industrial production, but rather to a weather front stalling over the region. Even if some people were to stay out of cars, there would still be major smog problems. Hence, eliminating "episodes" by simple reduction strategies usually would not work unless economic activity in the affected area and in a wide, multistate surrounding area came to a virtual standstill.

ⅢⅢ There are very great uncertainties as to appropriate strategies for protecting stratospheric ozone. They may take decades to have an effect, if ever. One complicating factor involves the long life of the chemicals that destroy the upper layer of ozone. Some last hundreds of years. Therefore, stopping production of harmful chemicals such as CFCs will not immediately stop the process of the destruction of global ozone. Molecules already released into the atmosphere over the years are in the process of drifting up into the stratosphere, where they will eventually become part of an ongoing chain reaction.

ⅢⅢ The issue, now, is not whether to cut CFC production, but how fast. All CFC producers initially resisted regulation because of weaknesses in the data. As it turns out, waiting made the problem much worse. While industry has become more proactive, user industries, like the automotive industry, argue that time is needed to make the transition smooth and painless for manufacturers and their customers. Activists argue that a slow process will make the next century's ozone troubles much worse.

ⅢⅢ All CFCs will eventually leak into the atmosphere. However, they can be captured and reused many times, or they can be abandoned after one use. The parties to the Montreal Protocol, along with some environmental groups, argue that existing CFCs should be destroyed while others argue that companies that switch to a non-CFC–using technology are not benefiting the environment more than companies that use exclusively second-time around CFCs.

ⅢⅢ Some CFC replacements are greenhouse gases which contribute to the problem of global warming. For example, some scientists have suggested that fluorocarbons (suggested as replacements for gases that destroy the earth's protective ozone shield) could add to the danger of global warming. While having no effect on the stratospheric ozone layer that shields living things, fluorocarbons do serve to trap the sun's heat. Other replacement gases represent fire/explosion hazards where they are produced. Reporters should always ask what is being used instead of the harmful substance to be eliminated, and what problems the new substance can cause.

ⅢⅢ The public is often confused about warming versus thinning. Chlorofluorocarbons, widely used as refrigerants, are the agent involved in the *thinning* of the ozone layer. CFCs also contribute to global warming. (See the brief on "Greenhouse Effect.")

ⅢⅢ CFCs are *no longer* used in aerosol cans. Sometimes journalists miss this point and continue to suggest that people can aid the environment by not using aerosol cans. This can make companies wonder whether or not to bother with environmental improvements when the public and journalists fail to take notice.

ⅢⅢ While high standards were written into the old Clean Air Act, and even tougher ones have been added to the 1990 amendments, they cannot be met without radical changes in the economy and our lifestyles. In the face of institutionalized noncompliance with ground-level ozone standards, Congress and the EPA can take credit for setting tough standards without any chance of enforcing them.

ⅢⅢ SOURCES FOR JOURNALISTS ⅢⅢ

ⅢⅢ LOWER OZONE

ⅢⅢ State departments of health can provide information on ozone alert days and the number of times ozone standards are surpassed. They can also lead you to other appropriate agencies within the state. State environmental protection agencies are another source of information.

ⅢⅢ The EPA's Office of Air Quality Planning and Standards in Research Triangle Park, North Carolina, can provide information on ground-level ozone. Its number is 919-541-5615.

ⅢⅢ The American Lung Association is located at 1740 Broadway, New York, New York 10019. Its number is 212- 315-8700.

ⅢⅢ UPPER OZONE

ⅢⅢ Check with the Global Change Division of the EPA. Its number is 202-260-7750.

ⅢⅢ The Environmental Defense Fund is located at 257 Park Ave. South, 16th Floor, New York, New York 10010. Its number is 212-505-2100

ⅢⅢ The National Oceanic and Atmospheric Administration's National Center for Atmospheric Research is another source of information.

ⅢⅢ The Natural Resource Defense Council is another good source of information. It is located at 122 E. 42 St. in New York. Its number is 212-949-0049.

||||||| The Alliance for Responsible CFC Policy is another source of information. In cooperation with the EPA, the alliance sponsors an annual conference on alternatives. It is located in Arlington, Virginia. Its number is 703-243-0344.

PESTICIDES

The U.S. Environmental Protection Agency estimates that approximately 100–250 cancers a year are caused by application of pesticides and growth regulators. This small number is meaningful because the number of farm workers and professional applicators is also relatively small. In addition, some scientists estimate up to 6,000 cancers a year in the general public, due to contamination of food with pesticides and growth regulators. This latter figure is controversial.

IIIII IDENTIFYING THE PROBLEM IIIII

The term pesticide covers a wide variety of chemical compounds that control unwanted plants, insects, rodents, and other pests. There are many categories of pesticides, such as herbicides, which kill plants, insecticides, which kill insects, and fungicides, which kill certain micro-organisms.

Pesticides have made it easier to protect crops from insects, weeds, and diseases, enabling society to produce ever larger amounts of fruits, vegetables, and grains free of blemishes and rot. The use of pesticides has served to dramatically increase crop yield and increase food production in an economical fashion. But as their use has increased, the hazards posed by these chemicals

IIIII This brief was written by Richard Fenske, associate professor, Department of Environmental Health, School of Public Health and Community Medicine, University of Washington. Additional comments were provided by Theodore Berger of Hoffmann–La Roche. IIIII has become more apparent: pesticides have drained into streams and lakes, killing wildlife; laboratory evidence has indicated that many pesticides fed to rats and mice are capable of inducing cancers. More recent evidence has suggested that trace levels of some pesticides on fresh food can become concentrated during the processing of such foods as jellies, catsup, tomato sauce, and grain mixes.

In addition, pesticide use poses concern with regard to the buildup of crop resistance over time and the need to use ever-increasing doses. Weeds resistant to herbicides, for example, are threatening wheat fields around the globe and could become a problem in the United States.

There are five major pesticide health/environmental issues of concern: 1. pesticide runoff into groundwater and surface water from farms and nonagricultural applications to lawns and golf courses; 2. occupational exposures of farm workers, commercial applicators, and others who work regularly with pesticides; 3. pesticide residue on or in foods; 4. exposures from drifting farm applications to adjacent communities; and 5. children's exposure during residential use of pesticides. While all five are significant controversies, technical experts would probably disagree on the importance of certain of them.

Many pesticides pose some form of risk to human health if not used correctly. Pesticides should be used only according to package directions. The most poisonous will be marked with a skull and crossbones symbol. Should these chemicals enter the body, they may cause illness, even death, in high concentrations. The chemical could destroy, for example, a liver cell and replace it with scar tissue. Herbicides, such as Agent Orange, can cause illness—particularly chloracne, a skin eruption similar to regular acne.

If pesticides are present in the food chain—in meat, dairy products, grain, fruits, and vegetables—humans can be adversely affected. All mammals are affected in similar ways, so livestock can be made sick before they become part of the food chain.

Pesticides control vegetable and animal pests in different ways. For example, a common herbicide such as 2,4-D causes rapid growth in a plant until it dies. Malathion, an insecticide, works on an insect's nervous system—the insect ingests the chemical, which then travels through the bloodstream and reacts with an enzyme that short-circuits the nervous system, causing death. Most insec-

Sally Forth

By Greg Howard

ticides in current use ultimately break down in the environment to the point at which they cause less harm to humans or livestock. However, this dictates that certain substances not be used on food crops just before harvest because the pest control products need a given amount of time to break down in the environment.

The following are major groups of insecticides.

⫼ Organophosphates contain carbon and phosphorus. They are usually used to kill insects and can affect the human nervous system in the same way. Early symptoms of poisoning in humans are flu-like, with a general malaise. The symptoms increase with the degree of exposure. In severe cases, there is a loss of bodily functions and other neuromuscular control, including pinpoint pupils of the eye. Some examples of organophosphates are: Chlorpyrifos (Dursban), Diazinon, Malathion, and Parathion.

⫼ Carbamates contain carbon and nitrogen and are similar to organophosphates in the way they affect the central nervous system of humans. The symptoms of poisoning are similar to those of organophosphates. Both break down relatively quickly in the human body but are acutely toxic, that is, symptoms occur within a few hours of exposure. Examples of carbamates are: Aldicarb (Temik) and Carbaryl (Sevin).

⫼ Organochlorines are organic compounds that have been chlorinated, usually with several atoms of chlorine per molecule. The organochlorines have been widely used in agriculture but are now mostly banned in the United States because of their persistence in the environment. Humans exposed to high levels of these chlorinated chemicals experience numbness and tingling of the mouth and face, dizziness, and tremors. They also report symptoms of memory and concentration loss as well as sleeplessness. The compounds remain in the body a long time, lodging in and damaging organs and fatty tissues. Some examples are: Aldrin, Dieldrin, Lindane, DDT, endrin, heptachlor, and chlordane.

ⅢⅢ **CORRECTING THE PROBLEM** ⅢⅢ

The organophosphates and carbamates can cause immediate illness (acute toxicity). They may also have long-term effects (chronic toxicity), as can most other pesticides. Levels of pesticide exposure needed to create these long-term effects are not well understood by scientists. With the exception of known cancer-causing substances, there are levels of exposure at which no measurable harm occurs. In toxicology, this is called a threshold. The human body can potentially deal with exposure without negative effects. In occupational health, these are sometimes called TLVs (threshold limit values) or lifetime daily exposure to the airborne substance with no negative result.

Occupational thresholds are different from general public threshold levels because there is a wider range of tolerance and intolerance to substances in the general population than in a group of workers. Workers are usually healthier than nonworkers. In toxicology, a similar level is called a no adverse effect level (NOAEL). Federal and state agencies attempt to minimize risk for the general population by keeping exposures well below the no-effect level. Occupational and environmental standards also differ because of social values that hold that because workers are compensated for their risk they are expected to bear some, but bystanders are not compensated and, therefore, should be as nearly risk-free as possible.

The notion of a threshold is hotly debated, in particular, thresholds for carcinogens. As a result, many pesticides are labeled as possible, not known, carcinogens, giving no indication of thresholds.

In 1992, a Federal Court of Appeals in San Francisco ruled that the EPA must remove from the market any pesticides that have both the potential of causing cancer and that leave residues in processed foods. According to this ruling, such pesticides are covered under the Delaney Amendment—a provision of the Food, Drug, and Cosmetics Act which prohibits even trace amounts of any potentially carcinogenic additive in juices, breads, jellies, flour, and thousands of other processed foods. Previously, pesticides were regulated by the EPA under a separate law that allowed small amounts of cancer-causing chemicals to be present in foods if the chemicals' benefits to farmers and consumers outweighed the risk to health and the environment. The EPA has found that at least 67 of the roughly 300 pesticides used on food crops cause cancer in one or more laboratory animals. The 1992 court ruling affects at least 35 of these cancer-causing farm chemicals that also concentrate in processed foods.

In some cases, safer pesticides have been substituted for more controversial ones, and the amount of pesticides used in agriculture has been reduced by the introduction of innovative approaches in agriculture including integrated pest management (IPM). IPM refers to the introduction of natural predators into fields to control crop-damaging pests. Efforts have been made to restrict occupational exposures by requiring workers to wear gloves, coveralls, and respirators during applications, for example. In addition, measures have been taken to restrict runoff.

Genetic engineering (introducing genes that endow an organism with specific properties that might make wheat, for example, inherently pest-resistant) is also being introduced by some agricultural chemical companies, in an effort to curtail dependence on chemical pesticides. Proponents of biotechnology promise to mitigate pollution by decreasing dependency on agricultural chemicals, to create crops that require less processing, thereby cutting costs and curtailing the need for chemical additives, and to provide a means for addressing the dilemma of world population growth.

ⅠⅠⅠⅠⅠ IMPORTANT POINTS FOR RESEARCHING A STORY ⅠⅠⅠⅠⅠ

ⅠⅠⅠⅠⅠ Always find out the name of the chemical involved in any exposure and whether the information was obtained from an employer or an employee. Although farm workers may be excluded under some states' worker and community right-to-know laws, the employer must make such information available to the consulting physician. In some cases, employers deliberately withhold pest control chemical information from workers.

||||| Determine whether a suspected victim of pesticide poisoning consulted a physician and, if so, be sure to get the diagnosis. A biological assay, such as measuring a certain enzyme in the blood and levels in the urine, can help confirm the diagnosis.

||||| Learn the extent of the exposure and how it happened. Find out how toxic is the pesticide involved. The accuracy of this information is crucial in assessing risk to human health. Keep in mind that spraying occurs accidentally on occasion.

||||| The federal government has banned the use of certain pesticides because of concern over their impact on health. However, pesticides no longer used in the United States are often used overseas; in many cases they are manufactured here, raising issues of colonialism and the double standard. In some cases, agricultural products are then imported back to this country, raising the issue of a "circle of poison." Of course it may make good cost-benefit sense for a third-world country with little cash and much hunger to use an effective, but hazardous, pesticide that the United States can afford to do without.

||||| See the brief on "Dioxin and PCBs."

||||| **PITFALLS** |||||

||||| The amount of chemical involved is important in communicating risk. There is an approved tolerance level, or limit, for pesticides to be used on food crops, that is considered as safe for public consumption. Eating two peaches dusted with an insecticide is eminently less risky than swimming in a vat of the same substance for an hour.

||||| The standards for approving pesticides have become tougher. For many years existing applications were grandfathered.

Now the government is reregistering long-approved pesticides and asking for new data to justify their safety, application by application. In many cases, pesticide manufacturers are declining to bother, not because they think the pesticide is hazardous, but because the cost of reregistration research exceeds the commercial value of the product application. Thus, the fact that a pesticide is already approved for use does not mean it is okay by today's standards—it might be grandfathered; conversely, the fact that approval is withdrawn does not mean that it is dangerous—reregistration might just be too expensive to bother.

||||| Bruce Ames, who developed the Ames test for mutagenicity, has done research on natural versus pesticide carcinogens, essentially arguing that nature puts more carcinogenic pesticides *in* vegetables than agribusiness puts *on* vegetables. His point is not that vegetables are dangerous, but rather that pesticide residues are safe. The irony here, if Ames is right, is that we are busy developing pest-resistant strains of plants so we will not need to apply so much pesticide; these strains may be more carcinogenic than the ones they replace. Thus, instead of residues on the apple (that can be washed off) we will wind up with carcinogens as part of the apple.

||||| Bioengineering is being used to develop both pest-resistant plants and pesti*cide*-resistant plants (so we can use more pesticides without damaging the crops themselves). There is controversy over the process, gene-splicing, and also over the goal. The deconstruction and reconstruction of DNA chains in edible plants and animals taps a well-spring of modern misgiving. The public is uneasy over genetic engineering as are some food technologists. A telephone survey of public attitudes toward biotechnology, conducted by researchers at North Carolina State University in Raleigh in 1992, found that people favored genetic tailoring of plants, but crossing species lines, particularly using genes from animals "got people nervous."

||||| The Alar controversy has had an impact on the scrutiny that pesticides receive from both the Food and Drug Adminis-

tration (FDA) and the EPA. Alar is, technically, a growth-promoter rather than a pesticide. However, it is an example of environmentalist overkill, since the risk was exaggerated in some of the anti-Alar propaganda, and certainly misunderstood by some frightened citizens. On the other hand, the EPA had already determined that Alar was a significant enough hazard and an unimportant enough product to get it off the market—slowly. The real battle was between the slow, bureaucratic action versus fast, populist action to get rid of mid-size risks. Many would argue that the threat of the latter has moved the FDA and the EPA a lot faster on pesticide issues since the Alar controversy.

|||||| SOURCES FOR JOURNALISTS ||||||

|||||| Each state has a lead agency, traditionally the pesticide control division in an environmental or agricultural agency, that has priority in investigating and bringing charges against companies that use banned pesticides, overexpose their workers, or pollute with pesticides. Several federal, state, and local health agencies may share jurisdiction over pesticides, including the EPA, the FDA, and the state agricultural office. Representatives of these agencies will keep extensive records on toxicity of pest control chemicals.

|||||| Local hospitals and state poison control centers are another possible source of information.

|||||| Another excellent source of information on pesticides is a toxicologist. Try locating one in the state health department or at a local university.

|||||| Texas Tech University in Lubbock maintains the National Pesticide Telecommunications Network (800-858-7378) for journalists and laypeople to get answers to pesticide questions.

RADON (INDOOR)

Scientists estimate the occurrence of 5,000–30,000 lung cancers annually from radon exposure in homes. Individual risks can be very high. The U.S. Environmental Protection Agency has set down "live with" levels of exposure to radon for humans at 4 picocuries per liter (pCi/l) or .02 "working levels." It is difficult to reduce indoor radon levels below this amount. This average may cause as many as 200 cases of lung cancer per 1 million people exposed for one year. This represents a huge risk compared to others discussed in this book. Elsewhere we talk about risks as low as one in a million lifetime risk—which is 200 x 70 or 14,000 times less serious. Most of those at risk are smokers. However, even nonsmokers in nonsmoking households face a considerably more serious risk from radon than from most of the other hazards discussed here. More press coverage centered around persuading people to monitor their homes and remediate high levels is desirable.

IIIII IDENTIFYING THE PROBLEM IIIII

Radon is a colorless, odorless, tasteless, radioactive gas found in low concentrations everywhere on the globe. It is formed by the disintegration of radium, a decay product of uranium. Radon's own decay products, known as radon progeny or radon daughters, are metals, such as radioactive lead and bismuth which

IIIII Comments on this brief were provided by Judith Klotz of the New Jersey State Department of Health, Theodore Berger of Hoffmann–La Roche, and senior attorneys at the Environmental Law Institute. IIIII emit beta particles, a type of radiation that can travel only short distances.

While Sweden recognized the problem early in the 1970s, concern in the United States began in the 1980s when a nuclear engineer set off a radiation detector as he entered his workplace. Tests were made of the radiation present in an air sample taken from the inside of his home. Results showed an extremely high concentration of radon gas emanating from the soil under his house.

Today, health officials have determined that if radon gas and its decay products are inhaled, alpha particles they emit can increase the risk of lung cancer. The radon progeny are more dangerous than radon gas itself, because they are chemically reactive with any surface, including the human bronchial lining. The progeny lodge in the upper lobes of the lungs, causing lung damage and, in some cases, cancer.

Because alpha particles can travel only a short distance, they do not penetrate the skin or move to other body organs. Scientists believe that lung cancer is the only significant health threat to humans from radon exposure. Most scientists say smoking can aggravate damage from radon decay products. Smoke carries the radon daughters to the lungs. For the same reason, living/working in any dust-filled environment (such as a mine) increases the radon risk.

Radon can be found in higher concentrations in certain geographical areas throughout the nation, although high concentrations can be present almost anywhere. One such geological formation is the Reading Prong, rich in uranium deposits, which underlies sections of New York State, New Jersey, and Pennsylvania.

‖‖‖‖ CORRECTING THE PROBLEM ‖‖‖‖

Homeowners can determine levels of radon in their residences by having a screening done by a qualified contractor. Local environmental agencies and departments of health can usually provide lists of approved radon testing businesses and laboratories. Sampling devices are also available at low cost from municipal governments, state agencies, and statewide lung associations. Test kits can be purchased from hardware stores for approximately $20. These devices are small, unobtrusive, and easy to use. After using, they can be sent back to a lab which returns the analysis results by mail. There are some reliability problems—with both the companies selling and reading the test kits and how homeowners use the kits, especially when real estate transactions are involved. There is no medical procedure for testing humans for radon exposure.

Once the level of indoor radon has been confirmed as unacceptable, efforts should be made to reduce exposure to within accepted levels. The risk—like all cancer risks—is chronic, not acute. It is total exposure over time that matters most.

Since radon usually drifts in through the basements, cracks in basement foundations should be filled, surfaces sealed, and ventilation systems installed so that radon from the soil can by-pass the house. If private well water radon concentrations are extremely high, the drinking water can be aerated outside the house before use.

Depending on the level of radiation, it is suggested that homeowners with very high concentrations temporarily make minimal use of contaminated areas. The higher the radon concentration, the sooner remediation should take place.

||||| IMPORTANT POINTS FOR RESEARCHING A STORY |||||

||||| Determine whether the level of radon has been confirmed by expert testing and analysis and what is that level. It is proper to note whether testing was done via a kit or by an outside testing agency.
||||| Find out whether there are smokers in the house.
||||| Always learn whether remedial measures have been recommended, if they've been made, and what cost is involved.
||||| Do not ignore other important sources of radon stories such as schools and the workplace. More and more these buildings are being testing for radon.
||||| The 4 pCi/l level at which the EPA recommends mitigation is a standard based on feasibility and triage. That is, there is a substantial cancer risk at 4 pCi/l, but it is harder to reduce

levels below this point, and there are many houses higher. There is much debate over what the standard should be; some think the EPA number is too conservative (most other countries use a higher number), while others think it should be more conservative.

⫿⫿⫿ Also see the brief on "Air Pollution (Indoor)."

⫿⫿⫿ **PITFALLS** ⫿⫿⫿

⫿⫿⫿ Do not make risk estimates based solely on screening tests. Risk can best be gauged using results of the average exposure. Screening is ideally done in a worst-case atmosphere in the winter when the house is tightly closed. Average concentration, obviously, will be smaller since it will include warm-weather conditions when the house is most open to the outside air. Furthermore, kits are placed in the basement, far away from where people usually are in the house. It is a mistake to assume basement levels are the level to which people generally have been exposed—and exposure is the issue here.

⫿⫿⫿ It is impossible for a house to have no radon; every house, workplace, and outdoor area has some radon, although it may be insignificant. The important question is how much?

⫿⫿⫿ Sometimes results of radon studies appear confusing and have to be thoroughly explained to readers. For example, in studying areas where uranium deposits are high, scientists recently found lung cancer rates were no higher than expected. However, other variables to consider include the long latency period for lung cancer, up to 30 years; the lack of urban industrial air pollution in a rural area; and the fact that people migrate frequently, so they may not have been exposed for many years. Likewise, do not assume that radon is the cause of lung cancers when there is a lung cancer case in a home with high radon levels. Check for smoking and occupational exposures.

⫿⫿⫿ It is impossible to avoid some exposure to radon in one's lifetime, and scientists believe that no level of exposure is without health risk.

IIIIII If a radon problem is discovered and corrected, property values may recover and even possibly rise. Fears about property value are the core of an issue like Superfund—where it is not possible to simply "fix" your home. However, for radon, they may be a false issue.

IIIIII While the risks from radon are relatively much greater than those of other hazards discussed here, radon generates relatively little concern. This is due, in part, to the nature of radon; it is natural and individually controlled; there is no villain to blame or sue here; and the home is a familiar place. Radon is like seat belts and cholesterol, a major health issue that is not a major controversy. It lacks the outrage characteristics that make people take it seriously. It is a bigger hazard and a smaller outrage than most of the issues discussed here. This point is particularly relevant to journalists. Unlike many issues we discuss, radon provides few new pegs on which to hang a story. The story, most of the time, is just that the radon is still there, it is still dangerous, and most people still have not tested. There are no lawsuits, no controversies, no villains, and no victims squaring off against each other. Journalists may not feel it is their job to persuade people to test for radon, or even to remind people that radon is still an issue. However, it is important to realize in covering a radon story, that the outrage (and, therefore, the newsworthiness) is much lower and the hazard much higher than for most environmental stories covered.

IIIIII There is wide variation in radon levels from house to house within a neighborhood. Thus, everyone has to test in order to know their house's level. People often mistakenly assume a neighborhood is either "hot" or "safe."

IIIIII Until 1992, risk estimates provided by the EPA combined smoker and nonsmoker risk. Since the latter is much lower than the former, the combined estimates understated smoker risk and overstated nonsmoker risk—significantly. Reporters should beware of radon figures that do not separate smokers from nonsmokers.

IIIIII Radiation professionals acknowledge that radon is more serious than most other radiation risks, but they tend to be reluctant to treat it too seriously, because they worry that the public will extrapolate from radon risks to radiation risks in general. The Department of Energy has led the fight to push the EPA to deemphasize radon. On the other hand, some feel the EPA seized upon radon as the ideal environmental issue for a Republican administration to push (since it offends no industry) and overplayed it, much as it did with asbestos mitigation in the schools. No one questions that radon is more serious than most environmental health threats, but there is real debate over whether the problem has been taken too seriously, not seriously enough, or about right.

||||||| Most radon mitigation occurs in connection with real estate transactions. And most government action is confined to educating the public and certifying contractors. The "hot" upcoming issue is whether government (federal or state) should require some kind of radon action, at least for new construction and public buildings.

||||||| SOURCES FOR JOURNALISTS |||||||

||||||| State and federal environmental and health regulatory agencies throughout the country have set up radon offices. Other information is available from universities and medical schools where radon or indoor air-pollution research is being conducted. Another good contact is the local chapter of the American Lung Association.

||||||| To find related stories, reporters should be aware of abandoned factory sites in industries which used radium, such as watch dial companies. These may be Superfund sites. Another related story is uranium miners' health and disposal sites for uranium mine tailings. Sources are miners' unions and community groups that monitor lung diseases connected with uranium mining. Health studies of residential radon are also being conducted in many other countries. Determine if your area as a whole, or in parts, has a high level of background radiation.

RECYCLING

Widespread recycling would reduce the impact of solid and hazardous waste facilities on public health, although there would remain a need for such facilities to handle materials that are not recycled, and to handle the residuals from recycling, reuse, and resource-recovery facilities. The major health hazard associated with recycling is to workers who must breathe recycled materials.

IIIIII IDENTIFYING THE PROBLEM IIIIII

I n our throw away society, the average U.S. resident produces more than half a ton of solid waste each year—4 pounds per day. Together, our annual trash output is 200 million tons. What do we do with all this waste? Historically, most has been landfilled and/or incinerated. But landfills are problematic for many reasons: they represent air and water pollution problems; they waste potentially valuable resources; and they are expensive. (See the brief on "Landfills.") Waste-to-energy incinerators also raise environmental and economic problems. (See the brief on "Incinerators.") In

IIIIII   This brief is based on an earlier version by Liz Fuerst, Department of Journalism and Mass Media, Rutgers University for the first edition of *The Environmental Reporter's Handbook.* Additional comments were provided by Glen Belnay of the Hillsborough Township Health Department in New Jersey, Timothy Forker of the Environmental Coalition, David Boltz of Bethlehem Steel Corporation, Robert Perry of Water Environment Federation, Ron Burstein of National Starch and Chemical Corporation, Paul Zakriski of BF Goodrich, and senior attorneys with the Environmental Law Institute.   IIIIII recent years, interest has grown in reducing the amount of waste that needs either to be landfilled or incinerated. Source reduction is the best way to do this, of course; but another promising solution is recycling.

In growing numbers, cities, suburbs, and rural communities, faced with concerns about the environment and the cost of solid-waste disposal (which is growing at an exponential rate, second only to education in many municipal budgets) are turning to recycling as one way to reduce the amount of waste going to landfills and incinerators. The National Solid Waste Management Association estimates the number of curbside collection programs has grown from 600 in 1989 to 3,500 in 1992, reaching 15 million households and thousands of office buildings. Approximately 40 percent of curbside programs are mandatory, according to *Biocycle* magazine. Most of these are in the Northeast, California, and Minnesota. In addition to curbside programs, many cities have programs through which recyclables can be brought to a central location. In 1988, the U.S. Environmental Protection Agency estimated that 25 percent of all the paper and paperboard, almost 31 percent of aluminum, 15 percent of steel cans, and 12 percent of glass generated was recovered. However, only 1.1 percent of plastics generated was recovered. Many cities have expanded beyond conventional items to include such troublesome waste as batteries, motor oil, antifreeze, paint, toner cartridges from laser printers, tires, concrete, and asphalt.

There are many levels of recycling. The highest level of the recycling hierarchy involves reusing the same object for the same purpose: wash out the bottle and fill it again. A variation on this involves reusing the materials in an object for the same purpose: crushing glass, melting it, and making new bottles out of it. However, it is harder to make new bottles out of old ones than to just refill the old ones: more energy is needed and more materials. At a lower level of recycling is the reuse of one product to make another. Glass can be crushed to make glasphalt for road surfacing. Plastic milk bottles can be used to make plastic park benches. This too takes greater inputs of energy and materials. In many cases, it also produces something less useful or easier to produce, lower down on the materials "food chain." If milk bottles are made into park benches, more milk bottles need to be produced from scratch, and there is only so much need for park benches. At a much lower level of recycling is the process of incinerating products to create energy. This is less satisfying because the product can only be reused once, so this is at the bottom of the materials "food chain." The only other alternative is to throw the object away (or burn it and not use the heat for energy). This gets nothing out of the material. It is important for reporters to know that everything in this hierarchy is called recycling by its supporters—so the group that fights for the right to burn waste in cement kilns (that is, use the waste to cook cement) is called the Cement Kiln Recycling Coalition.

Recycling is not without problems. While the supply side of America's recycling revolution has been growing at an explosive rate, the demand side is still barely under way. Manufacturers simply are not geared up to absorb the huge volumes suddenly available. As a result, in the 1990s collection centers in many cities and towns are buried in old newspapers, green and brown bottles, and plastic milk jugs that nobody wants. Aluminum cans bring only a pittance, victims of the former Soviet Union's desperate effort to raise hard currency by dumping bauxite ingot on the market. And rising shipping and labor costs have combined with the recession to squeeze waste haulers, materials brokers, and processors. A lack of manufacturers who will buy recycled materials and convert them into new products or packaging is also a problem.

In places where strong after-recycling markets have not kept pace with recycling, some haulers who have run out of storage space have begun dumping or burning recyclable materials. Others have gone out of business. The oversupply is so great in some places that state officials now report instances of separated trash being mixed together again and hauled to dumps and incinerators at the taxpayer's expense.

The "softness" of the market for recycled goods is a serious problem. The question is whether this is a transitional problem or a permanent one. Many obstacles to the growth of recycling remain. Currently U.S. de-inking facilities are few in number. Siting disputes make it difficult to build major recycling facilities: people do not want the piles of waste or the factory in their neighborhoods. Lower freight rates for raw materials than for manufactured goods means that it is more costly to transport cans to be recycled than to transport bauxite to be made into cans.

Supporters of recycling argue that imbalances are only temporary and understandable. They warn that overreaction to these temporary problems will kill recycling because the public needs to continue to demand recycling. Recycling puts an extra burden on municipal finances at a time when budgets are strained to the limit. If the public does not demand recycling, then politicians will quickly lose interest.

Critics of recycling argue that recycling is a craze driven by panic over vanishing landfills. They equate recycling with the push for synthetic fuels under the Carter administration and propane in automobiles under the Bush administration—dubious environmental boons that captured the public's imagination and created an industry with strong lobbying support. This has led to government subsidies (federal, state, and local) without which most recycling efforts would have disappeared.

Many critics question the economic assumptions upon which recycling is based, arguing that the recycling of many products ultimately costs more in time, labor, energy, and transportation than they are worth. It is one thing to argue for a transfer of savings from mining, tree-growing, landfilling, or pollution-cleanup to underwrite recycling efforts; it is very different to argue for recycling if its net economic benefits are less than its net cost. The question they pose is whether society should be recycling when some recycled products may cost more and/or perform worse?

|||||| **CORRECTING THE PROBLEM** ||||||

The EPA and many individual states have developed an integrated waste management strategy that encourages (in order of priority) source reduction, recycling, resource recovery, incineration, and residuals landfilling for municipal solid-waste management.

Most states now require solid-waste management plans. Mandatory recycling laws have been adopted in many states (e.g., California, Connecticut, New Jersey, Pennsylvania, and Rhode Island) and in some large cities such as New York City and Philadelphia. In Pennsylvania, for example, local governments are required to identify what must be recycled from a list of options, allowing flexibility in targeting. In a few states, governments are being required to buy half their paper needs from recycled goods and, in New Jersey, bid specifications for highway construction have to include such recycled materials as rubber, asphalt, and glass.

Other states, such as Oregon and Washington, have successful voluntary recycling programs for homes and industries. These are operated by private agencies and nonprofit groups. For the past five years, Oregon has given tax credits to manufacturers who use recycled materials. In Seattle, approximately 22 percent of all trash is recycled through a network of one hundred and fifty collection centers. City officials say recycling will save residents millions in refuse-disposal costs over the next ten years. The city has a goal of 60 percent waste reduction by 1995.

More and more states, such as Massachusetts, are financing regional mechanized recycling facilities (MRFs) to separate and process bulk loads of recyclables into crushed or shredded form. MRFs employ large amounts of manual labor. In this form, recyclables are more attractive to large-scale glass, steel, and aluminum manufacturers and to paper mills, which, under pressure from the public, activists, and government, are actively seeking recycled goods. Paper goods are also shipped overseas where markets are growing in the Far East. Owing to some of the obstacles to recycling discussed above, developing new domestic markets for increasing amounts of recycled materials remains the primary challenge for the foreseeable future.

Many states have emphasized the development of bottle laws. "Bottle bills" require customers who purchase soft drinks and beer in bottles and cans to put a deposit on the containers. The deposit is refunded when the container is returned to the original place of purchase. In 1971, Oregon was the first state to pass a bottle bill. In Oregon, 90 percent of all bottles and cans are returned and recycled through the deposit system. Bottle bills have been proposed in many other states, but there is much controversy over their adoption. Many claim the bottle deposit system is too unwieldy and too expensive a price to pay for what amounts to a very small portion of the waste stream.

Plastics are recycled less often than glass and metals. Many are technically harder to recycle. However, there are always important trade-offs that must be weighed in making the decision to use a product that is technically harder to recycle. In the case of plastics, they are lighter, which means lower transportation costs, less gasoline used, and fewer CFCs for refrigerated trucks, in addition to questions of safety, hygiene, and convenience. Large-scale recycling of plastics is an emerging frontier as private companies (e.g., Union Carbide and Du Pont) have begun recycling programs for plastics. While the number of plastic recycling programs is growing quickly, the amount being recycled continues to remain small. Many plastic products, such as disposable diapers, film cartridges, and disposable razors continue to present problems.

Today, approximately 25 percent of all soft drinks are sold in bottles made from the plastic polyethylene teraphthalate (PET). Milk bottles are made of high density polyethylene, and other plastics bottles are made from polyvinyl chloride and polypropylene. These plastics cannot be reused as glass can because they cannot be sanitized without melting. So they have to be shredded and sent to factories that manufacture pillows, pellets for packaging protection, and padding for jackets and sleeping bags. The recycled plastic is also used for synthetic lumber, paint brushes, and carpet backing. Scientists are now looking into ways to prevent different plastics from losing their properties when fused together. That way, plastics can be remolded for use as fence posts and even light furniture and park benches.

Styrofoam cups, plates, and packaging materials have been long a concern. Recently the National Starch and Chemical Company developed and began selling commercially a packaging material to replace styrofoam. Called "Eco-foam," it is composed mainly of corn starch. The material totally dissolves in water when fully saturated.

Other emerging recyclables include waste oil and mixed paper bundled together, including magazines; hardcover books; paperback books such as telephone directories; junk mail; and used office paper and envelopes. In general, mixed substances are harder to recycle. Mixed substances might include paper mixed with ink, staples, and glue; juice boxes mixed with cardboard, aluminum foil, and plastics; bimetal cans; and composite plastics.

A variety of recycling measures have been proposed for addressing the growing waste problem. Reductions in the volume of packaging is critical (source reduction). Other approaches include the use of recycled materials in products manufacturing and products designed with recyclability in mind. This may require the replacement of certain plastic polymers and designing packaging with the idea of re-use. In addition, some environmentalists have proposed a user tax on packaging.

IMPORTANT POINTS FOR RESEARCHING A STORY

Determine whether recycling is mandatory or voluntary in your city or state. Some states, like New Jersey, require every municipality to offer recycling and citizen participation is mandatory. In states like Oregon, municipalities must offer curbside pickup of recyclables but citizen participation is not mandatory. In Massachusetts, a community that wants to use the state's new processing center for recyclables must first pass a mandatory recycling ordinance.

If citizen participation is mandatory, learn what the penalties are for noncompliance. Interview homeowners in communities that recycle. Find out how they viewed the demands of recycling. Did they find it routine, fun, or unpleasant. Identify local leaders promoting recycling for both the residential and business sectors.

Reporters need to be aware of the total life-cycle analysis of all factors involved in a decision to recycle a particular object. Recycling should not be a substitute for environmental virtue. All things being equal, the more recycling the better. But a product that takes more energy and produces more pollution when manufactured and transported might be considered environmentally inferior to another that is cleaner to make and easier to move around—even if it is harder to recycle. To determine where recycling is a boon and where it is a boondoggle, try tracing the life cycle of recycled products. Then ascertain the cost of landfilling and incineration by calculating tipping fees, both at in-state and out-of-state landfills. Putting these two pieces together will give you some idea of the cost of landfilling versus recycling in specific cases.

|||||| Consider recycling program components that make recycling convenient or inconvenient for the participant.

|||||| If some communities save money by not using as much landfill space and also receive a direct payment from their states for collecting recycled products, determine the economic benefits to local governments in your area.

|||||| Also see the briefs on "Landfills" and "Incinerators."

|||||| **PITFALLS** ||||||

|||||| Do not ignore private industry and the public sector in stories about recycling. Most private companies are recycling office paper, computer printout, aluminum cans, corrugated paper, and other products. School districts, universities, hotels, restaurants, correctional facilities, and hospitals, under pressure to reduce disposal costs, have set up elaborate recycling plans.

|||||| Find out where your community's recyclables are going. Too many reporters take it for granted that the recycled items are being resold at a profit. There could be a market glut in one item or another.

|||||| If private agencies or nonprofit groups are running recycling programs, you may want to know where the money that is collected from the sale of recycled goods is going. Did the agencies or firms bid competitively for the contract?

|||||| It is important for reporters to know that the wisdom of recycling, both in general and in particular cases, is debatable, not obvious. In some cases the savings from recycling is real and subsidies just represent a transfer of funds (paying the paper-user instead of the landfill operator). But the economic dilemma comes when the net cost to society is higher for recycling some products than landfilling them.

In such cases, critics argue that it would be wiser to landfill and apply the savings to other environmental problems deemed important by society.

IIIIII Recycling has become a cultural shibboleth, dangerous to attack; opponents of recycling, or of some particular varieties of recycling, are disparaged as cranks, no matter how sound their data and arguments. Recycling has come to symbolize the (small) sacrifices we feel we should make in our lifestyles for the sake of the environment. Recycling, therefore, does not get the skeptical coverage that every environmental topic deserves. This is not to say recycling is not important—only that it is a sacred cow and should not be.

IIIIII The meaning of recycling is very distorted. Reporters should help the public distinguish between the various levels— reusing the object, versus making another one, versus making something else, versus burning it for energy; all are called recycling, but all are not equally desirable. Similarly, reporters should point out that "recycled" and "recyclable" are different—all paper is recyclable, but only recycled paper was paper once before. And among "recyclable" products there are the ones that are frequently recycled (metal cans, newsprint) versus the ones that are technically recyclable but very infrequently recycled (many plastics).

IIIIII The economics of recycling are not separable from its environmental costs and benefits. Landfills and incinerators are not a huge health risk. So the arguments for recycling are not necessarily the direct risks of throwing stuff away; instead they are the indirect risks, such as the environmental costs (largely energy) of mining new raw materials instead of reusing old materials. It is important to consider the entire life cycle of products and their alternatives. If landfilling is cheaper, it would be possible to landfill and use the money thus saved on serious environmental problems, including the manufacturing problems entailed in replacing the materials we landfill. The cost of recycling paper includes the cost of de-inking factories and the hazardous waste they generate; the cost of using recyclable glass bottles instead of less recyclable plastic bottles includes the cost of transporting the heavier glass.

||||| There are many serious misunderstandings about recycling including the notion that recycling paper saves trees. This is similar to suggesting that eating fewer carrots will save carrot plants. The lower consumer demand for carrots, the fewer carrots farmers plant. The same is true for paper and trees. Some lumber is made from old growth, but paper is made from farmed trees, and they farm to meet demand. When we recycle paper, paper companies see that demand is down, plant fewer trees, and sell off the unused land for housing developments or whatever else makes the most economic sense. The values served by trees (from aesthetics to the oxygen/carbon dioxide balance) are thus *damaged*, not aided, by paper recycling. The misinformed connection made between recycling and biodegradability is another example. Consider the transportation of orange juice. Of all the media for transporting orange juice, the worst, environmentally, is the orange itself. People who drink fresh orange juice throw away the peel; it goes into a landfill, biodegrades, and produces methane and other risky wastes. In a compost heap, the outcome is better, but still better are the commercial processors who make animal feed out of the peel. The best way to transport orange juice is probably the condensed frozen package since the water and waste do not have to be transported. However, this packaging is not easily recycled. Next best may be the juice box because it does not require refrigeration (energy and CFCs) and it takes up so little space in a landfill—it would take 100 percent glass or metal recycling to match the low volume and low weight of the juice box. But it, too, is hard to recycle. Big glass bottles—ideal for recycling—are somewhere in the environmental middle.

||||| A great deal of recycling is done just because of public relations—companies and industry associations often subsidize recycling programs to make themselves look good and to prove they can. Reporters should look very carefully at these programs: Are they economically viable, or

heavily subsidized? Is the material really recycled, or treated as waste when no one is looking? (This requires investigative reporting: ask to talk to customers who buy the recycled product.) Is the program symbolic (a small fraction of the total) or meaningful—and if it is symbolic, is it growing or being kept merely symbolic?

‖‖‖ SOURCES FOR JOURNALISTS ‖‖‖

‖‖‖ The EPA's Office of Public Affairs in Washington, D.C. (202-260-4361) has a lot of information about recycling and bottle bills. Its Office of Municipal Solid Waste (202-260-6261) also has information on recycling.

‖‖‖ The National Recycling Coalition/Recycling Advisory Council, 1101 30th St. N.W. Washington, D.C. 20007; 202-625-6406.

‖‖‖Most states now have recycling associations. For specific states check with the National Recycling Coalition.

‖‖‖ National Resource Recovery Association of the U.S. Conference of Mayors, 1620 I St. N.W., Washington, D.C. 20006; 202-293-7330.

‖‖‖ The National Soft Drink Association is another source of information on recycling. The soft drink association is against bottle bills but is very interested in recycling of soft drink bottles and cans. It is located in Washington D.C. at 1101 16th St. N.W.; 202-463-6771.

‖‖‖ Institute of Scrap Recycling Industries, Inc., 1325 G Street, N.W. Suite 1000, Washington, D.C. 20005; 202-466-4050.

‖‖‖ To learn more about plastics recycling, contact the Society of the Plastics Industry, 1275 K St. N.W. Washington, D.C. 20005; 202-371-5200.

‖‖‖ Another source of information on recycling plastics is the Council on Plastics and Packaging in the Environment, 1001 Connecticut Ave. N.W., Washington, D.C. 20036; 202-331-0099.

‖‖‖ The federal government–funded Center for Plastics Recycling Research at Rutgers University is a leader in research in plastics recycling. It is located in Building 3529, Busch

Campus, Rutgers University, Piscataway, New Jersey 08855-1179; 908-932-3683.

ⅢⅢ The Can Manufacturers Institute (202-232-4677), the Steel Can Recycling Institute (800-876-SCRI), and the Glass Packaging Institute (202-887-4850) are trade associations for their industries. The American Paper Institute (212-340-0600) handles press inquiries on newspaper and paper recycling.

ⅢⅢ Industry leaders in aluminum recycling are Alcoa (412-553-4545) in Pittsburgh, Pennsylvania, and Reynolds (804-281-4788) in Richmond, Virginia.

RIGHT-TO-KNOW (SARA TITLE III)

SARA Title III or right-to-know, is the legacy of industry and government failure to voluntarily communicate important risk information to workers and the public. Under SARA Title III, industries are required to provide massive amounts of information on the risk of the materials they use and produce, much of which information is never used. Eventually, if the public becomes more trusting, we think a smaller data set of the most dangerous materials (tied directly to emergency planning) may become the focus of the program.

IIIIII IDENTIFYING AND CORRECTING THE PROBLEM IIIIII

S ARA Title III establishes requirements for federal, state, and local governments and industry for emergency planning and "community right-to-know" reporting on certain chemicals defined under the legislation as hazardous and toxic.

The release of methyl isocyanate at a Union Carbide Corporation plant in Bhopal, India, in 1984 was the driving force behind the passage of SARA Title III. SARA refers to the Superfund Amendments and Reauthorization Act of 1986, administered by the U.S.

IIIIII Comments on this brief were provided by Albert Larotonda of the New Jersey Department of Environmental Protection and Energy, Jon Holtzman of the Chemical Manufacturer's Association, Nora Lopez in Region II of the U.S. Environmental Protection Agency, and Theodore Berger of Hoffmann–La Roche. IIIIII

242 THE REPORTER'S ENVIRONMENTAL HANDBOOK

Environmental Protection Agency. Title III is the third part of SARA, also known as the Emergency Planning and Community Right-to-Know Act (EPCRA) of 1986.

Title III requires that detailed information about the nature of hazardous chemicals in or near communities be made available to workers and the public. The law provides stiff penalties for companies that do not comply, and it allows workers and citizens to file lawsuits against companies and government agencies to force them to comply.

SARA Title III contains four major provisions: planning for chemical emergency (sections 301–303); emergency notification of chemical accidents and releases (section 304); reporting of hazardous-chemical inventories (sections 311, 312); and reporting of the toxic-chemical release inventory ([TRI] section 313).

⁞⁞⁞⁞ **EMERGENCY PLANNING**

This section of the law is designed to help communities prepare for and respond to emergencies involving hazardous chemicals. Every community must be part of a comprehensive plan. Governors must appoint state emergency response commissions (SERCs). In some cases, the SERCs have been formed from existing organizations, such as state environmental, emergency, or public health agencies. In others, they are new organizations with representatives from public agencies and departments, along with various private groups. SERCs establish emergency planning districts and appoint, supervise, and coordinate local emergency planning committees (LEPCs).

LEPCs develop emergency response plans and review them, test them, and update them, at least annually. Facilities notify SERCs and LEPCs if they have extremely hazardous substances present above "threshold planning quantities" and participate in emergency planning. LEPCs must consist of representatives of all of the following groups and organizations: elected state and local officials, law enforcement, civil defense, fire fighting, first aid, health, local environmental and transportation agencies, hospitals, broadcast and print media, community groups, and representatives of facilities subject to the emergency planning and community right-to-know requirements.

⦚⦚⦚⦚ **EMERGENCY RELEASE NOTIFICATION**

Facilities are required to notify SERCs and LEPCs immediately of accidental releases of hazardous substances in excess of "reportable quantities" and to provide written reports on actions taken and on medical effects. Chemicals covered by this section include 366 "extremely hazardous substances" identified by the EPA as having immediate health effects and hazardous properties as well as more than seven hundred hazardous substances subject to the emergency notification requirements of the Superfund hazardous-waste cleanup law. In turn, the SERCs and the LEPCs make accidental-release information available to the public.

⦚⦚⦚⦚ **HAZARDOUS-CHEMICAL REPORTING**

In addition to accidental releases, communities have a right to information about the amounts, locations, and potential effects of hazardous chemicals present within the community. Facilities must report on hazardous chemicals in two different ways. Facilities are required to submit to SERCS, LEPCs and local fire departments, a material safety data sheet (MSDS). MSDSs are descriptions of the risks of particular chemicals maintained on-site at above "threshold quantities" and of how to handle them. An MSDS contains information on a chemical's physical properties, flammability, explosion hazard, and health effects including acute and chronic toxicity information. In addition, facilities must report annual inventories of these same hazardous chemicals to the same organizations. SERCs and LEPCs must then make hazardous chemical information available to the public.

⦚⦚⦚⦚ **TOXIC-CHEMICAL RELEASE REPORTING**

Communities also have the right to know if certain manufacturing plants are routinely releasing any of some 320 toxic chemicals into the air, water, or soil of the community. This section of the law is the aspect of SARA Title III that generates the most news (and the greatest public interest.)

Toxic-chemical release reporting applies to facilities with ten or more employees that manufacture, process, or use more than "threshold" amounts of these chemicals. An estimated thirty thousand facilities nationwide are subject to reporting. Covered facilities must submit annual reports on yearly toxic-chemical releases to states and the EPA by July 1 of each year. Facilities must report which toxic chemicals were released into the environment during the previous year; how much went into the air, water, and land; how much was transported away for treatment and disposal; how chemical wastes were treated on-site; and the efficiency of that treatment.

Using these reports, the EPA develops a national toxic-chemical release inventory available to the public on a national computerized database. Many toxic chemicals covered by this section, although not all, are listed because they are suspected of posing long-term (chronic) health and environmental hazards such as cancer, disorders of the nervous system, and reproductive disorders from ongoing routine exposure. The TRI is only a list of how much of what chemicals was released where. The TRI data are not risk data or exposure data—just toxic-release data. Actual risks and subsequent health effects are determined elsewhere through sophisticated testing procedures. (See "The Language of Risk" for a discussion of toxicology.)

TRI totals without risk assessment data can be misleading. Much depends on the type of release. The highest volume releases of chemicals, for example, are often deep well injections into brackish water; unless there is a leak in the pipe or in the aquifer, no one is exposed to the material. This is very different from releasing the same amounts of the same chemicals into a river immediately upstream of a water supply. In addition, some of the chemicals listed are much more toxic than others. A news story that reports a release of ten thousand pounds of toxics from company A and the release of twenty thousand pounds from company B does not necessarily show that company B endangered people twice as much as company A; it depends on what was released, how and where it was released, and who was exposed. Similarly, a company that reduced releases from twenty thousand to ten thousand pounds may or may not have improved by 50 percent, depending on the answers to the same types of questions.

Title III/TRI requires only reporting, not reductions. The emissions are all legal, and nothing in SARA changes their legality.

Nonetheless, the law has had considerable impact. First, it is of value to future regulation—telling regulators what the big volume emissions are that they might want to pursue next, pointing out possible combinations (of substances or facilities) that might be collectively hazardous. Also, the information gives citizens and activists information they need to apply pressure on companies and regulators. In fact, with or without pressure, many companies have voluntarily responded to the TRI data with pledges and major programs to reduce their emissions. This is being done as companies try to get further down on the following year's list. Some companies have pledged up to 90 percent reductions; some have already achieved 50 percent and more. In many cases, SARA Title III served a useful function in forcing companies to establish the exact amount of their emissions. The law, therefore, is not only about the community's *right* to know; it is also about the company's *responsibility* to know.

A handful of states have more stringent community right-to-know laws. The federal law does not preempt these state requirements. For example, in California, the Toxic Hot Spots Act or A.B. 2588 goes beyond SARA Title III in two important ways. Actual risk calculations are required and, for high-risk emissions, notification of neighbors is required. The New Jersey Worker and Community Right-to-Know Act, passed in 1983, creates a statewide program to collect chemical information from certain industrial facilities. Each year, every facility covered by the law must complete a survey listing certain chemicals and conditions at the facility that may be dangerous to community residents if released into the environment.

▌▌▌ **PITFALLS** ▌▌▌

▌▌▌ SARA Title III does not preempt states or local communities from having more stringent or additional requirements. It is important for the reporter to know whether a particular state has more stringent requirements than the federal laws.

▌▌▌ SARA Title III contains a "two-tier" approach for annual inventory reporting. Under Tier I, a facility must report the amounts and general location of chemicals in certain hazard categories. A Tier II report contains this information plus the names of specific chemicals. Congress gave companies flexibility to choose whether to file Tier I or Tier II forms, unless Tier II are required by the SERC, LEPC, or fire department.

|||||| While information from companies is available to the public, companies can request that the locations of specific chemicals within the facility be kept confidential. Find out if a facility has requested confidentiality or not. Under certain conditions, facilities can withhold the name of a chemical on a "trade secret" basis (other information must be provided). Trade secret claims, however, can be challenged by submitting a petition to the EPA.

|||||| Citizens can sue the owner or operator of a business or facility that does not comply. In addition, citizens can sue the EPA, the SERC, or the governor of the state if any of them fails to provide information that must be made public under the act.

|||||| LEPCs vary widely in strength, budget, level of activity, and extent of industry domination. Reporter's should find out how their LEPC compares with others around the state.

|||||| There is some game-playing with the TRI list. In comparing a company's TRI numbers for two years to see if they are making progress, consider some of the factors that could affect the numbers. For example, consider what substances went on or off the list from one year to the next. Consider how definitions of what sorts of emissions that are covered or not covered may have changed (e.g., when are emissions nonreportable because they are considered "recycling"?). Consider whether the company has changed the size of its overall operation. During a recession, most TRI numbers improve because production is down.

|||||| SOURCES FOR JOURNALISTS ||||||

|||||| The toll-free EPA Emergency Planning and Community Right-to-Know Information Hotline number is 800-535-0202. In

Washington, D.C., call 202-479-2449. It is available between 8:30 A.M. and 7:30 P.M. eastern time.

⦚⦚⦚⦚⦚ State environmental agencies usually have a division or bureau of hazardous-substance information that is a good source of information with regard to a state's specific right-to-know program.

⦚⦚⦚⦚⦚ Detailed information on the various provisions of the Emergency Planning and Community Right-to-Know Act can be found in the *Federal Register,* which is available at public or university libraries. Sections 301–303 can be found in April 22 and December 17, 1987; February 25, 1988 (40 CFR 300 and 355). Section 304 can be found in April 22 and December 19, 1987; February 25, 1988 (40 CFR 300 and 355). Sections 311–312 can be found in October 15, 1987, and August 4, 1988 (40 CFR 370). Section 313 can be found in February 16 and June 20, 1988 (40 CFR 372).

⦚⦚⦚⦚⦚ Local emergency plans, materials safety data sheets, and emergency and hazardous chemical inventory forms are available through the LEPCs and SERCs.

⦚⦚⦚⦚⦚ Toxic release data are available on microfiche from the state office where forms are filed, federal depository libraries, and the Local Emergency Planning Committees. The TRI should be accessible within the community. Copies of the actual reports can be obtained from the state or the EPA. The national database can be accessed on personal computers through the TOXNET computer system (a nominal access fee is charged). This is a user-friendly database. Information about accessing the system can be obtained by calling the National Library of Medicine (301-496-4000).

⦚⦚⦚⦚⦚ Companies often provide their own TRI data before it is available from the government, often with their interpretation provided. Be sure to check their interpretation of the data.

⦚⦚⦚⦚⦚ TRI reports include a contact name at the facility. This is usually a technical person who has compiled the data and is supposed to stand ready to explain it. This is a good source.

⦚⦚⦚⦚⦚ Information (emissions data) can also be obtained from the regional offices of the EPA. Each regional office has a press contact person. See the "Key Telephone Numbers" for the

EPA and FEMA (Federal Emergency Management Agency) regional offices and for the commission in each state.

IIIIIII Activists often develop a list of "the ten worst polluters in Smithville" using TRI data. Be sure to check their interpretation of the data.

IIIIIII Additional information can be obtained from the Chemical Manufacturers Association, 2501 M St. N.W., Washington, D.C. 20037; 202-997-1100.

TOXIC METALS: LEAD, MERCURY, AND CADMIUM

While a great deal of mass media attention is focused on new synthetic organic chemicals with complicated names, naturally occurring toxic metals were, and continue to be, ubiquitous threats. Like asbestos, the legacy of past widespread exposures to these metals will be felt for decades. Major efforts are being made to limit new exposures, but safe and inexpensive substitutes for these metals are not always available.

IIIII IDENTIFYING THE PROBLEM IIIII

Metals are chemical elements that do not breakdown or degrade. Unlike many organic pollutants that breakdown with exposure to sunlight or heat, metals persist. They can be buried in landfills or washed into sediment, but they never disappear entirely. They always remain a threat to be remobilized in the future. For decades, manufacturers have used metals in the production of numerous products. As a results, the soil, the ocean, the sediments of lakes and rivers, and the atmosphere have become contaminated with toxic metals.

Trace metals are metals that are present in the environment or in the human body in very low concentrations, such as copper,

IIIII Comments on this brief were provided by Robert Hazen of the New Jersey Department of Environmental Protection and Energy and Norbert Steiner of Degussa Corporation. IIIII iron, and zinc. Heavy metals are those trace metals whose densities are at least five times greater than water, such as lead, mercury, and cadmium. Toxic metals are all those metals whose concentrations in the environment are now considered to be harmful, at least to some people, in some places.

Some metals are essential for good health, and their deficiency can lead to disease. Some metals, essential to good health, can be harmful if ingested in large quantities. Finally, some metals, such as lead, mercury, cadmium, arsenic, and beryllium, have no known functions in the body and any internal exposure may be harmful. We focus here on these metals since they are widely used toxic metals and represent a current threat to public health and the environment.

|||||| LEAD

Lead is a soft bluish or silvery grey metal usually found in sulfite deposits in association with other minerals, particularly zinc and copper. The widespread use of lead in industrial applications has made it omnipresent in the environment.

Lead is a highly toxic metal. As an element, it is essentially indestructible. Once released into the environment, it remains available to living organisms. It does not biodegrade or breakdown into other substances. It accumulates in the soil over months and years. Exposure to lead can occur in all areas of the United States—rural and urban.

Delays in neurological and physical development of children are the main health effect of lead exposure. Other possible effects include nervous and reproductive system disorders, cognitive and behavioral changes, hypertension, and anemia. In extreme cases, effects include mental retardation and death. The effects of exposure to lead occur at low doses—doses to which many children are exposed. In other words, the public health threat is very widespread. However, because symptoms, at very low doses, are invisible or universal (e.g., headaches), it is very difficult to arouse public concern. Furthermore, because it is omnipresent and hard to clean up, it is often difficult to mitigate.

Lead exposure is primarily a problem for poor, urban children, however there are many exceptions. Children in the suburbs can be poisoned by the leaded dust created during the process of rehabilitating older homes. Scraping old paint from walls releases lead-contaminated dust which then settles within the home and poses a health risk. Even rural areas can sometimes have significant exposures. Furthermore, adults can show symptoms, though at higher doses. For adults, lead exposure has been associated with increased risk of cardiovascular disease, elevated blood levels, and hypertension. Lead is stored in bones and can become a factor in overall health during periods of stress, pregnancy, and among people suffering from osteoporosis. Lead may also play a role in miscarriages and in damage to the male reproductive system.

Blood lead measurements are a way to estimate recent exposure. Adverse effects have been found at lower and lower levels. In 1991, the federal government sharply lowered the "threshold" level for lead in blood—the amount thought to be safe—from 25 micrograms of lead per 100 milliliters of blood, to 10 micrograms. Some experts argue that 10 micrograms is still too high a standard—that it is not health-based but rather a triage standard set because so many children have lead poisoning.

For blood levels lower than the 45 microgram range, removal of the source of the poisoning is usually sufficient to lower lead levels. Removal of the source of contamination, of course, is not an easy thing. Lead paint decomposes into dust even where it is not chipping and being eaten. Soil and dust near highways and major roads have been contaminated with lead gasoline for decades.

For elevated levels, chelation—a medical procedure in which EDTA, a compound to which the lead binds, is intravenously injected into the body—may be necessary. It is then flushed from the blood and excreted in urine.

Lead has been called the nation's number one environmental threat to the health of children by the Secretary of Health and Human Services who recommended that all children six or younger (not just those living in dilapidated housing) be tested for lead in their blood.

New sources of lead in the environment have been stopped. Lead is no longer added to gasoline, paint, or pesticides. Lead pipes and lead solder are no longer allowed in plumbing systems. However, the Environmental Protection Agency's enforcement of this ban has been limited. Furthermore, the legacy of past practices will be with us for decades—old paint, lead in drinking water caused by old pipes and solder that are still in place, and incredible volumes of dust and soil near roads and highways (including many playgrounds) that are contaminated with lead from gasoline. These sources continue to provide moderate exposure in large populations.

At the same time, another source of exposure has potentially big effects on relatively few people. Stationary point sources such as smelters continue to affect small, localized populations, causing elevated lead levels. It is estimated that approximately 230,000 children live near enough to smelters to be exposed to smelting by-products.

Additional sources of continued lead exposure include:

IIIIII Superfund National Priority List (NPL) sites that have lead as an important contaminant (more than 1,200);

IIIIII municipal waste combustors;

IIIIII sewage sludge disposal (primarily incineration concerns);

IIIIII occupational exposures (including secondary exposure of children whose parents are exposed); and

IIIIII exposures at mining sites.

Lead is still used in the manufacture of certain products or for purposes that could result in high exposures, including the use of lead in brass plumbing fixtures, in hobby products, and in ceramic glazes that coat many kinds of china and dinnerware. The severity of lead exposure from these sources is unclear.

IIIIII **MERCURY**

Mercury is a stable, naturally occurring element that is refined from cinnabar (the mineral—mercuric sulfide). It forms a variety of compounds. At room temperature, in its pure form, it is a silvery liquid that vaporizes easily. It is probably best known as the silver-white substance in thermometers. It is the only metallic element that is liquid at room temperature.

Because of its unique properties, which include its ability to conduct electricity, its liquidity at room temperature, its ability to alloy with almost all common metals, and its ease in vaporizing and freezing, mercury is widely used in industrial applications. Over three thousand industries utilize mercury in manufacturing and processing. It is used to make batteries, paints, electrical switches, and hundreds of other products. It is also used as an industrial catalyst in the production of urethane and polyvinyl chloride. Because of its inherent toxicity it was widely used in pesticides until the mid-1970s. Mercury is also used with other metals in an amalgam in dentistry for tooth fillings. Because of its significance in industrial applications, large amounts of mercury are being redistributed and concentrated in the environment.

Mercury compounds in the atmosphere can come from both natural sources, such as volcanos, and from industrial sources. Industrial sources include mining; the burning of oil and coal; metal smelting, steel and cement making; agricultural products; pharmaceuticals; pulp and paper manufacturing; and incineration of batteries, paint, and other products containing mercury. Approximately 80 percent of the mercury used in manufacturing is eventually released back into the environment.

Air emissions are a major source of human exposure, especially near sewage treatment facilities. The largest contributors to air emissions are chlorine-alkali plants, municipal incinerators, and mercury mines and smelters. And since mercury is a trace constituent of coal and petroleum products, burning fossil fuels also releases mercury into the air where it can be suspended for several years. Scientists now believe that mercury is being swept into the upper atmosphere from cement and phosphate plants as well as power plants and incinerators. Mercury is also evaporating from contaminated lake and ocean sediments and falling back to earth as toxic rain.

Mercury enters waterways through wastewater discharges from industrial plants and municipal sewage. Mercury waste is discharged by industries into sewer systems. Sewage treatment plants cannot filter out the metals, so they are discharged into waterways as liquid or sludge. Here it is collected in sediment and passed up the food chain from plankton, to minnows, to large fish, to birds of prey and large mammals—and human beings.

Landfill disposal of wastes contribute to the soil buildup of mercury. There is growing concern that the use of municipal sewage sludge as fertilizer may be contributing to the problem of mercury contamination of the soil.

Although all mercury compounds are toxic, mercury is most

dangerous when it is converted into methyl mercury. Scientific evidence points to the existence of a mercury cycle, where elemental mercury and various mercury compounds are transformed in the environment into methyl mercury—the organic form of mercury that is readily absorbed by fish. This process is known as methylation. Since mercury is an element and, therefore, cannot be broken down into harmless components once it is released into the environment, mercury remains available for methylation for many years.

Mercury when taken into the body through air, water, or food is absorbed in varying amounts. The major food sources for mercury are fish and shellfish. The body cannot metabolize monomethyl mercury forms and thus it remains in the body for a relatively long time. Mercury accumulates in the liver, kidney, brain, and blood and causes both acute and chronic health effects, depending on the form of mercury. Acute poisoning can result in gastrointestinal damage, cardiovascular collapse, and acute kidney failure, all of which can result in death. Chronic symptoms of inorganic and organic mercury compounds (seen most often in workers and cases of food contamination) include birth defects, and central nervous system and kidney damage. Genetic damage is also suspected. Loss of appetite and weight loss are often the first signs of chronic mercury poisoning. There have been few studies of the extent to which people have been harmed by mercury poisoning.

In the 1950s, more than one hundred people living in Minimata, Japan, were poisoned after eating fish contaminated with high levels of mercury. Across the United States and Canada, mercury contamination of fish in lakes and harbors continues to poison wildlife and threaten human health. Mercury has been confirmed as the cause of death of panthers and loons in Florida, and it is suspected of causing reproductive failures seen in eagles, minks, otters, and other animals in the Great Lakes region.

In the 1990s, concerns were raised about the use of mercury in silver amalgam used by dentists to fill teeth. However, in 1991, both the Food and Drug Administration and a committee of experts at the National Institutes of Health concluded that this use of mercury posed no threat to health. Nevertheless, some dentists have stopped using filling containing mercury and are substituting more expensive materials like gold and other composites.

IIIIIII   **CADMIUM**

Cadmium is a soft, silvery metal found in sulfide deposits primarily in zinc ores, and to a lesser extent in lead and copper ores and high sulphur coal. Most industrial cadmium is produced as a by-product of zinc refining. Although U.S. production of cadmium is relatively low, large amounts are imported annually for manufacturing purposes. Cadmium is used for electroplating; in pigments for higher quality plastics, paints, and inks; as alloys in batteries and in other industrial processes; as well as for other industrial uses. Cadmium pigments are used to manufacture such products as football helmets and automobile dashboards. Artists also use cadmium paints. However, they represent only about 5 percent of the country's cadmium pigment use.

As a natural element, cadmium accumulates in soils. It does not break down or decompose into less toxic components over time. Cadmium is of concern because of its known toxicity at very low levels, its ability to accumulate in soils, its potential as a human carcinogen, and the widespread exposure of the public to cadmium. Industrial production has redistributed the metal throughout the environment, causing widespread cadmium contamination. Sewage sludge, used as fertilizer and soil conditioner, may contain high levels of cadmium. Electroplating accounts for nearly 75 percent of waterborne cadmium wastes. The largest single source of cadmium air contamination is zinc smelters. However, zinc smelters, which are few in number and generally isolated from the general public, may pose a smaller risk than do other sources, such as iron and steel mills and municipal incinerators, which contribute a smaller percentage of the total emissions but affect a greater number of people. Cadmium is released into the environment when products colored with cadmium pigment are incinerated. If the ash is not properly contained, experts say, the cadmium can seep into groundwater. The pigments can also cause contamination in the recycling process. Cadmium is also released into the environment through its use in pesticides.

Humans absorb cadmium by inhalation of airborne cadmium and ingestion of food and water containing cadmium. Cadmium is hazardous to human health both in high concentrations for short periods of time and in low doses for prolonged periods. Some scientists now believe the health hazards associated with the latter may be more serious and more widespread than previously suspected. In the natural environment, localized cadmium ore deposits would pose little threat to public health. Acute poisoning, while rare, produces respiratory or gastrointestinal symptoms. Chronic exposure to low levels is much more widespread. Inhalation of cadmium over prolonged periods of time can cause serious damage to the respiratory system. When humans consume cadmium, it concentrates in the kidneys and liver where damage may occur. Elevated concentrations can cause problems ranging from kidney malfunction to death. Some studies indicate cadmium may also be a human carcinogen. While some studies suggest a link between cadmium exposure and human birth defects, this link has not been fully documented.

Smokers, particularly smokers who work in industries using cadmium or live near industries discharging cadmium emissions, run a higher risk of cadmium-related diseases than do nonsmoking segments of the population.

⫼⫼⫼ **ARSENIC, BERYLLIUM, AND OTHER METALS**

Arsenic exposure comes from the burning of coal and oil and the smelting of nonferrous ores such as copper. Arsenic has been an additive to glass, was used as a pesticide, and is found in mine tailings. It is a cumulative poison at high concentrations and a carcinogen. It is an extremely toxic substance.

Beryllium exposure also results from the burning of coal and oil. It is used as an additive to harden alloys and ceramics. It is often found at cement plants. Exposure to this metal can also cause skin cancer lesions, ulcers, respiratory disease (berylliosis), and cancer.

Chromium has been used in the metallurgical industry, particularly to make stainless steel and alloys. Chromium compounds are used in the manufacture of bricks, glass, ceramics, and certain iron-containing metals. Chromium is also used in the pigment, paint, tanning, and dyeing industries. It has been associated with lung cancer in exposed workers. Exposure to nickel in the workplace has been associated with cancer of the sinuses and respiratory passages. Radioactive uranium produces ionizing radiation and is discussed elsewhere.

ⅢⅢⅢ CORRECTING THE PROBLEM ⅢⅢⅢ

ⅢⅢⅢ LEAD

Reducing the amount of lead we put into the environment is one of society's biggest environmental achievements; what to do about all the lead we already put there is one of our biggest environmental problems. It is possible to make industry clean up the lead in Superfund sites, and it is possible to identify and mitigate individual pockets of high lead exposure. However, a huge number of people continue to be exposed to moderate, but still hazardous, levels from water, dust, and paint. Cleaning up these sources in a cost-effective manner is problematic.

Efforts have been underway since the 1970s to limit the use of lead-based paint. In 1971, the U.S. Department of Housing and Urban Development (HUD) began restricting Federal Housing Authority mortgages for new dwellings to those with paint that did not contain more than 1 percent lead. The level was further reduced in 1973 to 0.5 percent. In 1987, the Housing and Community Development Act required HUD to prepare plans for the abatement of lead-based paint hazards in housing. To date, the control of lead-based paint in residential units remains the responsibility of homeowners. However, HUD is responsible for public housing.

Getting the paint off of the walls can be problematic as well. For example, in Boston, it is illegal for landlords to rent to families with children if there is lead paint on the walls. At the same time, it is illegal to refuse to rent to families with children if you are in the rental business. And yet it is prohibitively expensive to get the lead off the walls.

The EPA has a number of programs underway to address soil contamination and has issued interim guidance on lead soil cleanup levels at the 1,200 Superfund NPL sites. The EPA also is conducting pilot programs under the Superfund Amendments and Reauthorization Act (SARA) to evaluate the effects on children's blood lead levels of removing lead-contaminated soil and dust in Boston, Baltimore, and Cincinnati.

Amendments to the Safe Drinking Water Act (SDWA) in 1986 banned the use of lead solder from public water supply systems, and from plumbing in residential or nonresidential facilities connected to a public water supply system. The use of pipes containing more than 8 percent lead was also banned. However, EPA enforcement of this ban has been limited. The EPA is also considering efforts to ban the sale of lead solder. The Lead Contamination and Control Act of 1988 banned the use of lead-containing materials in drinking water systems and water coolers. In 1988, the EPA's Office of Drinking Water proposed further revisions to the National Primary Drinking Water Regulation for lead under the Safe Drinking Water Act. These revisions are designed to reduce the maximum contaminant level (MCL) from 50 parts per billion (ppb) MCL to 15 ppb at the tap.

Other control measures include efforts by the EPA to increase battery recycling and phase out current uses of lead that pose unreasonable risk. Measures being considered include restrictions on the following:

|||||| disposal of lead, including restrictions on land disposal of waste containing lead;

|||||| incineration of sludge with high lead content; and

|||||| the introduction of new uses of lead posing unreasonable risks.

The Centers for Disease Control and Prevention directs the targeted lead-screening program that identifies lead-poisoned children.

In additional to these federal programs, there are state and local programs for getting rid of lead in the environment and for testing children.

While removing lead from the environment is difficult and can be costly, there are solutions that can be effective. For example, washing down the walls every few weeks and cleaning the dust off of sills can significantly reduce exposures at very little cost. However, there has been very little interest in promoting these low-tech, voluntary, half-way solutions.

|||||| **MERCURY**

The federal government has taken steps to reduce public exposure to mercury and its compounds, including provisions under the Clean Water Act and the Resource Conservation and Recovery Act. In addition, the EPA has banned the production, sale, and use of pesticides containing mercury. Because of risks to workers in industries that use mercury, the U.S. Occupational Safety and Health Administration (OSHA) has set occupational exposure standards.

The U.S. Food and Drug Administration has set a maximum limit of one-thousandth of a gram of mercury per kilogram in fish. Some state health departments have set even more stringent limits. For example, the Minnesota Department of Health has set a limit of 0.16 thousands of a gram per kilogram that is thought to be the nation's strictest.

Disposal methods that keep discarded batteries and paint from incinerators help to reduce mercury in the atmosphere. Battery manufacturers, concerned about possible new regulations, have significantly reduced their use of mercury.

In 1990, the EPA banned the use of mercury in interior latex paints. Paints manufactured before the ban can be sold but they must contain warning labels. Oil-based paints do not contain mercury. Even prior to the ban, many paint manufacturers had not used mercury in paints for years.

Sewage treatment facilities have been required to regulate industrial discharges since 1978. However, the number of industries continuing to discharge metals remains high and the amount of lead and mercury entering the plants has actually increased. In 1990, the EPA set limits to toxic discharges of mercury from sewage treatment plants and industries in New York and New Jersey, including 14 sewage treatment plants in New York City. This was done to ensure that water quality standards for those substances were met by 1993. New York Harbor shellfish have some of the highest levels of toxic metal contamination in the nation.

Utility companies and incinerator builders estimate that the costs to remove mercury from emissions could be high. Utilities have estimated the cost at $5 billion nationally, while incinerator builders estimate costs between $10 and $30 million per plant.

|||||| **CADMIUM**

Workplace exposure to cadmium has been regulated for some time because of its known toxic properties. The standards set by OSHA for exposure are designed to protect workers against the development of kidney damage which has been reported at low levels.

Federal regulation has since been expanded to include cadmium contamination of land, water, air, and food. The EPA has established criteria for the disposal of sewage sludge containing cadmium on agricultural lands. To reduce cadmium levels in water, the EPA has used the authority of the Clean Water Act to set effluent guidelines that limit the amount of cadmium in waste water discharges. Similarly, the EPA has used the authority of the Clean Air Act to set guidelines that limit cadmium emissions from industry.

‖‖‖‖ **PITFALLS** ‖‖‖‖

‖‖‖‖ Even as extensive efforts are underway to stop the *introduction* of lead into the environment, the problem of "in-place" lead exposure continues. There are millions of tons of lead in the soil from the previous use of lead in gasoline and in paints and an estimated 15 percent of children still have blood lead levels over 10 micrograms/dl—considered still high by many. Elevated blood levels today are largely due to exposures to this lead that was previously deposited. With so much lead "in place," the poor think (rightly) that they do not have all that much choice. On the other hand, the rich think (wrongly) that it is not a problem for their kids. While lead affects mostly poor urban children, there are many exceptions (e.g., the leaded dust created during the process of rehabilitating older homes).

‖‖‖‖ The media (and readers) are typically more interested in environmental risks like lead present at Superfund sites than in individual-level risks like lead paint. But with lead (as with many other hazards), the individual lead paint risk is much greater and more widespread than the lead contamination from a Superfund site or an incinerator. Readers need to know about lead paint and how to cope with its effects in their lives. They need to know about the importance of getting their children tested. Therefore, reporters need to consider the relative priority of a big lead controversy (and subsequent outrage) versus a big lead hazard (lead exposure in paint) without much outrage. Certainly both deserve coverage but too often the latter is short-changed.

ⅢⅢ We tend to divide environmental risks into big ones that should be dealt with immediately and small ones that should be forgotten. Lead is a big risk, but there is no fast way to remove all the lead from our walls, our pipes, and the soil around us. Reporters have to help readers create a third category of big risks that cannot be eliminated immediately. Given that we have put lead everywhere, the big lead questions are how fast to clean up and how to pay for cleaning up?

ⅢⅢ SOURCES FOR JOURNALISTS ⅢⅢ

ⅢⅢ State health departments are good sources of information on lead exposure and exposure to other toxic metals.

ⅢⅢ The state environmental protection department is a good source of information on toxic metals. It usually has an office that can provide technical background information. Its right-to-know programs can provide information on occupational and community exposures.

ⅢⅢ The Office of Pesticides and Toxic Substances within the EPA is another source of information on toxic metals. Its number in Washington, D.C. is 202-260-2902.

ⅢⅢ Information is available on toxic metals from companies that manufacture paints.

ⅢⅢ See the briefs on "Occupational Exposure to Toxic Chemicals" and "Nuclear Power Plants (Commercial)."

WATER POLLUTION

Scientists estimate that 400–1,000 cancer cases annually result from long-term exposure to contaminated drinking water. In other words, water pollution is less of a problem than exposure to asbestos, radon, and lifestyle risks such as smoking tobacco and alcohol abuse. However, water is a vital resource to protect for present use as well as for future generations. Groundwater, in particular, is vulnerable to contamination. Once contaminated, it is difficult, if not economically infeasible, to clean it sufficiently for use as drinking water. Protection of well-head and aquifer recharge areas is important.

|||| **IDENTIFYING THE PROBLEM** ||||

Water, like the air, is a dynamic system that has received enormous environmental insults as the result of human activities. Over the last few decades, industrialization and population growth have led to a nationwide deterioration in groundwater and surface water quality. The discharge of pollutants,

|||| This article is based on an earlier version by Liz Fuerst, Department of Journalism and Mass Media, in the first edition of *The Environmental Reporter's Handbook*. Additional information was provided by Daniel J. Van Abs of the New Jersey Department of Environmental Protection and Energy, Hazel Groman of the U.S. Environmental Protection Agency's Office of Wetlands Protection, Ralph Tiner of the U.S. Fish and Wildlife Service, Robert Perry and Maureen G. Novotne of the Water Environment Federation, Wilfried Eul of Degussa Corporation, and Peter Hannak of Union Carbide Chemicals and Plastics Company, Inc. ||||

unchecked development, and shrinking quantities of water all disturb the aquatic environment and threaten its existence. This poses several problems. Human life depends on drinking water taken from rivers, streams, and reservoirs. Water is necessary to grow and prepare food, operate the sanitary waste process, and continue industrial activities such as the manufacture of paper, textiles, chemicals, metals, and foodstuffs. Clean water is vital as well to the inland fishing industry. The discharge of oxygen-consuming and toxic substances harms fish and makes them less suitable for human consumption.

Groundwater includes all water beneath the land surface where the water saturates the rock or sediments and is free to flow. Water that is bound to soil particles or does not saturate the rock or sediments is not generally considered groundwater. Much groundwater is derived from precipitation onto the land surface.

Groundwater is the main, but not the only, source of drinking water. Therefore, potability is the main, but not the only, groundwater issue.

Surface water refers to water at the surface of the earth, including lakes, rivers, ponds, and streams. It is the source of much groundwater through the larger hydrologic cycle as water moves from the surface to aquifers below ground.

The process whereby water moves, under the influence of gravity, from the surface to aquifers, is called aquifer recharge. Most recharge to aquifers occurs very close to, or even directly above, the aquifer itself, through soils that readily allow water movement. Such areas are called recharge areas. When water fills all pore spaces or fractures in a geologic unit, that level is called the water table. The height of the water table is the depth needed to reach groundwater (or saturated areas). The higher the water table, in general, the easier it is to get at the water, but the harder it is to keep it unpolluted.

Groundwater may be found in pores between sand, gravel, or silt particles, or it may be found in fractures and channels in rock. These water-bearing units may be uniform or very complex. When groundwater is found in quantities sufficient to be withdrawn by pumping wells, the groundwater and the unit in which it is found are together called an aquifer. Even when the groundwater is not in an aquifer, it may provide valuable flow to surface waters (called base flow) or to surface ecosystems such as wetlands. Much groundwater is closely connected to surface water systems.

In some areas aquifers are confined; that is, they lie underneath one or more thick beds of clay or silt across which water cannot easily flow. These confining layers may be thick or thin, extensive or limited in area. Confined aquifers receive much of their recharge from areas where the aquifer reaches the surface, called outcrop areas. Because of the pressure, the water level in wells drilled into these aquifers may rise much higher than the top of the actual aquifer; such wells are called artesian wells. In some cases, water may actually flow from the well without being pumped.

Pollution of surface water can come from both point sources and nonpoint sources. Point source refers to the discharge from one pipe or leak. Included here are municipal (home and business) and industrial sources. Nonpoint source means the source is broad and cannot be easily pinpointed as can a wastewater pipe draining into a stream.

Primary nonpoint sources of water pollution are pesticide, fertilizer, and other chemical runoffs from farmland. Forestry practices, construction, and mining are also important contributors to nonpoint pollution. According to the EPA, nonpoint sources are responsible for 65 percent of pollution in degraded rivers and for 76 percent of pollution in degraded lakes. In estuaries, nonpoint pollution makes up 45 percent of the problem.

In 1990, the U.S. Environmental Protection Agency completed its national survey of pesticides and identified over one thousand possible drinking-water contaminants, including inorganic substances such as cadmium, mercury, selenium, and arsenic; and organic materials such as paint thinner, glues, dyes, and pesticides. In general, the EPA reported that the percentage of wells containing pesticides was low, but rural domestic wells, in particular, were often affected by one or more pesticides.

The dumping of phosphates from laundry detergents has severely damaged lakes and rivers over the years. This dumping encouraged excessive, uncontrolled growth of plankton or algae blooms. This is known as eutrophication during which the water turns green or brown. Some species of algae, when growing uncontrollably, can produce toxic substances, causing death to livestock that drink from the surface water. Improved wastewater treatment plants and bans on phosphate detergents have decreased phosphate output significantly.

Thermal pollution occurs from the release of heated waters from power stations using surface water for cooling purposes. While the water is returned without chemical additives, its temperature is higher. This can lead to a decrease in dissolved oxygen levels that can interfere with migration habits and the spawning of fish.

Many of the same pollutants that foul surface waters make their way underground by many routes. Landfills, surface lagoons, spills, underground and aboveground storage tanks, and septic systems have caused much of the groundwater pollution found to date. Other sources include stormwater infiltration basins, fertilizer and pesticide use, indiscriminate dumping, and material stockpiles. Some states allow deep well injection of hazardous wastes into geologic units isolated from groundwater. However, leaks can contaminate the groundwater.

Most groundwater pollution is localized and does not readily spread throughout the region. It moves slowly, does not mix readily, and stays in discrete areas called plumes. This is both good news and bad news. The good news is that pollution in groundwater does not spread rapidly. The bad news is that, because it does not spread rapidly, the pollution does not dilute; it remains more concentrated than it would in surface waters. The concentrations of hazardous and toxic pollutants in groundwater may be hundreds or thousands of times higher than the range of concentrations in surface water.

This makes it urgent to know when it occurs. For instance, where volatile organic chemicals, such as trichloroethylene (TCE), a common solvent, will readily dilute in surface waters or will move into the air, TCE stays concentrated in groundwater. In New Jersey, for example, over one hundred public community water supply wells and many thousands of domestic wells have been polluted. Even so, vast areas and volumes of the state's, and nation's, aquifers meet all drinking water quality standards, and large volumes are pristine, or nearly so.

IIIIII CORRECTING THE PROBLEM IIIIII

There are three ways to treat water pollution problems: treatment, containment, and prevention. Treatment is difficult, expensive, and sometimes, impossible, though much research is being done in this area. The other two approaches are easier and less expensive. Drinking water standards can involve all three—if the groundwater does not meet standards, then it cannot be used (containment), or it must be cleaned up (treatment). But, most importantly, what remains must be protected.

Containment technologies include barriers to prevent pollution migration and to control heavily contaminated soils. Treatment technologies include removal of concentrated pollutants through drainage-type collection systems, and pumping and treatment of polluted groundwater. In addition, new technologies are being developed that use bacteria to consume pollutants, or that use chemicals or heat to transform the pollutants into less harmful substances.

Although containment can be effective, pollution is extremely hard to remove from groundwater. More than one pollution case has had a price tag of well over $20 million to mitigate groundwater pollution. Even at such high cost, in many cases, complete remedies cannot be assured because sufficient technologies often do not exist.

Preventing pollution is far less costly to society, in the long run, than trying to mitigate its effects. Although pollution prevention may require up-front expenditures, responding to major pollution problems after the fact can bankrupt companies, take limited public funds from other uses, and disrupt citizens' lives and the economic health of a state. By their nature, preventive activities can be planned so that facilities can budget time and money in a way that minimizes cost while maximizing protection.

Pollution prevention efforts in the United States are increasing. Recycling of solid wastes and collection and disposal or recycling of household and industrial hazardous wastes are increasing. Keeping land uses that contaminate water away from well head areas and aquifer recharge areas through land-use ordinances is an important prevention strategy.

Pollution can be controlled and even prevented by getting at the source before it enters the water system. Pollutants can be withheld from the environment when it is understood that purification techniques will not do the job. At-source control means that industry has to set up production processes that produce minimal pollution, either by using fewer or different raw materials, or by minimizing the loss of raw materials during production When using at-source control, methods have to be implemented to evaluate pollutants.

Since the Clean Water Act was passed in 1972, the standards for drinking water quality have improved. The act requires secondary water treatment to remove 85 percent of the major pollutants and suspended particles in used water and sewage. Today many sanitary waste treatment plants are being upgraded so that through treatment, 90 percent or more of the organics and solids can be removed before discharge.

The Safe Drinking Water Act (SDWA) was passed in 1974. The SDWA defined standards of quality for potable water, free of waterborne diseases. Standards for drinking water were based on best available technology, taking cost into account. Amendments to the act were passed in 1986 to address contamination of drinking water by synthetic and naturally occurring compounds. These amendments gave the EPA the ability to regulate eighty-three different contaminants such as cyanide, PCBs, and benzene in public drinking water systems by 1989. The list includes pesticides and herbicides, nine inorganic substances, and radium and overall radioactivity. Secondary standards were set for nontoxic materials that affect taste and tooth color and cause pipe corrosion.

|||||| IMPORTANT POINTS FOR RESEARCHING A STORY ||||||

|||||| When dealing with sanitary waste facilities, find out where the waste originates, what body of surface water will carry the effluent away, and what communities consume the water downstream.

|||||| It is important to note what type of agency (a commission, authority, municipal governing body, private agency, or

developer) will operate the water treatment plant and how it intends to charge customers.

⠿ All water treatment plants have varying levels of purification. Determine whether the plant you are writing about is a primary, secondary, or advanced treatment facility. Some waste facilities are nothing more than a large pond in which solids drop to the bottom and the liquids above are treated with purifying chemicals. In many cases, the treated water is further purified through aeration and spread on local agricultural fields near the facility. This is known as spray irrigation of waste.

⠿ Where point-source pollution is involved, try to determine what the pollutant is and what its consequences to the aquatic environment are. Fish kills and disappearance of certain varieties of aquatic life are clues that surface waters have become polluted. Press the industries to tell you what is being done to combat point-source pollution and how much money is being spent in the process.

⠿ Where runoff is the major source of pollution, be sure to talk with local agricultural agents, land-use planners, river basin commissions, and other groups that would know the extent of runoff. Try to determine if the local government has made efforts to protect well head areas and aquifer recharge areas. If not, ask why not.

⠿ PITFALLS ⠿

⠿ A great deal of uncertainty is associated with groundwater contamination. Stories should avoid hiding this uncertainty. The identification, investigation, and mitigation of groundwater pollution is an expensive, lengthy, often uncertain, and highly technical undertaking. The top experts may disagree in complex sites. There may be an honest difference of opinion.

⠿ Pollution sources may be old, with no remaining records or evidence at the site—except the pollution that remains behind. The responsible sources for some well pollution incidents are never found.

‖‖‖‖‖ Water may be aesthetically unpleasant and yet not actually harmful to drink. Likewise, groundwater which to all appearances is pure, may contain carcinogens in high concentrations. When in doubt, test! Many states have lists of laboratories that can properly analyze groundwater and drinking water samples.

‖‖‖‖‖ The cost of water pollution investigations can be very high. Therefore, most information will be developed by government agencies and the responsible parties themselves. Find out who (if anyone) is actively investigating a site. Work with them to understand the local circumstances. Verify analyses with other experts.

‖‖‖‖‖ Chemicals differ enormously in the health risks they present. Know what chemicals have been found and their concentrations. Some health effects have thresholds below which no effect is expected, while others are primarily a concern during long exposures. Be careful in your use of health-effect terms. Also, health effects may be debatable. Use more than one source of scientific information, and make sure that your source actually has expertise in the appropriate field.

‖‖‖‖‖ Pay attention to the effect of water quantity on water quality. When communities fail to control flooding, high waters may inundate polluting industries built near river and stream banks, causing extensive contamination of those bodies of water. In 1982, severe floods on the Meramec River, a tributary of the Mississippi River, brought dioxin-contaminated soil into flooded homes in Times Beach, Missouri. The dioxin was contained in waste oil spread on local roadways as much as ten years earlier. After the floods, the river was also found to contain dioxin. In addition, there is typically a water pollution problem in periods of drought, because the amount of clean water in the streams available to dilute contaminated discharges is reduced. When there is a water shortage, the small amount of surface water in an area may be treated water from an upstream sewage treatment plant.

‖‖‖‖‖ Focus on the good pollution stories as well as the bad. Many companies have taken drastic steps to clean up production waste, thereby making water less hazardous. Industry efforts to police itself should be covered by the environmental reporter, possibly with assistance from the business reporting staff.

ⅢⅢⅢ It is important to realize how slowly groundwater pollution migrates. It is a common mistake to imagine an underground river that will spill pollution into the neighboring county by Tuesday.

ⅢⅢⅢ Industrial chemicals are not the only contaminants in water. Bacteria and other organic contamination have always been the main risk—and still are, not just in Third World countries but also in the United States. In addition, there are other natural risks—such as radon—that are serious waterborne problems. (Regulations on testing for radon in water supplies were developed in 1993.) Chlorination is an extraordinarily cost-effective way to make water potable by killing bacteria. But the chlorine combines with organic materials (dead leaves and the like) in water to produce trihalomethanes, which are carcinogens. While there are other ways to kill waterborne diseases without this drawback, they often cost more.

ⅢⅢⅢ SOURCES FOR JOURNALISTS ⅢⅢⅢ

ⅢⅢⅢ The EPA regulates public water supplies, including setting the standards for drinking water quality. Information on new developments in drinking water standards can be obtained by calling the EPA's drinking water hotline. It's number is 800-426-4791.

ⅢⅢⅢ Water quality is monitored by state environmental, health, or natural resource departments. Information on water pollution problems and regulatory programs is available from these departments. State environmental agencies invariably have a division of water quality which deals with point-source and diffuse-source pollution and construction and funding of sanitary sewer systems. Local or regional health agencies may also have site-specific information.

ⅢⅢⅢ Information on groundwater and aquifers is available from the U.S. Geological Survey's Water Resources Division.

ⅢⅢⅢ University departments of environmental sciences, environmental engineering, and geology often have experts in the field.

ⅢⅢⅢ Information is available on pollution treatment from local sewerage authorities.

ⅢⅢⅢ Water quality is often monitored by private water resource groups, often called conservation or watershed associations. They are usually grouped by region, such as the Chesapeake Bay Foundation in Maryland (301-268-8816) or Lake Erie Clean-Up Committee in Michigan (313-271-8906).

ⅢⅢⅢ The Water Environment Federation in Alexandria, Virginia, is another source of information. Its telephone number is 703-684-2492.

ⅢⅢⅢ See the section on lead in the brief "Toxic Metals: Lead, Mercury, and Cadmium."

RESOURCES

TRACKING DOWN A COMPANY'S ENVIRONMENTAL RECORD

Reporters are frequently assigned stories about companies or institutions that have been involved in an environmental controversy. How do you find out the environmental track record of a company? How do you find out whether a chemical spill caused by a company is unusual or whether the firm has a long history of pollution problems?

IIIIII **NEWSPAPERS**

One of the first things you should do is check with your newspaper's librarian to dig out all of the clips about the company that have appeared in your own paper over the past five or ten years. By reviewing these clips you may see a pattern (i.e. the company has been cited for numerous air pollution problems but appears to have had a good record concerning water pollution). If your own library has no clips, visit the libraries of other papers that may have done stories about the company and review their clips.

IIIIII **COMMUNITY ACTIVISTS**

From these clips you may find out the names of community activists who have complained about the company in the past. Call these people to learn their perspective. If there are environmental

IIIIII This chapter was written by James Detjen, a science and energy reporter for the *Philadelphia Inquirer* in Philadelphia, Pennsylvania. IIIIII organizations in your community, such as the Sierra Club or Audubon Society, give their officers a call to see what they know about a company's environmental record.

|||||| **NEIGHBORS**

Talk to neighbors of the plant. You can walk through the neighborhood knocking on doors. Or you can check city directories to find out the names, addresses, and phone numbers of people living near the plant. And don't forget to talk to officials in police and fire departments They have tremendous street knowledge about companies and institutions in their neighborhood

|||||| **LABOR UNIONS**

Track down the local offices of labor unions that have workers employed at the company. Sometimes union officials are unwilling to talk publicly about a company's environmental record because of fear that jobs will be lost. Others may be very helpful because they are concerned about workers who are being exposed to unsafe levels of toxic chemicals. Unions may be able to track down the names and phone numbers of workers for you. Companies with poor occupational health records often have poor environmental records as well.

|||||| **CHECKING ENVIRONMENTAL AGENCY FILES**

Most state and federal environmental laws require that permits be issued to companies intending to discharge pollutants to the air and water or to send toxic waste to disposal facilities. Review the agency files on these companies looking at permits, inspection reports, enforcement actions, environmental impact statements, and correspondence. Different records may be kept in different offices of these agencies. If you have the time, check the files in environmental agencies in neighboring states as well. Be firm and ask to see the complete files yourself, not just a few documents that a public relations officer pulls for you.

If officials refuse to let you see these files, be firm and say you have a right to see them. File an open records request with state and local agencies and a Freedom of Information Act request with federal agencies if you have to.

IIIIII   **USING THE FREEDOM OF INFORMATION ACT**

One of the most powerful tools available to journalists is the Freedom of Information Act or the FOIA. This law enables you to look at records that officials in federal agencies may not want you to see. Before sending a letter, find out the name of the FOIA officer and address the request to that person. When requesting records, be as specific as possible. (You can obtain a good introductory booklet on the FOIA by writing to the Reporters' Committee, 1125 15th Street, Washington, D.C. 20005.)

A sample letter might look something like this:

Freedom of Information Officer
U.S. Environmental Protection Agency
Your regional office

Dear Mr. Cleanwater:

This request is being made under the federal Freedom of Information Act, 5 U.S.C. 552. Please send me copies of, or make available to me for review, the following records: all permits, inspection records, enforcement actions, and correspondence between your agency and the XYZ corporation concerning their Backwater factory, from the years 1970 to the present. As you know, the FOIA provides that if portions of a document are exempt from release, the remainder must be segregated and disclosed. I reserve the right to appeal your decision to withhold any materials.

Please notify me in advance if the total fees for this request exceed $ (*fill in the amount you are willing to pay*). Please call me at my office if you have any questions pertaining to this request.

Thank you for your assistance. I look forward to receiving your reply within ten working days, as required by law.

Very sincerely,
Your name

If you don't hear from the agency within a reasonable amount of time, call and ask them why there has been a delay. You have the right to file an appeal and ultimately to sue them for the records if you think they are being illegally withheld.

⫿⫿⫿⫿ CHECKING OTHER RECORDS

Check court records to see if people living near the plant or government agencies have sued the company for environmental problems. Check records kept by your county health department, your local sewer district, and any other government agency that might have records on the company's environmental problems. If it is a publicly held corporation, ask the federal Securities and Exchange Commission to look at the company's 10-K reports, which list any actions such as enforcement actions by environmental agencies that could adversely affect the company's profits.

And don't forget to talk to the company or institution. Once they know how much information you have gathered they will be less likely to try to snow you. Try to talk to those company officials with direct knowledge of pollution incidents.

⫿⫿⫿⫿ DO YOUR OWN TESTING

If no records about a pollution problem exist, but people think that a company is illegally discharging pollution into a stream, consider taking your own samples and conducting laboratory tests on these samples. These tests can be expensive, but, often, they are the only way you can get answers. Sometimes a local college will run these tests for you for free or at a very low cost.

⫿⫿⫿⫿ FINDING AN EXPERT

After reviewing records and documents, you may need to track down experts who can help translate some of the technical information or answer questions. The Scientists' Institute for Public Information in New York City will help you track down experts quickly. Its toll-free number is 800-223-1730. See the section on "Finding an Expert."

ⅢⅢ **PITFALLS** ⅢⅢ

ⅢⅢ Make sure you have checked with the company or institution about each pollution incident you are covering. Be fair to the company or institution. Let them respond to any negative statements that environmental activists or environmental agency officials may have made.

ⅢⅢ Don't try to "prove" connections that do not exist. If ten neighbors of a plant say their relatives have died of cancer because of the air pollution a company emits, be very cautious. Such cancer connections are almost impossible to prove. People die of cancer for many reasons, such as smoking tobacco and eating improperly.

ⅢⅢ Make sure your reporting is technically accurate. Double-check all of your facts, calculations, and quotations.

FINDING AN EXPERT

HOW DO YOU FIND AN EXPERT?

Experts are not always easy to find. You will develop your own lists of individuals whom you trust and with whom you feel comfortable.

A major state university that has active graduate programs is a good source of experts. Graduate programs tend to emphasize specialization while undergraduate programs are more apt to emphasize generalization. Consult university catalogs that describe graduate courses and faculty.

Most professional organizations have statewide and local offices, and they often will provide the right expert. If the situation is one of health risk, try contacting organizations that raise money for the disease at risk, for example, the American Cancer Society for cancer, the March of Dimes for birth defects. The Scientists' Institute for Public Information (SIPI), based in New York City, maintains a file of experts, and they will choose experts for you within your deadline pressures.

In certain situations, state and local government can be helpful, as can industry associations. Obviously, they may have their own biases. Try to get an unbiased opinion or a range of opinions,

|||||| This chapter was written by Bernard D. Goldstein, director, Environmental and Occupational Safety and Health Institute, Piscataway, New Jersey. ||||||

especially on controversial topics where objectivity is rare. Since experts tend to know one another, ask an expert in one area to refer you to an unbiased expert in another area, but make sure that the first expert does not have a vested interest in the second area.

||||||| **IS THE EXPERT REALLY AN EXPERT?**

How do you find out if a person has the credentials to make an expert statement? Gentle probing can elicit information about educational background and current affiliation. However, there are potential pitfalls, for example, someone addressed as doctor could be a doctor of optometry or a PH.D. in an unrelated field.

An affiliation claimed by, or attributed to, a person also should not be taken at face value. Ask these questions:
- ||||||| What do you do at the university?
- ||||||| Do you work there full-time?
- ||||||| What precisely is your field?
- ||||||| Have you been involved in a situation like this before?

Avoid asking experts about something outside of their immediate area. There is the human tendency not to be willing to admit ignorance. This age of technology often requires that a person's knowledge be highly specialized. Thus, an engineer who is an expert in hydraulics may know little or nothing about hazardous-waste control technology. A physician does not necessarily know about the risks of environmental pollutants or workplace chemicals.

||||||| **IS THE EXPERT PROVIDING FACTUAL INFORMATION OR OPINION?**

It is perfectly legitimate for an expert to provide an opinion based on knowledge. However, it is important to determine if the expert is stating fact or opinion.

Fact can be defined as something that is known with certainty and is objectively verifiable. Opinion is an evaluation or judgment based on special knowledge and given by an expert. It is a conclusion not substantiated by positive proof or knowledge. Most experts know the distinction but could assume you are asking for their judgment or opinion.

Ask the expert if the information they are giving you is indeed fact. Also, be careful not to interpret an opinion and report it as a fact. Ask the expert for names of individuals with opposing points of view, and seek additional information from them.

‖‖‖‖ **IS THE EXPERT UNBIASED?**

There are two major sources of bias on the part of experts. One source is an obvious conflict of interest, such as owning stock in an affected industry, or a riverside home if flood control is the issue. The second source is more subtle and occurs when an expert's scientific reputation is involved in an outcome, leading to a willingness to jump to conclusions or to make unjustified pronouncements. Further investigation and the use of more than one expert are the best means of overcoming bias.

MAJOR DEVELOPMENTS IN FEDERAL LEGISLATIVE HISTORY

|||||| AIR QUALITY[1] ||||||

1955   Federal role emphasizes research and data collection and technical assistance to states.

1963   Grants awarded to states for air quality programs; federal-state conferences used for enforcement.

1965   Emission standards for new motor vehicles introduced.

1967   Mandates federal air quality criteria; provides for the states to set ambient air quality standards; designates air quality control regions for planning purposes.

1970:CAA   National Ambient Air Quality Standards (NAAQS); emission standards for new motor vehicles and facilities; emission standards for new sources (NSPS) and for hazardous substances for existing facilities; provisions for the development of state implementation plans (SIPS).

1977: CAA   More stringent controls on air quality degradation;
AMENDMENTS   prevention of significant deterioration provision added, construction of new sources contingent on state approved air quality plan.

|||||| This compilation was developed by Rae Zimmerman of New York University and is reprinted with the permission of the Guilford Press. An earlier version by R. Zimmerman appeared in *Public Health and the Environment*, ed. Michael Greenberg (New York, New York: Guilford Press, 1987), 237–240. ||||||

1978   Lead added as an element in national ambient air
quality standard.

1980s   Health effects studies developed for noncriteria air
pollutants; extensive delegation of permit programs for
new sources of air pollution and the development of hazardous air pollution standards to state agencies with continued federal oversight responsibilities; development of
regulations for an emissions trading policy; increased strin-
gency of standards for lead content of gasoline.

1990:CAA   Major changes made in emission and ambient
AMENDMENTS   standards for both stationary and mobile pollutant
sources, new emission levels and controls specified for
conventional or NAAQS; in a regulation preceding the 1990
amendments, one of the six criteria pollutants for total
suspended particulates is changed to particulates 10 microns or less in size (PM-10); sources of ozone, carbon
monoxide (CO), and PM-10 in areas not meeting ambient
standards are subject to emission controls such as best
available control technology (BACT), reasonably available
control technology (RACT), and lowest achievable emission
rate (LAER), depending on pollutants and air quality in the
area in which the emissions occur; special provisions introduced primarily for sulfur dioxide (SO_2) reductions to
achieve acid deposition control; SO_2 emissions regulated
through emission allowances tradeable among sources;
many more chemicals—beyond NAAQS pollutants—placed
under direct emission controls; NESHAPs replaced by 189
hazardous air pollutants (HAPs) to which technology-based
emission standards (for source categories) and, where necessary, residual risk-based standards, will apply; for stationary air pollution sources, these emission limits are to
be attained using maximum achievable control technology
(MACT), and for "major" sources, will be regulated via new
operating permits; accidental chemical release controls included; special solid-waste incinerator standards and planning provisions also covered; restrictions placed on
stratospheric ozone depleting substances.

Mobile air pollution controls aimed at CO, NO_x, VOC
reductions, including tailpipe emission controls, improved

refueling procedures, clean-fuels program, and various regulatory provisions for fuels; extensive reductions in motor vehicle emissions phased in between 1994 and 1998, calling for 30% hydrocarbon emission reduction and 60% for nitrogen oxides with subsequent reductions considered by 2003, and a CO standard for cold engine starts.

Enforcement provisions and citizen rights to sue have been strengthened.

‖‖‖‖ WATER QUALITY[2] ‖‖‖‖

Late 1800s–   Rivers and Harbors Act used for pollution.
early 1900s   control through the late 1960s; 1924 oil pollution control acts used similarly; both acts administered by the U.S. Army Corps of Engineers.

1948   Grants for state programs and facility plans; orientation of federal effort is toward interstate waterways.

1956   Authorized federal wastewater treatment facility construction grants (up to 30% of the costs) and grants for state programs; continuation of emphasis on data collection, research, and technical assistance to states; enforcement procedures use a federal-state conference and require that endangerment of health or welfare occur before action is taken.

1961   Expansion of federal jurisdiction from interstate waters to coastal waters; incentives for interjurisdictional projects for wastewater treatment; increases in funding in most areas.

1965:WQA   State to set and enforce water quality standards for interstate, navigable waterways; enforcement plans developed, conformance of projects with local area plans encouraged.

1966   Increased authorizations for construction grants up to 50% of costs; formulas for increases based on federal-state shares and other incentives; allotment formula becomes more complex.

1970   State certification of compliance with water quality standards as a condition for issuing wastewater discharge permits; strengthening of marine vessel and oil pollution controls.

1972:CZMA   Planning for the development of coastal areas, incorporating environmental and economic criteria.

1972:FWPCA   Extensive controls for industrial, municipal, and other sources of pollution; standards for ambient quality, effluent discharges; NPDES permit program for wastewater discharges; provision for area-wide planning; coverage of grants for wastewater facility construction increased up to 75% of costs.

1972:MPRSA   Permits for ocean disposal of wastes; provisions for establishing criteria for the quality of material for disposal.

1974:SDWA   Standards for public water supply systems; designation of sole-source drinking water aquifers; development of an underground injection control program.

1977:CWA   Extensive delegation of programs to the states;
AMENDMENTS   extension of construction grant funding and applicability to operation and maintenance; provision for 85% federal share for innovative projects; delegation of sec. 404 provisions for dredging and filling in wetlands assigned to the Corps of Engineers; expansion in the number of toxic substances covered under water quality standards and expansion in the use of pretreatment standards for wastes entering municipal wastewater treatment systems; compliance deadlines extended.

1977:MPRSA   Prohibition of ocean disposal of sewage sludge
AMENDMENTS   after 1981 (however, this provision was the subject of a number of court cases and subsequent revisions of the deadline); five classes of ocean disposal permits established.

1981   Reduction in the applicability and scope of construction grant awards for wastewater treatment plants and reduction in the federal share of such grants to 55% after 1985; extensive delegation of programs to state agencies, including construction grants program, NPDES program, underground injection control program and coastal management programs; prohibitions on ocean disposal of hazardous waste.

1986:SDWA   Standards-setting is considerably expanded; the
AMENDMENTS   number of standards to be set for drinking water
supplies is increased to 83 chemicals over three years: a list
of chemicals is to be developed from which chemicals are
drawn for standards-setting; monitoring and treatment requirements are expanded to meet the new standards; filtra-
tion or equivalent treatment method is required for surface
water supplies; underground injection program requirements and groundwater protection provisions added.

1987   Amendments strengthen previous CWA provisions,
especially in the waterborne toxics area; number of chemicals regulated and their numerical values are expanded in
both effluent (discharge) and ambient standards and guidelines; effluent guidelines for BACT include more industrial
categories and pollutants; states mandated to pass numerical criteria for toxic waterborne pollutants to meet state-
designated water usages; in areas exceeding criteria,
discharges are controlled via total maximum daily loads
(TMDLS); for "toxic hot spots" or areas that exceed standards after controls are imposed, sources must be identified and targeted for individual control strategies (ICSs);
wastewater discharge permit program (NPDES) still back-
bone of regulation of wastewater discharges; stormwater
discharge, sewage sludge, and pretreatment provisions expanded, reflecting emphasis on toxics; permit system introduced for certain storm water discharges; wastewater
treatment plant financing cut back and substituted, in some
cases, by state-revolving funds.

1988:LCCA   Amendment to SDWA targets control of lead in certain drinking water supplies, in particular, drinking water
coolers in schools.

1988:ODBA   Amendment to MPRSA requires withdrawal of sewage sludge from disposal in oceans and replacement with
land-based alternatives.

1990:OPA   The Oil Pollution Act includes revised provisions
of Section 311 of the Clean Water Act, primarily addressing
liability and damage recovery.

1992   CWA reauthorization tabled; provisions included
major water-related infrastructure.

|||||| **PESTICIDES**[3] ||||||

1910   General standards for insecticides and fungicides; specific standards for a couple of pesticides; basic purpose is protection from consumer fraud.

1938:FFDCA   Sections regulate pesticide residues in food.

1947:FIFRA   Registration and labeling system established.

1964   Safety considerations included in registration process; explicit references to registration, cancellation/suspension.

1972:FEPCA   Regulation orientation supplants registration orientation of earlier statutes; cost-benefit analysis included.

1975   Cost impacts of suspension and cancellation of registration required; formal RPAR process is adopted for premarket registration of pesticides; science advisory panel created to review regulations and product bans; amendments weaken overall cost/benefits and strengthen agricultural interests—agricultural economic impact statements required.

1978:FPA   Development of generic standards based on active ingredients rather than on each individual pesticide preparation.

1980s   Streamlining the registration process; review of existing pesticide process through registration standards program; expansion in the number of registration standards; expansion in the delegation of pesticide applicator and training programs to the states.

1988:FIFRA   Focus on pesticide use and production; require
AMENDMENTS   reregistration or cancellation of pesticides registered under earlier statutes (pre-1972) according to prescribed schedule and fee system to pay for reregistration process. Pesticide industry becomes responsible for disposal of pesticides whose registration has been withdrawn; heavy reliance on cost-benefit analysis; establishment of a fund to compensate industry for losses due to registration withdrawal.

ⅢⅢ MANUFACTURE OF TOXIC SUBSTANCES AND HAZARDOUS-WASTE DISPOSAL[4] ⅢⅢ

1976:RCRA   Permit program with a preventive orientation for hazardous-waste generators, transporters, and treatment storage and disposal facilities under a cradle-to-grave manifest system; development of performance standards for these regulations; mandatory solid-waste plan development by the states; grants and technical assistance to states; federal government authorized to perform emergency cleanup of sites by responsible parties.

1976:TSCA   Registration system for toxic substances prior to manufacture (PMN system); ban on the manufacture of PCBs.

1980:CERCLA   Mandatory cleanup of illegal hazardous-waste disposal sites by private parties or the federal government (with reimbursement provisions by responsible parties); authorizes both emergency removal actions and more long-term removal actions; financing of federal cleanup activities by a chemical feedstock tax; national contingency plan describing criteria and methods of cleanup; listing of hazardous wastes and reportable quantities above which cleanup is required.

1980:   Regulations under RCRA provide criteria for the designation of hazardous wastes and de-listing provisions; technical standards for incinerators and land disposal facilities adopted, such as percent removal efficiencies, liners for landfills, and groundwater monitoring.

1982:TSCAA   Expansion of the reporting requirements for chemicals; established rules on asbestos in schools and for manufacturers and handlers.

1984:HSWA   More stringent requirements for land disposal facilities; double liners and leachate control systems for land disposal facilities, restrictions on the land disposal of solvents, underground storage tank restrictions; requirements for resource recovery facilities, such as dioxin emission limits; increase in the number of wastes regulated; improvements in the test procedures for hazardous wastes; lowering of the limit of applicability of the permit program to facilities generating 100 kg/mo or more of hazardous wastes; restrictions on the burning of fuel containing hazardous wastes.

1986:AHERA (AMENDMENT TO TSCA) Provides for removal procedures for asbestos in schools, other abatement procedures for public and commercial buildings, and worker protection during removal.

1986:RCRA AMENDMENTS Establish trust fund for remediation of leaking underground storage tanks.

1986:SARA Authorized $9 billion for hazardous-waste site and underground storage tank cleanup; schedules are required for cleanup of sites on the national priorities list and for the preparation of cleanup plans; cost-effectiveness test is required for evaluating cleanup options and rules are developed to evaluate cleanup levels; health assessment studies are authorized for chemicals found at hazardous waste sites; liability protection is provided for hazardous waste contractors; emergency management through state emergency response commissions and emergency planning districts is provided; the provision of information by industry to communities (right-to-know provision) is required through inventory mechanisms for generators and treatment facilities; the method of providing funds under Superfund (the Hazardous Substances Superfund) is revised to include governmental appropriations as well as various taxes on industry; the chemical feedstock tax is supplemented by a corporate income tax; limits are placed on the use of Superfund monies for damage claims; authorizations are made from the fund for special cleanups; a connection is provided between regulation of chemicals under Superfund and under the HMTA; a special provision is made for radon gas research.

1990:PPA Requires source reductions in amount/hazards to public health and the environment associated with hazardous substances.

1992:FRLBPHRA Amendment to Housing and Community Development Act calls for abatement guidelines and notification by sellers of the existence of lead-based paint.

|||||| **REFERENCES** ||||||

Ackerman, B. A., et al. 1974. *The Uncertain Search for Environmental Quality.* New York: Free Press.

Advisory Commission on Intergovernmental Relations. 1972. *Multistate Regionalism.* Washington, D.C.: Advisory Commission on Intergovernmental Relations.

Anderson, R. F. 1973. *NEPA in the Courts.* Baltimore: Johns Hopkins University Press.

Andrews, R.N.L. 1976. *Environmental Policy and Administrative Change.* Lexington, Mass: Lexington Books.

Ashford, N. A., Ryan, C. W., and Caldart, C. C. 1983. "A Hard Look at Federal Regulation of Formaldehyde: A Departure from Reasoned Decisionmaking." *Harvard Environmental Law Review,* 7:297-370.

―――. 1983. "Law and Science Policy in Federal Regulation of Formaldehyde." *Science.* 122:894-900.

Association of State and Interstate Water Pollution Control Administrators and the U.S. Environmental Protection Agency. 1984. *America's Clean Water: The States' Evaluation of Progress 1972-1982.* Washington, D.C.: Association of State and Interstate Water Pollution Control Administrators.

Baldwin, J. H. 1985. *Environmental Planning and Management.* Boulder, Colo.: Westview Press.

Baram, M. S. 1982. *Alternatives to Regulation.* Lexington, Mass.: D. C. Heath.

Bardach, E. and Kagan, R. A. 1982. "Introduction." In *Social Regulation: Strategies for Reform,* ed. E. Bardach and R. A. Kagan. San Francisco: Institute for Contemporary Studies.

Bick, T. and R. E. Kasperson. 1978. "The CPSC Experiment: Pitfalls of Hazard Management." *Environment,* 20: 30-42.

Bishop, A. B., et al. 1974. *Carrying Capacity in Regional Environmental Management.* Washington, D.C.: U.S. Government Printing Office.

Bosselman, F., and Callies, D. 1971. *The Quiet Revolution in Land Use Control.* Washington, D.C.: U.S. Government Printing Office.

Bosselman, F., Callies, D., and Banta, J. 1973. *The Taking Issue.* Washington, D.C.: U.S. Government Printing Office.

Bosselman, F., Feurer, D., and Siemon, C. 1976. *The Permit Explosion*. Washington, D.C.: Urban Institute Press.

Boulding, K. 1971. "The Economics of the Coming Spaceship Earth." In *Environmental Quality in a Growing Economy*, ed. H. Jarrett. Baltimore: Johns Hopkins University Press.

Breyers, S. 1982. *Regulation and Its Reform*. Cambridge, Mass.: Harvard University Press.

Burton, I., Kates, R. W., and White, G. F. 1979. *The Environment as Hazard*. New York: Oxford University Press.

Caldwell, L. K., 1982. *Science and the National Environmental Policy Act*. University: University of Alabama Press.

Carter, S., et al. 1974. *Environmental Management and Local Government*. Washington, D.C.: U.S. Environmental Protection Agency.

Cole, H.S.D., et al., eds. 1973. *Models of Doom*. New York: Universe Books.

Conservation Foundation. 1982. *State of the Environment 1982*. Washington, D.C.: Conservation Foundation.

Commoner, B. 1971. *The Closing Circle*. New York: Alfred A. Knopf.

Cotgrove, S., and Duff, A. 1980. "Environmentalism, Middle-Class Radicalism and Politics. *The Sociological Review*, 28:333–351.

Council on Environmental Quality. 1981. *Environmental Trends*. Washington, D.C.: U.S. Government Printing Office.

———. *Twelfth annual report: Environmental Quality 1981*. Washington, D.C.: U.S. Government Printing Office.

———. *Thirteenth annual report: Environmental Quality 1982*. Washington, D.C.: U.S. Government Printing Office.

———. *Fourteenth annual report: Environmental Quality 1983*. Washington, D.C.: U.S. Government Printing Office.

———. *Fifteenth annual report: Environmental Quality 1984*. Washington, D.C.: U.S. Government Printing Office.

Dee, N., et al. 1973. *Environmental Evaluation System for Water Quality Management Planning*. Columbus, Oh: Battelle Columbus Labs.

Derthick, M. 1974. *Between State and Nation*. Washington, D.C.: The Brookings Institution.

Downs, A. 1972. "Up and Down with Ecology: The Issue-Attention Cycle." *Public Interest*, 28:38–50.

Ehrlich, P. 1970. *The Population Bomb*. New York: Ballantine Books.

Forrester, J. 1969. *Urban Dynamics*. Boston: MIT Press.

Gould, G. 1980. "Regulation of Point Source Pollution under the Federal Water Pollution Control Act." In *Water Quality Administration*, ed. B. L. Lamb. Ann Arbor, Mich.: Ann Arbor Science.

Harris, L. 1985. *Environmental Pollution Causes Deep Concern*. New York: Louis Harris.

Haskell, E. H. and Price, V. S. 1973. *State Environmental Management*. New York: Praeger.

Kaiser, E. J., et al. 1973. *Promoting Environmental Quality through Urban Planning and Controls*. Washington, D.C.: U.S. Environmental Protection Agency.

Keyes, D. L. 1976. *Land Development and the Natural Environment*. Washington, D.C.: The Urban Institute.

Kneese, A. V. and Schultze, C. L. 1975. *Pollution, Prices and Public Policy*. Washington, D.C.: The Brookings Institution.

Kundell, J. E. 1977. *Municipal Environmental Conservation Commissions in New York State*. Springfield, Va.: National Technical Information Service.

Lamb, B. L., ed. 1980. *Water Quality Administration*. Ann Arbor, Mich.: Ann Arbor Science.

Lee, D. B. 1973. "Requiem for Large Scale Models." *Journal of the American Institute of Planners*, 39:163–178.

Leontief, W. 1970. "Environmental Repercussions and the Economic Structure: An Input-Output Approach." *Review of Economics and Statistics*, 52:262–271.

Leopold, L. B., et al. 1971. *A Procedure for Evaluating Environmental Impact*. Washington, D.C.: U.S. Geological Survey.

Lisk, D. J. 1974. "Recent Development in the Analysis of Toxic Elements." *Science*, 184, no. 4142:1137–1141.

Marcus, A. 1980. "Environmental Protection Agency. In *The politics of Regulation*, ed. J. Q. Wilson. New York: Basic Books.

Marsh and McLennan Co., Inc. 1980. *Risk in a Complex Society*. Philadelphia: Marsh and McLennan.

McAllister, D. M. 1973. *Environment: A New Focus for Land-Use Planning*. Washington, D.C.: National Science Foundation.

McHarg, I. L. 1971. *Design with Nature*. Garden City, N.Y.: Doubleday.

Melosi, M. V. 1980. "Environmental Crisis in the City: The Relationship between Industrialization and Urban Pollution." In *Pollution and Reform in American Cities: 1870–1930*, ed. M. Melosi. Austin: University of Texas Press.

National Research Council. 1977–1978. *Analytical Studies for the U.S. Environmental Protection Agency*. Washington, D.C.: National Academy Press.

———. 1980. *Regulating Pesticides*. Washington, D.C.: National Academy Press.

———. 1983. *Risk Assessment in the Federal Government: Managing the Process*. Washington, D.C.: National Academy Press.

Noble, J., Banta, J., and Rosenberg, J. 1977. *Groping through the Maze*. Washington, D.C.: Conservation Foundation.

Office of Technology Assessment. 1983. *Technologies and Management Strategies for Hazardous Waste Control*. Washington, D.C.: Office of Technology Assessment.

O'Riordan, T., and Turner, R. K. 1983. *An Annotated Reader in Environmental Planning and Management*. Oxford, Eng.: Pergamon Press.

Pepper, D. 1984. *The Roots of Modern Environmentalism*. Dover, N.H.: Croom-Helm.

Schumacher, F. 1973. *Small is Beautiful*. London: Abachus.

Sorensen, J. C. 1971. *A Framework for Identification and Control of Resource Degradation and Conflict in the Multiple Use of the Coastal Zone*. Berkeley: Department of Landscape Architecture, University of California at Berkeley. Unpublished monograph.

Susskind, L., Bacow, L., and Wheeler, M. 1983. *Resolving Environmental Regulatory Disputes*. Cambridge, Mass.: Schenkman.

U.S. Environment Protection Agency. 1978. *National Water Quality Inventory: 1977 Report to Congress*. Washington, D.C.: U.S. Environmental Protection Agency.

———. 1984. *Risk Assessment and Management: Framework for Decision Making*. Washington, D.C.: U.S. Environmental Protection Agency.

U.S. General Accounting Office. 1981. *EPA Slow in Controlling PCB's*. Washington, D.C.: U.S. General Accounting Office.

———. 1982. *Cleaning Up the Environment: Progress Achieved but Major Unresolved Issues Remain.* Washington, D.C.: General Accounting Office.

———. 1982. *Environmental Protection: Agenda for the 1980's.* Washington, D.C.: General Accounting Office.

———. 1982. *Problems in Air Quality Monitoring System Affect Data Reliability.* Washington, D.C.: General Accounting Office.

———. 1982. *Implementation of Selected Aspects of the Toxic Substances Control Act.* Washington, D.C.: General Accounting Office.

———. 1983. *Delays in EPA's Regulation of Hazardous Air Pollutants.* Washington, D.C.: General Accounting Office.

———. 1983. *Interim Report on Inspection, Enforcement, and Permitting Activities at Hazardous Waste Facilities.* Washington, D.C.: General Accounting Office.

———. 1984. *EPA Could Benefit from Comprehensive Management Information on Superfund Enforcement Actions.* Washington, D.C.: General Accounting Office.

———. 1985. *EPA's Inventory of Potential Hazardous Waste Sites is Incomplete.* Washington, D.C.: General Accounting Office.

———. 1985. *Status of the Department of Energy's Implementation of the Nuclear Waste Policy Act of 1982 as of December 31, 1984.* Washington, D.C.: General Accounting Office.

———. 1986. *EPA's Strategy to Control Emissions of Benzene and Gasoline Vapor: Air Pollution.* Washington, D.C.: General Accounting Office.

Vig, N. J. and Kraft, M. E. 1984. "Environmental Policy from the Seventies to the Eighties." In *Environmental Policy in the 1980s: Reagan's New Agenda*, ed. N. J. Vig and M. E. Kraft. Washington, D.C.: Congressional Quarterly.

White, G. 1969. *Strategies of American Water Management.* Ann Arbor: University of Michigan Press.

White, L. J. 1981. *Reforming Regulation.* Englewood Cliffs, N.J.: Prentice-Hall.

Zimmerman, R. 1980. "The Administration of Regulation (PB 80-223647)." Springfield, Va.: National Technical Information Service.

————. 1980. 1982. *The Management of Risk*. Report of the National Science Foundation, 2 volumes and executive summary. New York: Graduate School of Public Administration, New York University.

————. 1983. "Risk Assessment and Environmental Health." *Environmental Planning Quarterly*, 3:5–7.

————. 1985. "The Environmental Impact Assessment Process and Urban Development in New York City." *New York Affairs*, 8:132–144.

————. 1985. "The Relationship of Emergency Management to Government Policies on Man-Made Technological Disaster." *Public Administration Review*, 45:29–39.

|||||| **NOTES** ||||||

[1] Adapted from the Council on Environmental Quality's 12th Annual Report—1981 and 13th Annual Report—1982.

[2] Adapted from the Council on Environmental Quality's 12th Annual Report—1981 and 13th Annual Report—1982 and from Lamb, 1980.

[3] Adapted from the National Research Council, 1980, and the Council on Environmental Quality's 13th Annual Report—1982.

[4] Adapted from the Council on Environmental Quality's 13th Annual Report—1982 and 15th Annual Report—1984. This section excludes the review of various statutes pertaining to hazardous substances that fall within the jurisdiction of the Food and Drug Administration, the Consumer Product Safety Commission, the Nuclear Regulatory Commission, and the Department of Transportation.

KEY TELEPHONE NUMBERS

⁞⁞⁞⁞⁞ **ENVIRONMENTAL HEALTH ISSUES—GENERAL**

U.S. Environmental Protection Agency, Public Information Center
   800-828-4445
U.S. Environmental Protection Agency, Referral Center
   800-334-8571

⁞⁞⁞⁞⁞ **HEALTH INFORMATION—GENERAL**

National Health Information Clearinghouse
   800-336-4797

⁞⁞⁞⁞⁞ **CANCER**

Memorial Sloan Kettering Cancer Information Service
   800-4-CANCER

⁞⁞⁞⁞⁞ **CHEMICALS**

Chemical Manufacturers Association/Chemical Referral Center
CHEMTREC Emergency Hotline
This is a telephone service set up by the chemical industry to
answer questions about the toxic properties of chemicals.
   800-424-9300
   800-262-8200

|||||| **CONSUMER PRODUCT SAFETY**

U.S. Consumer Products Safety Commission Hotline
    800-638-2772

|||||| **DOWN'S SYNDROME**

National Down Syndrome Society
    800-221-4602

|||||| **EMERGENCY PLANNING AND RIGHT-TO-KNOW HOTLINE**

U.S. Environmental Protection Agency service established to respond to questions related to toxic releases and community preparedness.
    800-535-0202

|||||| **ENERGY**

U.S. Department of Energy/Hotline—Renewable Energy
    800-523-2929

|||||| **PESTICIDES**

National Pesticide Telecommunications Hotline
Texas Tech University Health Sciences Center
    800-858-7378

|||||| **RCRC/SUPERFUND HOTLINE**

U.S. Environmental Protection Agency service to answer questions related to Superfund regulations, clean-up operations and toxic-waste cleanup laws.
    800-424-9346

|||||| **SAFE DRINKING WATER HOTLINE**

U.S. Environmental Protection Agency service to answer questions about water contamination and relevant legislation.
    800-426-4791

|||||| **SCIENTISTS' INSTITUTE FOR PUBLIC INFORMATION (SIPI)**

Media resource service for reporters. SIPI helps locate experts in various scientific fields to answer questions.
800-223-1730

|||||| **TOXICS**

Toxic Infoline/Natural Resource Defense Council (NRDC)
800-648-NRDC
212-687-6862 in New York state

|||||| **TOXIC SUBSTANCES CONTROL ACT INFORMATION**

U.S. Environmental Protection Agency
800-424-9065

|||||| **TOXIC-WASTE CLEANUP LAWS INFORMATION**

U.S. Environmental Protection Agency
800-424-9346

|||||| **REGIONAL ENVIRONMENTAL PROTECTION AGENCY OFFICES** ||||||

The Environmental Protection Agency has ten regional offices throughout the United States. Each regional office has a press contact person.

REGION 1 includes Connecticut, Maine, Massachusetts, New Hampshire, Rhode Island, and Vermont.
The regional office is located in Boston.
617-565-3420

REGION 2 includes New Jersey, New York, Puerto Rico, and the Virgin Islands. The regional office is located in New York City.
1-212-264-2657

REGION 3 includes Delaware, the District of Columbia, Maryland, Pennsylvania, Virginia, and West Virginia. The regional office is located in Philadelphia.

215-597-9800

REGION 4 includes Alabama, Florida, Georgia, Kentucky, Mississippi, North Carolina, South Carolina, and Tennessee. The regional office is located in Atlanta.

404-1347-4727

REGION 5 includes Illinois, Indiana, Michigan, Minnesota, Ohio, and Wisconsin. The regional office is located in Chicago.

312-353-2000

REGION 6 includes Arkansas, Louisiana, New Mexico, Oklahoma, and Texas. The regional office is located in Dallas.

214-655-6444

REGION 7 includes Iowa, Kansas, Missouri, and Nebraska. The regional office is located in Kansas City, Kansas.

913-551-7000

REGION 8 includes Colorado, Montana, North Dakota, South Dakota, Utah, and Wyoming. The regional office is located in Denver.

303-293-1603

REGION 9 includes Arizona, California, Hawaii, Nevada, Northern Mariana Islands, American Samoa, and Guam. The regional office is located in San Francisco.

415-744-1305

REGION 10 includes Alaska, Idaho, Oregon, and Washington. The regional office is located in Seattle.

206-553-4973

KEY REFERENCES

Brown, L.R. 1992. *Vital Signs 1992.* A Worldwatch Institute Report.
Brown, L.R. Annual *State of the World Report.* Worldwatch Institute.
Budavari, S. 1989. *The Merck Index,* 11th edition. Rahway, N.J.: Merck and Co., Inc.
Dooge, J.C., Goodman, G.T., la Rivìere, J.W., Marton-Lefèvre, J., O'Riordan, T., and Praderie, F. 1992. *An Agenda of Science for Environment and Development into the Twenty-First Century.* New York: Cambridge University Press.
Environmental Writer. (monthly) Environmental Health Center.
NIOSH/OSHA. 1990. *Pocket Guide to Chemical Hazards.* NIOSH Publication No. 017-033-00448-0. Washington, D.C.: U.S. Government Printing Office.
Sax, N.I. 1984. *Dangerous Properties of Industrial Materials.* New York: Von Nostrand Reinhold.
S. E. Journal. Quarterly. Philadelphia: Society of Environmental Journalists. (Society of Environmental Journalists, 7904 Germantown Ave., Philadelphia, Pennsylvania 19118, 215-247-9710.)
World Resources Institute. 1992. *Environmental Almanac.* Boston: Houghton Mifflin.

ACRONYMS AND ABBREVIATIONS

2,4-D	The pesticide 2,4-dichlorophenoxyacetic acid
A	Amp
AC	Alternating Current
ACS	American Chemical Society; also American Cancer Society
AEA	Atomic Energy Act of (1954)
AEC	Atomic Energy Commission (now Nuclear Regulatory Commission)
AHERA	Asbestos Hazard Emergency Response Act
AIHC	American Industrial Health Council
ARS	Agricultural Research Service
ASTM	American Society for Testing and Materials
ATSDR	Agency for Toxic Substances and Disease Registry
BACT	Best Available Control Technology
BADCT	Best Available Demonstrated Control Technology (for wastewater)
BAT	Best Available Technology (for wastewater)
BATEA	Best Available Technology Economically Achievable (wastewater)
BCPCT	Best Conventional Pollutant Control Technology (wastewater)
BEIR	Biological Effects of Ionizing Radiation (committee, report of NAS)
BLEVE	Boiling Liquid Expanding Vapor Explosion
BOD	Biological Oxygen Demand
BPT	Best Practicable Technology
BPCTCA	Best Practicable Control Technology Currently Available
CAA	Clean Air Act
CAS	Chemical Abstract Service

CDC	Centers for Disease Control and Prevention
CEC	Cation Exchange Capacity
CEQ	Council on Environmental Quality
CERCLA	Comprehensive Environmental Response, Compensation, and Liability Act (Superfund)
CERCLIS	Comprehensive Environmental Response, Compensation, and Liability Information System
CFE	Chlorofluorocarbon
CITES	Convention on International Trade on Endangered Species of Wild Fauna and Flora
CMA	Chemical Manufacturers Association
COD	Chemical Oxygen Demand
CPI	Chemical Process Industry
CPSC	Consumer Product Safety Commission
CSIN	Chemical Substances Information Network
CWA	Clean Water Act (became the FWPCA when amended)
CZMA	Coastal Zone Management Act
DC	Direct Current
DDT	The pesticide 1,1-dichloro-2,2-bis (p-chlorophenyl) ethane 1,1-dichloro-2,2-bis (p-chlorophenyl) ethylene 1,1,1-trichloro-2,2-bis (p-chlorophenyl) ethane
DEC	Department of Environmental Conservation (New York)
DEP	Department of Environmental Protection (Connecticut, Maine)
DEPE	Department of Environmental Protection and Energy (New Jersey)
DER	Department of Environmental Resources (Pennsylvania)
DHS	Designated Hazardous Substances
DNA	Deoxyribonucleic Acid
DO	Dissolved Oxygen
DOD	Department of Defense (United States)
DOE	Department of Energy (United States)
DOI	Department of the Interior (United States)
DOJ	Department of Justice (United States)
DOT	Department of Transportation (United States)
ECSL	Enforcement Compliance Schedule Letters
EDF	Environmental Defense Fund
EEPA	Electromagnetic Energy Policy Alliance
EIS	Environmental Impact Statement
ELF	Extremely Low Frequency

ELI	Environmental Law Institute
EMF	Electromagnetic Field
EPA	Environmental Protection Agency (United States)
EPCRA	Emergency Planning and Community Right-to-Know Act (of 1986)
EPI	Environmental Policy Institute
EPRI	Electric Power Research Institute
EQIA	Environmental Quality Improvement Act
ERNS	Emergency Response Notification System
FAO	Food and Agricultural Organization (United Nations)
FDA	Food and Drug Administration
FEMA	Federal Emergency Management Agency
FEPCA	Federal Environmental Pesticide Control Act
FFDCA	Federal Food, Drug and Cosmetic Act
FGD	Flue Gas Desulfurization
FHSLA	Federal Hazardous Substance Labeling Act
FIFRA	Federal Insecticide, Fungicide, and Rodenticide Act (of 1972)
F/M	Food to Microorganism Ratio
FOE	Friends of the Earth
FOIA	Freedom of Information Act
FPA	Federal Pesticide Act
FRLBPHRA	Federal Residential Lead-Based Paint Hazard Reduction Act
FTC	Federal Trade Commission
FWPCA	Federal Water Pollution Control Act (of 1972)
FWS	Fish and Wildlife Service
G	Gauss
GAC	Granulated Activated Carbon
GAO	General Accounting Office
GLC	Ground Level Concentration
G/M	Grams per Mile
HAP	Hazardous Air Pollutant
HCFC	Hydrochlorofluorocarbon
HERL	Health Effects Research Laboratory (EPA)
HM	Hazardous Material
HMTA	Hazardous Material Transportation Act
HRS	Hazard Ranking System
HSWA	Hazardous and Solid Waste Act
HUD	Department of Housing and Urban Development (United States)

HW	Hazardous Waste
HWM	Hazardous Waste Management
Hz	Hertz
IAB	Industrial Advisory Board
IAQ	Indoor Air Quality
ICS	Individual Control Strategy
IERL	Industrial Environmental Research Laboratory (EPA)
ILO	International Labor Organization (United Nations)
IPCC	Intergovernmental Panel on Climate Change
IPM	Integrated Pest Management
IRPTC	International Registry of Potentially Toxic Chemicals (United Nations Environmental Program)
IUCN	International Union for the Conservation of Nature
kV	Kilovolt
LAER	Lowest Achievable Emission Rate
LC	Lethal Concentration
LCCA	Lead Contamination Control Act
LD	Lethal Dose
LEPC	Local Emergency Planning Committee
L&I	License and Inspection
LUST	Leaking Underground Storage Tanks
MACT	Maximum Achievable Control Technology
MCL	Maximum Contaminant Level
MLSS	Mixed Liquor Suspended Solids
MLVSS	Mixed Liquor Volatile Suspended Solids
MPN	Most Probable Number
MPRSA	Marine Protection Research and Sanctuary Act (of 1972)
MPRSAA	Marine Protection Research and Sanctuary Act (Amendment)
MRF	Mechanized Recycling Facility
MSDS	Material Safety Data Sheet
MTA	Metric Tons Annually
MTB	Materials Transportation Bureau
NAAQS	National Ambient Air Quality Standards
NAS	National Academy of Sciences
NBS	National Bureau of Standards
NCHS	National Center for Health Statistics
NCI	National Cancer Institute
NCP	National (Oil and Hazardous Substances Pollution) Contingency Plan
NEA	National Energy Act

NEPA	National Environmental Policy Act
NESHAP	National Emission Standards for Hazardous Air Pollutants
NHLBI	National Heart, Lung and Blood Institute
NIEHS	National Institute of Environmental Health Sciences
NIH	National Institutes of Health
NIMBY	Not-in-my-backyard syndrome
NIOSH	National Institute for Occupational Safety and Health
NOAA	National Oceanic and Atmospheric Administration
NOAEL	No Adverse Effect Level
NPDES	National Pollutant Discharge Elimination System
NPL	National Priorities List (of Superfund sites)
NRC	Nuclear Regulatory Commission or National Research Council
NRDC	Natural Resources Defense Council
NRT	National Response Team
NSPE	National Society for Professional Engineers
NSPS	New Source Performance Standards
NTIS	National Technical Information Service
ODBA	Ocean Dumping Ban Act
OMB	Office of Management and Budget
OPA	Oil Pollution Act
OPP	Office of Pesticide Programs (EPA)
ORD	Office of Research and Development (EPA)
ORP	Oxidation Reduction Potential
OSHA	Occupational Safety and Health Act and Occupational Safety and Health Administration
OSW	Office of Solid Waste (EPA)
PAC	Public Advisory Committee
PBB	Polybrominated biphenyl
PCB	Polychlorinated biphenyl
PDR	Physicians' Desk Reference (a directory of medications)
PEC	Pennsylvania Environmental Council
PET	Polyethylene teraphthalate
P.L.	Public Law
PMN	Premature Notice
POTW	Public Owned Treatment Works
PPA	Pollution Prevention Act
PPB	Part per billion
PPM	Part per million
PSD	Prevention of Significant Deterioration (program)

QA/QC	Quality Assurance/Quality Control
QRA	Quantitative Risk Assessment
RACT	Reasonably Available Control Technology
RAD	Radiation Absorbed Dose
RCC	Resource Conservation Committee
RCRA	Resource Conservation and Recovery Act
RCRAA	Resource Conservation and Recovery Act (Amendment)
RDF	Refuse Derived Fuel
REM	RAD Equivalent Mammal
RPAR	Rebuttable Presumption Against Registration Program
RQ	Reportable Quantity
RRA	Resource Recovery Act
RSPA	Research and Special Programs Administration
SARA	Superfund Amendments and Reauthorization Act (of 1986)
SDWA	Safe Drinking Water Act
SDWAA	Safe Drinking Water Act (Amendment)
SERC	State Emergency Response Commission
SIP	State Implementation Plan
SIPI	Scientists' Institute for Public Information
SPCC	Spill, Prevention, and Control Countermeasures
SRM	Standard Reference Manual
SRT	Sludge Retention Time
SS	Suspended Solids
SSP	Species Survival Program
SW	Solid Waste
SWA	Solid Waste Administration
SWDA	Solid Waste Disposal Act
T	Tesla
TA	Technical Assistance
TCDD	Dioxin, specifically 2,3,7,8-tetrachlorodibenzo-p-dioxin
TCE	Trichloroethylene
TDS	Total Dissolved Solids
TLV	Threshold Limit Value
TMDL	Total Maximum Daily Load
TMI	Three Mile Island
TOADS	Temporarily Obsolete Abandoned Derelict Sites
TRI	Toxic Release Inventory
TRIS-TRIS	(2,3-dibromoprophyl) phosphate
TS	Total Solids

TSCA	Toxic Substances Control Act
TSCAA	Toxic Substances Control Act (Amendment)
TSDF	Treatment, Storage, or Disposal Facility (hazardous waste)
TSS	Total Suspended Solids
TVA	Tennessee Valley Authority
UIC	Underground Injection Control Program
UN	United Nations
USDA	United States Department of Agriculture
USDOL	United States Department of Labor
UV	Ultraviolet light
V	Volt
VDT	Video Display Terminal
VLF	Very Low Frequency
VOC	Volatile Organic Compound
WHO	World Health Organization
WIPP	Waste Isolation Pilot Project
WL	Working Level
WQA	Water Quality Act
WWF	World Wildlife Fund

GLOSSARY

2,3,7,8-TCDD   A form of dioxin, considered the most deadly synthetic substance known. It is one of 22 TCDDs and one of the overall family of 75 dioxins.

A   Amp

AC   Abbreviation for alternating current. An AC current, or an AC field, changes strength and direction in a rhythmically repeating cycle, unlike DC or direct current, which does not change. In the United States, AC power has a frequency of 60 Hz. In most European countries, AC power has a frequency of 50 Hz. *See* DC.

ACID   A compound that can neutralize a base. Acids have a high concentration of hydrogen ions. An acid is a compound that has a pH of less than 7 on a scale of 0 to 14. Common acidic materials include vinegar (pH 2.2), apples (pH 3.0), tomatoes (pH 4.2), clean rain water (pH 5.6), milk (pH 6.6). Strong acids, closer to 0 on the scale, are corrosive. Weak acids, closer to 7, are not. *See* base, pH.

ACID RAIN   Any rain, snow, fog, dust, or other precipitation with a pH less than that of clean rain (pH 5.6). *See* acid, pH.

ACTION LEVEL   The amount of contamination necessary before cleanup, containment, study, or other action is initiated. The action level is determined by many factors (e.g., cost, available technology, and potential health effects).

ACUTE DOSE   In toxicology, a large amount of exposure or infusion received in a short time (less than a week). Acute doses of some chemicals may be hazardous to health. Acute doses are often used to test a new product or unknown chemical mixture. *See* chronic dose.

ACUTE EFFECT   A reaction that occurs shortly after exposure. Sunburn is an acute effect of sun-bathing; skin cancer is a chronic effect. *See* chronic effect.

AEROBIC DECAY   Breakdown of organic matter by microorganisms that use oxygen.

AEROSOL   Small particles of liquid or solid suspended in a gas.

AGENT   (Also agent of disease.) The cause of a particular effect or disease. Agents may be biological (bacteria), chemical, or physical (radiation). An agent alone or in combination with other agents can cause a disease.

AGE-SPECIFIC RATE   A relative occurrence rate for a selected age group. An age-specific rate is calculated by dividing the number of events (deaths, cancer cases) in the selected age group by the total number of people in that group. For working convenience, this number is often multiplied by 100,000 or 1,000,000. For example, if there were 18 white male lung cancer deaths for the age group 55-59 during 1990 in county X, and there were 10,000 white males in county X in 1990, the age-specific rate is 18/10,000 or 180/100,000 population.

AGGREGATE RISK   The fourth step in the quantitative risk-assessment process. The aggregate risk is the risk from exposure to a particular substance to the total population and subpopulation. *See* dose-response assessment, exposure assessment, hazard identification.

ALLOTROPE   A molecule that contains three atoms. This structural difference leads to a difference in chemical reactivity—the tendency to combine or otherwise interact with other substances.

ALPHA PARTICLE   In radiation, a fast-moving helium atom nucleus often expelled from a radioactive source. Alpha particles can cause cell damage leading to cancer when the radioactive source is located inside the respiratory system.

AMBIENT   The surrounding environment. Ambient usually refers to the surrounding outdoor air, water, or land.

AMES TEST   A lab test using bacteria to determine a chemical's potential to cause genetic changes (mutations). *See* assay, mutagen.

AMP (A)   Unit used to measure current. *See* current.

ANAEROBIC   Oxygen is not present. Anaerobic conditions in bodies of water are often responsible for major fish kills. Anaerobic is sometimes confused with aerobic (oxygen is present). *See* thermal pollution.

ANIMAL BIOASSAY   A test using animals to determine a chemical's effect. *See* assay.

AQUIFER   An underground water source. *See* groundwater, aquifer recharge.

AQUIFER RECHARGE   The process whereby water moves from the surface to aquifers under the influence of gravity.

AROMATIC HYDROCARBON   A type of hydrocarbon related to benzene. Many aromatic hydrocarbons are health hazards. *See* hydrocarbon.

ASBESTOSIS   Scarring of the lung from inhalation of airborne asbestos fibers. This disease is often fatal.

ASSAY   Also bioassay. A test using plants, animals, or bacteria to determine a chemical's effect. Assays can determine acute or chronic effects, depending on the method used. *See* acute effect, Ames Test, chronic effect.

BACKGROUND LEVEL   In radiation and chemistry, the concentration that naturally occurs in the environment or is added through human activities. Activities such as mining, manufacturing, disposing, and testing of chemical and radioactive products add to background levels.

BAGHOUSE   A series of fabric filters used in the scrubbing mechanism.

BASE   A compound that can neutralize an acid. Bases have a large concentration of hydroxyl (one hydrogen atom plus one oxygen atom) ions. A basic compound has a pH of more than 7 on a scale of 0 to 14. Common basic materials include blood (pH 7.4), sea water (pH 8.3), milk of magnesia (pH 10.5), ammonia (pH 11.0), and lime (pH 12.4). Strong bases, pH closer to 14, are corrosive. Weak bases, pH closer to 7, are not. *See* acid, pH.

BENIGN   Noncancerous. *See* cancer, malignant.

BETA PARTICLE   In radiation, a fast-moving electron often expelled from a radioactive source.

BIOACCUMULATE   Also bioconcentrate. To build up a large amount of a substance in the body by ingesting small amounts of the substance over an extended period of time. *See* food chain, fat-soluble, heavy metal.

BIOAVAILABILITY   The extent to which living things, as opposed to laboratory procedures, can extract toxic chemicals from soil and other materials. Material that is not bioavailable is not available to cause toxic effects.

BIOCONCENTRATE   *See* bioaccumulate.

BIODEGRADE   To naturally break down in the environment. Biodegradation is decay caused by environmental factors such as light, temperature, humidity, and microorganisms. See environmental persistence.

BIOREMEDIATION   A clean-up process, in pollution events, that involves providing nutrients to damaged areas. The nutrient can break down the pollutant.

BIRTH WEIGHT   Neonatal weight at time of birth; 2,500 grams (5.5 pounds) or less is considered a low birth weight and an indicator of potential health problems.

BOTTOM ASH   In the incineration process, bottom ash is that part which falls to the bottom of the incinerator, following burning. It is distinguished from fly ash which goes up the stack. Bottom ash must be disposed of at a hazardous-waste landfill or processed and recycled into usable materials such as building or road paving materials.

CADMIUM   A soft, silvery metal found in sulfite deposits, primarily in zinc ores. A highly toxic metal, cadmium does not break down over time.

CANCER   An uncontrolled local cell growth that can migrate to, and appear in, other parts of the body. *See* malignant, benign.

CANCER CLUSTER   An abnormally high incidence of cancer in a given area. *See* cluster.

CARBAMATEM   A category of pesticides that contains carbon and nitrogen.

CARCINOGEN   A cancer-causing agent.

CARDIOVASCULAR DISEASE   Disease pertaining to the heart and blood vessels.

CASE   In epidemiology, a person with a condition (disease, birth defect) that is being studied.

CASE-CONTROL STUDY   Also retrospective study. Research that compares people with a condition (disease, rash) with similar people who do not have the condition. *See* control group.

CATALYTIC CONVERTER   A pollution exhaust-control device installed on post-1975 model cars. Using metals and metallic oxides as the effective agents, it is designed to improve combustion and lower hydrocarbon and carbon monoxide output.

CHARGE   The electrical property of matter that is responsible for creating electric fields. There are two kinds of charge—negative and positive. Electric fields begin on positive charges and end on negative charges. Like charges repel each other. Unlike charges attract each other.

CHELATION   A medical procedure in which EDTA, a compound to which lead binds, is injected into the body to remove lead. It is then flushed from the blood and excreted in urine.

CHLORACNE   A disfiguring skin condition cause by exposure to any one of a variety of polycyclic halogenated aromatic compounds, including, but not limited to, the dioxins, the dibenzofurans, and some of the PCBs. A virtual carpet of blackheads that can cover areas of the skin, particularly on the face. Cysts and pustules develop and must often be removed surgically. Permanent scarring is common. Most cases heal, leaving scars, in 1-2 years. Some persist for over 30 years, with new eruptions occurring periodically.

CHLORINATED   Containing chlorine.

CHLORINATED HYDROCARBON   A compound that contains chlorine, hydrogen, and carbon. Pesticides (e.g., DDT) are often chlorinated hydrocarbons. Chlorinated hydrocarbons can bioaccumulate and are environmentally persistent. *See* bioaccumulate, environmental persistence, hydrocarbon.

CHLORINATION   The process of adding chlorine to sewage or water to kill pathogens.

CHLOROFLUOROCARBON (CFC)   People-made compounds containing chlorine, fluorine, and carbon used as propellants in aerosol cans and as refrigerants and insulators. CFCs act as a greenhouse gas in the troposphere.

CHROMOSOME   Gene carrier. *See* DNA, gene.

CHRONIC DOSE   In toxicology, small amounts of an agent received over a long period of time (months, years). *See* acute dose.

CHRONIC EFFECT   A long-term or repeated reaction that occurs after an exposure. Skin cancer is a chronic effect of sun-bathing, while sunburn is an acute effect. *See* acute effect.

CLUSTER   In epidemiology and statistics, an abnormally high number of events (diseases) with a common pattern in a given area. Diseases in a cluster may or may not have a common cause. *See* cancer cluster.

COGENERS   Chemical compounds. *See* isomers.

COHORT   In epidemiology and statistics, a group of people in a study who have something in common. All people born in the same year, town, or ethnic group, or all those working in the same industry would be cohorts. *See* cohort study.

COHORT STUDY   Research that follows a group over time to determine how the group responds to events such as chemical exposure, living conditions, or nutrition. Also concurrent study, follow-up study, incidence study, longitudinal study, prospective study.

COMEDONES   Blackheads, often exhibited by persons who have been exposed to certain types of chemicals. *See* chloracne.

COMMUNICABLE DISEASE   A contagious, infectious disease.

CONCENTRATION   A relative amount of material to a given substance. For example, ten parts of benzene to a million parts air. *See* dose.

CONCURRENT STUDY   *See* cohort study.

CONFOUNDING FACTOR   Something that complicates or confuses the outcome of a study. For example, smoking confounds studies of occupational exposures to other agents.

CONGENITAL   A condition existing from birth. Congenital conditions are acquired during development in the womb. They are not inherited from the parents.

CONSERVATIVE RISK ESTIMATE   An estimate that ensures that risk is not underestimated—by overestimating risk.

CONTROL GROUP   A comparison group. A group that is statistically identical to the study group except that it does not suffer from the condition (disease, chemical exposure) that is being studied. Scientifically valid studies have control groups.

CORRELATION   In statistics, a number ranging from 1 to -1 that describes the extent to which two variables are related—increase or decrease together. It is a measure of the strength of the relationship between variables.

CRITICAL HABITAT   Areas of land, water, and air needed by a species for survival.

CURIE   A unit used in measuring radioactivity. A curie is equal to the quantity of any radioactive material in which the number of disintegrations per second is 3.7 times 10 to the tenth power. A curie is a measure of the number of radioactive decays per unit of time. One picocurie is one trillionth of a curie. One picocurie per liter of indoor radon is usually assumed to result in 0.005 working levels under typical conditions in a building. So, that means that 100 picocuries per liter (pCi/l) equals 0.5 working levels.

CURRENT   An organized flow of electric charge. Current in a power line is similar to the rate of flow of fluids in a pipeline. All currents produce magnetic fields. Currents are measured in amps (A). *See* Amps (A).

DAUGHTER PRODUCTS   Also decay products. Material that is left after a radioactive substance decays. Radioactive uranium decays into radon. Daughter products, including radon daughters, may or may not be radioactive themselves. Radon daughters can cause lung cancer.

DC   The abbreviation for direct current. A DC current, or a DC field, is steady and does not change strength or direction over time unlike an AC current, (field) which does change. *See* AC.

DECAY PRODUCTS   *See* daughter products.

DECOMMISSIONING   In the nuclear industry, a term used for the process of eliminating radioactivity from a nuclear power plant, thereby making it accessible for public use.

DELANEY AMENDMENT   The portion of the Food, Drug, and Cosmetic Act that prohibits adding a known carcinogen to food.

DIFFUSION   Movement of molecules of gas or vapor from a source, such as a bottle or can, to a receptor, such as the human nose and respiratory tract.

DISTRIBUTION LINE   A power line used to distribute power in a local region. Distribution lines typically operate at voltages of somewhere between 5–35kV. While the voltage on distribution lines is much lower than the voltage of transmission lines, the currents on some distribution lines can be comparable to transmission line currents. *See* transmission line.

DNA (deoxyribonucleic acid)   The carrier of genetic information in cells. *See* chromosome, gene.

DOSE   A measured amount. The amount of exposure of a kind that produces effects. In the case of chemical pollutants, dose is usually the amount of chemical that gels into the body. *See* concentration.

DOSE-RESPONSE   A response that changes as the dose, duration of exposure, and intensity of exposure changes. For example, a few sleeping pills (a small dose) may cause drowsiness, the whole bottle (a large dose) may cause coma or death. *See* aggregate risk, exposure assessment, hazard identification.

DOSE-RESPONSE ASSESSMENT   The second step in the quantitative risk-assessment process. In dose-response assessments, human and animal studies are used to determine the human health effects of varying amounts of exposure to substances. *See* assay, animal bioassay.

DRUM, 55-GALLON   A standard size industrial barrel used for storing and transporting raw materials, products, and wastes.
  To convert 55-gallon drums to:
      cubic feet, multiply number of drums by 7.3524
      cubic meters, multiply number of drums by 0.20820.
  To convert cubic feet to:
      number of 55-gallon drums, divide by 7.35243.
  To convert cubic meters to:
      number of 55-gallon drums, divide by 0.20820.

ECOLOGY   The study of the relationship between living organisms and the environment.

EFFLUENT   Outflow from a manufacturing or treatment process. Effluent is usually liquid waste products and often toxic. *See* influent.

ELECTRIC FIELD   A representation of the forces that fixed electric charges exert on other charges at a distance. The electric field has a strength and direction at all points in space, which is often represented diagrammatically by field lines. Electric field lines begin on positive charges and end on negative charges.

ELECTROMAGNETIC FIELD   A field made up of electric and magnetic fields.

ELECTROMAGNETIC RADIATION   Electromagnetic waves that travel through space. Waves differ in wave length and frequency. The full range of lengths and frequencies is called the electromagnetic spectrum. Gamma rays and x-rays are at the high frequency end of the spectrum while electric and magnetic fields are located at extremely low frequencies.

ENVIRONMENT   In public health, everything external to a person that influences his or her health. Environment includes biological, cultural, physical, and mental factors.

ENVIRONMENTAL PERSISTENCE   The ability to last, or survive, in the environment. Environmentally persistent substances are long-lasting; they do not biodegrade quickly, if at all. For example, DDT is an environmentally persistent substance. *See* biodegrade.

EPIDEMIC   A rapidly spreading disease. The occurrence in a community or a region of cases of an illness, specific health-related behavior, or other health-related events clearly in excess of what would be expected normally.

EPIDEMIOLOGY   The study of diseases in society. Epidemiology includes the study of mortality, morbidity, prevalence, and distribution of diseases. Epidemiology is sometimes confused with etiology.

ETIOLOGY   The study of causes of disease. Etiology is sometimes confused with epidemiology.

EXPOSURE   Contact. Exposure may be oral (by mouth), dermal (through the skin), or by inhalation (breathing).

EXPOSURE ASSESSMENT   The third step in the quantitative risk-assessment process. In exposure assessment, a determination is made on the concentration of substances to which humans are exposed. *See* aggregate risk, dose-response assessment, hazard identification.

EXTRAPOLATION   Educated guesses regarding the impact of a substance on human health based on currently available data.

FAT-SOLUBLE   Can be stored in fat (lipid) tissue. Substances that are fat-soluble are easily passed up the food chain. *See* bioaccumulate, food chain, water-soluble.

FLY ASH   In the process of incineration, fly ash is the form of emissions that goes up the stack as opposed to bottom ash, that part that falls to the bottom following burning. Emission of fly ash is strictly regulated by most states.

FOLLOW-UP STUDY   *See* cohort study.

FOOD CHAIN   A sequence of organisms where the higher form in the chain uses the lower for food. *See* bioaccumulate, fat-soluble.

FOOD WEB   Interlinking food chains.

FOSSIL FUEL   Coal, natural gas, oil, or any other fuel that developed from the remains of prehistoric plants and animals.

GAMMA RAYS   High-energy waves often produced when a radioactive source decays. Gamma rays do not contain particles but may be emitted along with both alpha and beta particles.

GAS CHROMATOGRAPH   A machine that may be used to detect very low concentrations of a gas.

GAUSS (G)   A common unit of measurement used for assessing magnetic field intensity. Gauss is a relatively large unit so magnetic field intensity is reported in thousandths of a gauss of "milli" gauss (mG). There are 10,000 gauss in one tesla. See tesla.

GENE   A code for an inherited trait. See DNA, chromosome.

GENETIC ENGINEERING   The introduction of genes into an organism in a laboratory that endow the organism with specific desirable properties.

GERM CELL   A reproductive cell. Reproductive cells are the sperm (spermatozoon) and egg (ovum) cells. See somatic cells.

GREENHOUSE GASES   Heat-trapping gases that cause global warming. They include water vapor, carbon dioxide, methane, nitrous oxide, and halocarbons, including chlorofluorocarbons.

GROUNDWATER   Water that moves slowly underground in an aquifer. Once groundwater has been contaminated, it is nearly impossible to return it to its pure state. Groundwater is the main, but not the only, source of drinking water. See aquifer.

HALF-LIFE   In radiation and chemistry, the time needed for half of the material or effect to decay, react, or dissipate. Materials and agents that have a long half-life are environmentally persistent. See environmental persistence.

HAZARD   Exposure to the chance of loss, injury, risk, or danger. Hazard is magnitude times probability times the number of people exposed.

HAZARD IDENTIFICATION   The first step in the quantitative risk-assessment process. In hazard identification, human and animal studies are used to determine whether a substance can cause human health effects. See aggregate risk, assay, animal bioassay, dose-response assessment, exposure assessment.

HAZARDOUS WASTE   As defined by the Resource Conservation and Recovery Act (RCRA), a waste that may cause, or significantly contribute to, illness or death, or that may substantially threaten human health or the environment when it is not properly controlled.

HEALTH   A state of physical, mental, and social well-being.

HEAVY METAL   A class of metals having a high density. Heavy metals include lead, mercury, arsenic, beryllium, cadmium, cobalt, and chromium. They can bioaccumulate and many are toxic. *See* bioaccumulate.

HERTZ (Hz)   A unit used to measure frequency of power. In the United States, AC power has a frequency of 60 Hz. In most European countries, AC power has a frequency of 50 Hz. *See* AC.

HYDROCARBON   A compound that contains only hydrogen and carbon. Hydrocarbons are found primarily in petroleum, natural gas, and coal products. *See* aromatic hydrocarbon, chlorinated hydrocarbon.

HYDROLOGICAL CYCLE   The cyclical movement of water on the earth, including surface movements, evaporation, precipitation, and underground movement.

HYPOTHESIS   A supposition arrived at from observation or reflection that leads to refutable predictions.

IMMUNE RESPONSE   A protective action against illness. Antibody production is an immune response.

IMMUNOCOMPETENCE   The ability to develop an immune response. *See* immune response.

IMPACT   In ecology, the effect of human activities on an ecosystem.

INCIDENCE   The number of new events (cancer cases, deaths) in a given time period. Incidence is usually calculated for a one-year time period.

INCIDENCE STUDY   *See* cohort study.

INCINERATION   High temperature combustion or oxidation of carbon and hydrogen to form carbon dioxide and water.

INDUSTRIAL HYGIENE   The study and practice of creating a safe workplace.

INFLUENT   Materials that flow into a manufacturing or treatment system. Raw materials are often called influents, as opposed to effluents which are finished products. *See* effluent.

INORGANIC SUBSTANCE   Substances that do not contain carbon. Metals are inorganic chemicals.

INSULATION   Material used to prevent a heat loss or gain from the outdoor environment.

INTEGRATED PEST MANAGEMENT (IPM)   The control of crop-damaging pests through the introduction of natural predators.

IN VITRO   Outside the body. In vitro usually refers to a test in a laboratory. *See* in vivo.

IN VIVO   Inside the body. *See* in vitro.

ION   An atom or molecule with an electric charge. A cation has a positive charge. An anion has a negative charge.

IONIZING RADIATION   Energy that breaks a compound into ions. The high energy produced by ionizing radiation can cause severe damage to plants and animal tissue. Sources of ionizing radiation include uranium and x-ray machines. See nonionizing radiation.

ISOMERS   *See* cogeners.

KILOVOLT (kV)   A thousand volts.

LATENCY PERIOD   Delay between exposure to a disease-causing agent and the appearance of manifestations of the disease. The term may be used synonymously with induction period.

LD50   The dose needed to kill half an experimental animal population. A small LD50 indicates a highly toxic substance because only a small dose is needed to kill half the test animals. A large LD50 indicates low toxicity because a large dose is needed for the same effect.

LEACHATE   Liquid, such as rainwater, passed through the contents of a landfill. This polluted water percolates through the layers of refuse at a landfill. Leachate can travel out of a landfill and is often toxic.

LEAD   A soft, bluish or silvery grey metal usually found in sulfite deposits in association with other minerals, particularly zinc and copper. Lead, a metal that does not biodegrade or breakdown into other substances, is the toxic metal present in the atmosphere in the largest concentration.

LONGITUDINAL STUDY   A study of effects over time. *See* cohort study.

LOW BIRTH WEIGHT   A birth weight of 2,500 grams (5.5 pounds) or less is used as an indicator of potential health problems in newborns.

MAGNETIC FIELD   A representation of the forces that a moving charge exerts on other moving charges because they are moving. The magnetic field has a strength and direction at all points in space, which is often represented diagrammatically by field lines. All currents produce magnetic fields.

MALIGNANT   Cancerous. *See* benign, cancer.

MASS SPECTROMETER   A machine that may be used to detect very low concentrations of a chemical. A mass spectrometer separates compounds by mass.

MERCURY   Refined from cinnabar to form a variety of compounds, mercury is a stable-occurring toxic trace metal.

MESOTHELIOMA   Cancer in the mucous membrane lining of the chest, heart, or abdomen directly related to inhalation of asbestos fibers.

METALS   Chemical elements that do not break down or degrade.

MICROWAVES   Electromagnetic waves that have a frequency of between roughly 1 billion and 300 billion Hz (a wavelength of between roughly 30 centimeters and 1 millimeter). Microwaves have a frequency higher than normal radio waves but lower than heat (infrared) and light waves. They are a form of nonionizing radiation.

MODEL   A description of a process, often in the form of a mathematical equation and/or computer simulation. Models are sometimes used to predict an event. For example, a model of an oil spill can show how far a slick may spread. An air-quality model can predict where a plume may travel.

MORBIDITY   Sickness. Morbidity is often confused with mortality (death).

MORTALITY   Death. Mortality is often confused with morbidity (sickness).

MUNICIPAL SOLID WASTE   Garbage, refuse, sludge from waste treatment plants, water supply treatment plants, or air pollution control facilities, and other discarded material resulting from industrial, commercial, mining, agricultural operations, or community activities.

MUTAGEN   An agent that can permanently alter genetic material. *See* Ames test.

NATAL   Pertaining to birth.

NEURONS   Cells that carry nervous impulses.

NEUROTOXIN   Nerve poison.

NO ADVERSE EFFECT LEVEL (NOAEL)   The maximum amount of exposure to a toxic substance at which there is no detectable adverse effect on human health.

NONIONIZING RADIATION   Radiation without sufficient energy to transfer large amounts of energy to individual atoms in the region through which it passes. *See* ionizing radiation.

NON-POINT-SOURCE POLLUTION   Refers to pollution where the source is broad and cannot be easily pinpointed.

NUCLEAR FISSION   The splitting of an atomic nucleus.

NUCLEAR MEDICINE   Branch of medicine concerned with diagnostic, therapeutic, and investigative uses of radioactive materials.

OFF-GASSING   Process lasting from a few days to over a month by which irritating gases and particles, such as formaldehyde, are emitted into the indoor environment by new furniture, rugs, covers, wallboard, and similar items.

ONCOLOGY   Branch of medicine dealing with tumors.

ORGANIC   Of, pertaining to, or derived from living organisms.

ORGANIC CHEMICAL   A chemical containing carbon. Many organic chemicals are fat-soluble and can bioaccumulate. They are usually relatively insoluble in water. *See* bioaccumulate, fat-soluble, water-soluble.

ORGANOCHLORINES   A category of pesticides. Organic compounds that have been chlorinated, usually with several atoms of chlorine per molecule.

ORGANOPHOSPHATES   A category of pesticides that contains carbon and phosphorus. They are usually used to kill insects.

PARTICULATE   Minute particle. A particulate can be toxic. If inhaled, a particulate can interfere with the respiratory and other defense systems of the body.

PARTICULATE MATTER   Airborne materials that can, depending on their size and composition, lodge in various areas of the human respiratory tract. A good comparison is several levels of screening with holes of increasing size. The finest particles can descend into the deepest regions of the lung; the largest particles stop within the nasal passages.

PASSIVE SMOKE   Exposure of nonsmokers to smoke.

PATHOGEN   A disease-causing microorganism.

PESTICIDE   A general term covering a wide variety of chemical compounds that control unwanted plants, insects, rodents, or other pests. Pesticides include herbicides, which kill plants; insecticides, which kill insects; and fungicides, which kill micro-organisms.

pH   A measure of the strength of an acid or base. It is measured on a scale of 0 to 14 where 7 is considered neutral (neither acidic nor basic). Acids measure less than 7 on the scale. Bases measure greater than 7 on the scale. pH is related to the quantity of hydrogen ions present in a solution. *See* acid, base, ion.

PHARMACOLOGY   The study of drugs.

PICOCURIES (pCi/l)   A measurement used to assess indoor radon levels. It is usually reported as pCi per liter or pCi/l.

POINT-SOURCE POLLUTION   Refers to discharges from a particular pipe or leak.

POPULATION   The entire collection of people, houses, counties, animals, or other elements under study.

PPB (part per billion)   The occurrence relative to a base of one billion. One part per billion is 5 people out of the total world population (5 billion) or four drops of water in an Olympic-size pool (64,000 gallons). 1 ppb = 0.001 ppm = 1 nanogram/gram = 1,000 nanograms/liter.

PPM (part per million)   The occurrence relative to a base of one million. One part per million is 200 people out of the total population of the United States (200 million) or one penny in $10,000. 1 ppm = 0.0001 percent = 1 milligram/kilogram = 1 milligram/liter.

PREVALENCE   A measure of how widespread a disease is in a certain population at a certain time. Prevalence is usually greater than incidence because it not only includes new cases, but all old cases as well.

PROSPECTIVE STUDY   *See* cohort study.

QUANTITATIVE RISK-ASSESSMENT   A multi-step process used to evaluate chronic human health risks associated with chemical, biological, and physical substances.

RAD (radiation absorbed dose)   The unit denoting the amount of absorbed radiation.

RADIATION   Any of a variety of forms of energy generated through space. Radiation can be in the form of particles (e.g., alpha rays or beta rays) or waves (e.g., x-rays, light, microwaves, or radio waves). Ionizing radiation, such as x-rays, carries enough energy to break chemical and electrical bonds. Non-ionizing radiation, such as microwaves, does not.

REACTOR VESSEL   In a nuclear reactor, the great steel pots that hold the fuel.

RELATIVE RISK   Also risk ratio. The disease rate in an exposed group compared to that in an unexposed group.

REM (RAD equivalent mammal)   The amount of radiation required to produce the same biological effect as one Roentgen of high penetration x-rays. *See* Roentgen.

RESIN   A class of organic chemicals. Resins can be mixed with other chemicals to form plastics. *See* organic chemical.

RESOURCE RECOVERY   This term refers to the separation of recyclable glass, paper, and metals from the refuse before it is buried at a landfill. It also refers to the usable energy generated from solid-waste incineration or from the recoverable methane gas, a by-product of decomposition, for fuel.

RESTORATION ECOLOGY   Attempts by ecologists to rebuild ecosystems in new locations (e.g., relocating wetlands to allow development of existing wetlands).

RETROSPECTIVE STUDY   *See* case-control study.

RISK   The chance of an injury, illness, or death caused by exposure to a hazard.

RISK ASSESSMENT   A process that evaluates the risk of a hazard, estimates the population exposed to the hazard, and assesses the relative importance of the public health risk.

RISK FACTOR   Correlation of causation within a risk. For example, smoking, which increases the risk of getting lung cancer, is a risk factor.

RISK RATIO   *See* relative risk.

ROENTGEN   A standard unit of radiation.

SAMPLE   A portion of the population selected for study. *See* population.

SANITARY LANDFILL   A covered facility for municipal solid waste that meets the criteria published under Resource Conservation and Recovery Act, section 4004. It may result in leaching into the environment.

SCRUBBER   A filtering mechanism that removes acids and chemical particles from incinerator emissions. Scrubbers can be wet or dry, depending on the model.

SLUDGE   A nonpumpable mixture of solids and liquids, usually referring to a waste material.

SLURRY   A pumpable mixture of particles and liquid. A term used to describe a form of waste material.

SOLVENT   A liquid capable of dissolving a material and holding it in solution. For example, paint remover is a paint solvent.

SOMATIC CELLS   All cells in the body, except the reproductive cells. Cells in the body concerned with the maintenance of the individual, as distinguished from the reproduction of the species. *See* germ cell.

SOURCE REDUCTION   A method of eliminating waste by the reduction of the overall amount of solid waste that needs to be disposed and the limitation of amounts of potentially hazardous materials in products.

STATISTICAL SIGNIFICANCE   An estimate of the likelihood (probability) that an observation or finding occurred by chance.

STRATOSPHERE   The upper atmosphere located above the troposphere.

SURFACE IMPOUNDMENTS   Pits or areas encircled by dikes that are used to store liquid, sludge, or slurries. Impoundments usually lack liners which prevent seepage. *See* sludge, slurry.

SURFACE WATER   Water at the surface of the earth, including lakes, rivers, ponds, and streams. It is the source of much groundwater through the larger hydrologic cycle as water moves from the surface to aquifers below ground.

SYNERGISM   When substances acting together have an effect greater than that of any component taken alone.

TERATOGEN   A cause of a defect in a developing fetus. If a pregnant woman is exposed to the teratogen German measles, for example, the fetus may be born mentally retarded.

TESLA (T)   A unit of measure for magnetic fields. There are 10,000 gauss in one tesla. *See* gauss.

THERMAL POLLUTION   Contamination caused by heat. Thermal pollution may cause an anaerobic condition in water and result in a fish kill. See anaerobic.

THRESHOLD   The minimum amount needed for a given effect to occur. For example, an odor threshold is the smallest amount of a substance needed to produce an odor. The level of exposure below which risk is absent. The level below which no measurable harm occurs.

THRESHOLD LIMIT VALUE (TLV)   The lifetime daily exposure to an airborne substance with no long-term negative effect. Occupational levels are different from public levels, since there is a greater range of threshold in the general population than in a group of workers, who are considered to be relatively healthy.

TOXIC   Poisonous.

TOXIC METALS   Those metals whose concentrations in the environment are now considered to be harmful, at least to some people, in some places.

TOXICOLOGIST   A scientist who studies how chemicals interact in a harmful way with the body.

TRACE METALS   Metals that are present in the environment or in the human body in very low concentrations, such as copper, iron, and zinc. Heavy metals are a subset of trace metals having densities at least five times greater than water.

TRANSFER STATION   Site at which smaller truckloads of solid waste are compacted and loaded into a larger vehicle, which then takes it to a landfill. At many transfer stations, recyclable materials, particularly cardboard, are separated from the refuse before it is taken to a landfill.

TRANSMISSION LINE   A power line used to carry large quantities of electric power at high voltage, usually over long distances. Transmission lines usually operate at voltages of somewhere in the range of 70–765 kV. They are usually built on steel towers called pylons or very large wooden poles. *See* distribution line.

TRIHALOMETHANES   A group of chemicals formed when sewage or water is chlorinated. Trihalomethanes are potential health hazards. Chloroform is an example of a trihalomethane. *See* chlorination.

TROPOSPHERE   That part of the atmosphere within approximately five miles of the surface of the earth.

VAPOR RECOVERY NOZZLES   Nozzles installed on gas pumping equipment for the purpose of capturing gas vapors that normally escape when gas tanks are filled.

VENTILATION   The active movement and distribution of air within a building.

VITAL RECORDS   Governmental records of births, deaths, marriages, divorces, etc.

VOLATILE   Able to change quickly to a gas.

VOLTAGE   A measure of electric potential. It represents the amount of work that must be done to move a charge from ground to a location in space such as a power line conductor. It is similar to the pressure in a pipeline. Voltage is measured in volts.

VOLTS (v)   A measurement used to assess the strength of electric fields, reported in volts per meter. When the field is strong, larger units of a thousand volts per meter or "kilo" volts per meter (kV/m) are used.

WASTE   Refuse matter. Left over parts in a manufacturing process.

WATER-SOLUBLE   Capable of being dissolved in water. Water-soluble chemicals can contaminate water supplies and aquifers. However, they do not bioaccumulate well and can pass quickly through the body. See aquifer, bioaccumulate, fat-soluble.

WORKING LEVEL (WL)   For radioactive products, a working level is a measure of how much alpha particle energy eventually will be released into the air by the short-lived decay products.

X-RAYS   A form of electromagnetic waves similar to light but with a shorter wavelength (higher frequency). X-rays are a form of ionizing radiation. *See* ionizing radiation.

|||||| **FOR FURTHER INFORMATION** ||||||

Frenay, A. 1959. *Understanding Medical Terminology*, 4th edition. St. Louis: Catholic Hospital Association.

Friel, J., ed. 1974. *DOrland's Illustrated Medical Dictionary*, 25th edition. Philadelphia: W.B. Saunders Company.

Last, J. 1983. *A Dictionary of Epidemiology*. New York: Oxford University Press.

ABOUT THE AUTHORS

IIIIII **BERNADETTE WEST** is executive director with Mid-State Health Advisory Corporation in New Brunswick, New Jersey. Dr. West studies public health issues of significance to New Jersey and is coauthor of *Public Health and Public Health Services* (1992).

IIIIII   **PETER M. SANDMAN** is adjunct professor of human ecology at Rutgers University. The creator of the "Hazard + Outrage" formula for risk communication, Dr. Sandman has worked on the communication aspects of a wide range of environmental problems. He is the founder of the Environmental Communication Research Program at Rutgers in 1986 and is the author of numerous articles and books on various aspects of risk communication.

IIIIII **MICHAEL R. GREENBERG** is professor and codirector of the New Jersey Graduate Program in Public Health of Rutgers University and the University of Medicine and Dentistry of New Jersey, studies the impact of urbanization and industrialization on public health and the environment. His books include *Urbanization and Cancer Mortality* (1983), *Hazardous Waste Sites: The Credibility Gap* (1984), *Public Health and the Environment* (1987), and *Environmental Risk and the Press* (1987). Dr. Greenberg has contributed more than 250 publications to scientific journals such as *Cancer Research*, *The American Journal of Epidemiology*, and *The New England Journal of Medicine* and such public interest journals as *Society, The Sciences*, and *Public Interest*.   He is currently working on a book tentatively titled *Neighborhood Quality in Environmentally Devastated Neighborhoods*.

INDEX

INDEX

Securities and Exchange Commission, 278
Selenium, 265
Sevin, 217
Sick building syndrome, 40, 41
Smog, 56, 129, 205
Smoking, 6, 48, 226; and benzene, 61; and birth defects,
65–70, 67; and cadmium, 256;
deaths from, 5; and radon,
223, 224, 227; secondary
smoke, 39, 40
Society of the Plastics Industry,
239
Sources for journalists: acid rain,
37–38; air pollution, 38;
asbestos, 53–54; benzene, 64;
birth defects, 69–70; cancer
clusters, 77, 297; chemical
emergencies, 24, 26, 27,
85–87, 297; dioxin, 98;
electromagnetic fields,
107–109; endangered species,
118; greenhouse effect,
135–136; green marketing, 134;
hazardous waste, 150–151, 298;
incinerators, 158–159; indoor
air pollution, 43–44; landfills,
167; nuclear power, 184–185;
oil spills, 202–203; ozone,
213–214; pesticides, 222, 298;
pollution from automobiles,
60; polychlorinated biphenyls, 98; radon, 228; recycling, 239–240; right-to-know
laws, 246–248, 298; storage
tank leaks, 173; toxic chemical exposure, 193–194, 298;
toxic metals, 261; water
pollution, 271–272, 298
Species Survival Program, 116
Spills: bioremediation in, 198;
chemical, 80–81; cleanup, 198,
200, 202; climactic effect on,
197; land, 82; location effect
on, 197; oil, 87, 195–203;
prevention, 201; water, 82

Statistics, 10; extrapolation from,
13; limits of, 73
Steel Can Recycling Institute,
240
Storage tanks, underground:
benzene, 62; and drinking
water, 170; fiberglass, 58;
leakage from, 6, 169–173;
stainless steel, 58
Studies: animal, 10, 11–12, 49;
cluster, 75–76; cohort, 74;
contradictory, 14; epidemiological, 9–12; fiberglass, 49;
human, 10; implantation, 49;
inconclusive, 75–76; sample
size, 10
Sulfur, 36, 153, 198; removal, 36,
37
Sulfur dioxide, 33, 34, 36, 37
Sulfuric acid, 34, 42
Superfund, 140, 141, 171, 200, 252,
257; Amendments and
Reauthorization Act, 140,
241–248, 257; sites, 139, 228
Symptoms of exposure: air
pollution, 39; benzene, 62;
carbon monoxide, 56; dioxin,
91–92; lead exposure, 250;
mercury exposure, 254;
polychlorinated biphenyls, 94

|||||| **T** ||||||

TCDD dioxin, 90, 91, 92, 93, 96,
97
Technology: best available
control, 8, 284; fluidized bed
combustion, 36–37; gasification, 36, 37; hazardous waste
cleanup, 144–145; maximum
achievable control, 284; oil
spill, 201; reasonably available control, 284; risk-
reduction, 8; storage tank leak
detection, 172; water pollution
containment, 267
Tellico Dam Project, 112, 114, 117
Temik, 217